THE·LIVING·ISLES

A NATURAL HISTORY OF BRITAIN AND IRELAND

PETER CRAWFORD

THE·LIVING·ISLES

A NATURAL HISTORY OF BRITAIN AND IRELAND

CHARLES SCRIBNER'S SONS   NEW YORK

CONTENTS

First published by the British Broadcasting Corporation 1985

Library of Congress Catalog Card number 86–28053
ISBN 0–684–18801–5
Copyright © 1985 Peter Crawford

Set in 11/13pt Monophoto Photina by Jolly & Barber Ltd, Rugby
Colour separation by Bridge Graphics, Hull
Printed and bound in the Netherlands
by Royal Smeets Offset b.v. Weert

First American edition 1987

PREFACE

I have written this book as a companion to the BBC television series, *The Living Isles*. In their different ways, the book and the film series tell the fascinating story of the natural history of the British Isles from the end of the last Ice Age; I hope that one will enhance the other.

As with its predecessors from the Natural History Unit of the BBC, this project has been several years in the making; my original outline for the series and the book was drafted in 1981. During those four or five years of research and preparation, many people have helped with their specialist knowledge. Particular acknowledgement is due to the scientific staff of the Nature Conservancy Council and its regional officers and wardens. The BBC has also received invaluable help from the staff of the forty-six local Nature Conservation Trusts and their parent body, the Royal Society for Nature Conservation. Together with many other organisations in Britain and Ireland, including the Royal Society for the Protection of Birds and the National Trust, they have given constant advice and support. I and the producers of the programmes are very grateful to them all.

The experts with whom we have worked have been generous with their specialist knowledge and research. Several of them have kindly advised on particular chapters of the book: Dr John Birks, John F. Burton, Frank S. Dobson, Alistair Johnstone, Dr Peter Moore, Dr Stephen Nicholls, Dr Franklyn Perring and Ruth Tittensor. I am indebted to them for their guidance and enthusiasm, and hope that they will recognise in the chapters the fruits of their influence.

Acknowledgement is also due to colleagues at the BBC, especially the four producers of the television programmes: John Downer, Roger Jones, Robin Prytherch and Paul Reddish, and the series researcher, Mark Jacobs. At BBC Publications Sheila Ableman, Linda Blakemore, Valerie Buckingham and Jennifer Fry have produced this book with great flair and judgement.

Finally, I wish to record my personal gratitude to David Tyldesley, who, as landscape historian, not only helped to draw up the historical framework for the series and the book but also undertook the work of compiling the gazetteer of nature reserves that is an integral part of this volume. From a shortlist of 5000 sites, including those in Ireland suggested by Eamon de Buitlear and Dr Roger Goodwillie, he and I chose the 450 which we consider best illustrate the story of 'The Living Isles'. David Tyldesley's descriptions of the twenty regions and their selected nature reserves add a very fitting complement to this natural history of Britain and Ireland.

Peter Crawford Bristol, June 1985

To Pat

PROLOGUE

TEN THOUSAND YEARS AGO, at about the time the
men of Jericho were building their walls for the
first time, the last Ice Age ended in the land that we
now know as the British Isles. After thousands of years
locked in the grip of ice, which in places had been
more than a mile deep, there emerged a bare
and almost lifeless landscape.

Today, Britain and Ireland share an archipelago of
islands and seas which, considering its size, has a
greater diversity of scenery and wildlife than perhaps
any other part of the globe.

This story traces that epic transformation which
has taken place in the brief timespan of
two hundred human lives.

CHAPTER ONE

AFTER THE ICE

Imagine the view from a satellite high above the Earth. Our orbit has brought us to the point where we would expect to recognise the distinctive outlines of the British Isles. But by the marvels of modern technology we have been transported back in time and are scanning the scene as it was 18,000 years ago. In place of the familiar shapes of Britain and Ireland there is a single land mass linked firmly to the mainland of Europe; there are no islands. In place of the green land we had expected, our eyes are dazzled by the brilliant whiteness of snow and ice. We are witnessing the peak of the most recent major advance of the arctic ice-cap. We are back in the last Ice Age.

Looking north, we can see a massive ice-sheet that covers all of Scotland and, in the distance, one that engulfs Scandinavia. Further north, the sea is frozen and to the west great icebergs have broken free from the glaciers and are floating away, chilling the Atlantic Ocean. The ice-sheet engulfs nearly all of Ireland – only the most southern and some western mountains seem free of ice, while the Irish Sea and most of Wales are frozen solid. In England, glaciers cover the Lake District and extend down the west side of the Pennines to cover the Cheshire Plain. Where this giant tongue of the ice ends, we can see a great lake which overflows at its southern end to form the recognisable course of the River Severn beneath us. To the east there are even larger lakes at the southern boundaries of another massive sheet of ice that covers most of eastern England down as far as the Wash and north Norfolk. From our privileged vantage point high up in the satellite, the rest of southern Britain and the land mass to the east appears to be barren arctic waste. From this height there seems to be no life.

Ice Ages have been coming and going for millions of years – as far back perhaps as 2300 million years. About 670 million years ago, it is believed, most of our planet was covered by ice. Two hundred and fifty million years ago, when much of the world was a steamy swamp, the subcontinent of India was drifting across the South Pole entombed under glaciers. Other corners of the world have experienced their own Ice Ages at different stages in the long history of the Earth. Scientists have even suggested that there has been a regular pattern to these glaciations – such epochs occurring every 150 million years or so. There have been many attempts to explain the onset of these Ice Ages. It is fairly certain that the phenomenon of continental drift and the change in ocean currents have contributed to the long-term pattern of Ice Ages, culminating in the arrival of the Antarctic continent at the South Pole and the onset of another global freeze. One popular theory designed to explain the repeated glaciations of the last one to two million years is that there have been irregular wobbles in the axis of the Earth and in the plane of its orbit around the Sun. These variations may well trigger the growth of the polar ice-caps. Whatever their cause, we know that there have been several very long periods in the geological history of the Earth when global temperatures were much lower than today and the two polar ice-caps much greater in area and thickness. Since the Earth cooled after its creation, there has probably always been ice at the poles; we should perhaps simply think of an 'Ice Age' as a period in our planet's history with more ice than usual.

We are in an 'ice-epoch' now – a period of four Ice Ages which began about two million years ago and which has been named by geologists as the Pleistocene. At the coldest time in this long epoch, the polar ice-sheets covered a third of the world's land surface compared with about a tenth today. In that respect we are better off, but there have also been periods warmer than today when the ice-sheets retreated back towards the poles. During the Pleistocene ice-epoch, there have been several advances and retreats of the ice as the world's climate fluctuated, for reasons still unclear. We now appear to be living within one of the warm interglacial periods, which has so far lasted about 10,000 years. Geologists have optimistically given this most recent era a separate name – the Post Glacial or Holocene. Previous interglacial respites in this ice-epoch were even warmer than today and our islands were inhabited by such animals as the elephant, hippopotamus, rhinoceros, lion and spotted hyena. As the ice returned each time, Britain became colder and such warm-loving species were once more confined to the more tropical parts of the world which we now think of as their normal home.

The Cairngorms in winter today echo ice-age times.

About 25,000 years ago, the climate began to deteriorate. At that time, the British Isles had a very cosmopolitan fauna which included mammoth, woolly rhinoceros, horse, bison, reindeer, brown bear, wolf and arctic fox. People of the Old Stone Age lived here, hunting the herds of game that roamed the grasslands of southern Britain. Yet only 5000 years later, most of the British Isles were under ice and the grasslands had gone. This sudden, dramatic Ice Age chilled the surface of the Earth. Much of the extra ice was deposited on the great land masses of the northern hemisphere. With the increase in ice the level of the seas fell until they were two to three hundred feet lower than they are today. It has been calculated that this worldwide freeze created an extra 25 million cubic miles of ice and that the average thickness of the ice-sheet was 2500 feet. It covered the sites of Chicago, Boston, Glasgow, Stockholm and Moscow; and over Canada and Scandinavia was as much as 8000 feet deep, comparable to the ice-sheets of Greenland and the Antarctic today. Here, in the British Isles, the ice was up to a mile thick in the north, and in the ice-free regions of the south conditions were probably as inhospitable as in central Alaska today. These unglaciated parts of Britain were not only very cold but also very dry. There were no trees or other conspicuous plants, although there were parts of southern Ireland and Britain which acted as refuges for some hardy plant and animal species. In the summers of this last ice-age glaciation, occasional herds of reindeer might have crossed from continental Europe into the bleak tundra of southern Britain, to seek out the scant vegetation of lichens, mosses, grasses, sedges and dwarf willow – so, too, would ptarmigan and other birds that, although adapted for life in the cold, were still more at home in parts of Europe further away from the harsh grip of the glaciers. The British Isles had become one of the least hospitable places on Earth.

The recent glaciation in the north of Europe produced a series of different climatic conditions down through the continent – from north to south, and in some cases from west to east. Each climatic band favoured a different way of life – and most species naturally ended up where they were best suited to survive. Average summer temperatures throughout the main part of Europe were ten degrees Celsius lower than they are now; the tree-line of the Alps and Pyrenees stopped at a point nearly 5000 feet below where trees grow today. On the other hand, the area we now know as the Sahara Desert had a much heavier rainfall; north Africa must have been a hospitable place for many of the plants and animals that now thrive in temperate zones. When the world's climate changed again – this time becoming warmer – these environmental bands moved north once more. Within each band moved the species of plant and animal favoured by its particular climatic conditions. The great migration north had started.

Here in Britain the terrain left behind by the retreating glaciers must have been an unearthly landscape before it was given its green mantle. Many of the features that make up the topography of the British Isles were fashioned by the ice. Ireland is particularly notable for its glacial history and geologists have adopted several Irish names to describe the features of the landscape created by the glaciers that once covered nearly all that land. An advancing glacier sweeps with it a mass of rocks and boulders, clay and sand – a 'till' that, wherever the glacier changes course or eventually stops, is deposited as heaps or mounds called 'moraines'. Sometimes this till accumulates in oval masses beneath the flow of the glacier. When the ice melts, little hills are revealed – called 'drumlins' – a corruption of the Irish name for such features, which are characteristic of the central plain of Ireland and of Antrim and Armagh. Elsewhere in Ireland you will find 'eskers' – often the natural causeways that carry roads across boggy country. These raised banks of gravel also had their origins beneath the ice. The melting waters sometimes carved channels and ice caverns within the glacier itself. Such watercourses would have carried away much of the debris trapped within the ice, and most of this was deposited on the floor of the channel – as happens with rivers today. The Irish name for such intriguing features – 'eiscir' – has passed into the international language of geology.

The massive ice-sheets retreated from the British Isles more than 10,000 years ago – but the relentless passage of the glaciers, as they forged a path down from the ice-sheet, can still be seen in the face of the modern landscape. Wherever there were glaciers, you will find the U-shaped valleys left in their wake.

Drumlins – an ice-age mystery. No one knows exactly how they were formed, but they certainly had their origins under the ice-sheet and are characteristic features of the Central Plain of Ireland and the flatter areas of Scotland.

Scotland and Wales also have their own fascinating geological relics of the recent glaciation – notably the deep hollows or 'corries', known as 'cwms' in Wales, which were excavated by the constant freezing and thawing effects of the ice as it accumulated near the peaks of mountains. Sometimes this lens of ice remained contained within the corrie it had formed. When the ice melted, it left a corrie lake or tarn, one of the most beautiful natural features of our upland scenery. Other lenses of ice expanded so much during the Ice Age that they overflowed as glaciers – great powerful tongues of ice that forged their way down mountainsides, creating the U-shaped valleys which are so familiar in the Lake District and the Scottish Glens. Here you can see how the power of these glaciers has scoured, scratched and polished the hard rocks. Throughout the British Isles, wherever there was ice, the landscape is witness to the tremendous force and impact of the ice-sheet.

When it eventually melted, the ice left a bare landscape. The 'soil', where it existed, was probably a light greyish-white in colour, having no humus but being very rich in lime. Such raw soil was suitable only for a few hardy plants – species that were already adapted to the cold, dry climate of the tundra to the south, or which could tolerate poor soils and the short growing seasons of upland areas. Where the ice had scraped bare the rock and left no trace of soil in which even the hardiest of flowering plants could take root, it was the primeval-looking lichens that began the slow process of colonisation. These curious plant associations between fungus and alga are often the first life forms to etch a foothold on the hard surface of the rocks. Most familiar are the lichens that encrust the bare face of ancient stone – slowly eroding away the smooth surface as their colonies spread with time. The patches of lichens you often see colouring the stone roofs and tombstones of churches have probably been there ever since the raw rock was hewn from the landscape centuries before. It is on the rock that the spores and other fragments of the lichen, carried by the wind, begin their slow encrusting growth. Many such colonies are not visible to our eyes until they have been growing for ten years or so – but then the bright colours of these lichens bring obvious life to the seemingly barren stone. One such lichen is the map-lichen, so-called because of the distinct black margins which outline its patches of vivid yellow growth. So predictable is its rate of spread over new rock that geologists use it to give a timescale to their studies of glacier-retreat in parts of the world on the edge of today's ice-sheets. Lichens are perhaps the slowest growing organisms that we know; some patches may be as old as 5000 years, perhaps much more. It is not impossible that some lichens began their lives 10,000 years ago as soon as the ice-sheet had retreated.

Much of our first flora was recruited from the arctic plants that had survived just beyond the reach of the ice-sheet. We can get an impression of this pioneering vegetation from the way it grows today near the snow-fields of Scandinavia. In the summer, some of the snow melts, exposing areas of the ground for varying lengths of time during the brief growing season. Near the edge of the remaining snow patch, where the soil is only briefly exposed to the sun and air, there are lichens and mosses. Further out are flowering plants

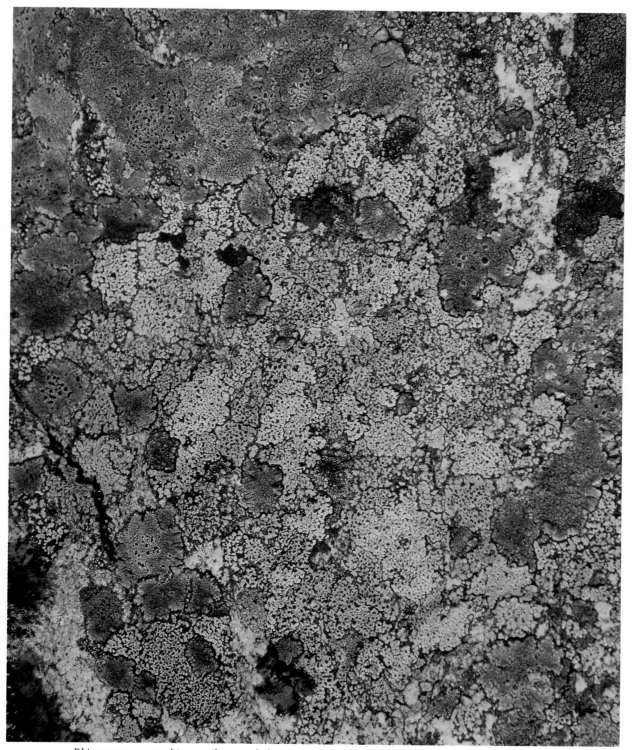

Rhizocarpon geographicum – the map-lichen – the largest of these plant growths may be the oldest living inhabitants of the British Isles, true relics of the Ice Age.

such as glacier buttercup, snow saxifrage and alpine lady's-mantle, which all grow and bloom quickly in the damp, shallow soil above the impenetrable permafrost; soon they become covered again by a protective blanket of snow. In the more exposed areas further out, many plants such as moss campion form compact cushions of growth which protect the young buds from the severe cold and dryness of the long winter. Alternatively, some plants, like the mountain avens, have a woody structure which creeps low to the ground out of the full impact of the wind. Whatever the adaptive device, these arctic colonisers are almost invariably perennials; there simply is not enough time to grow to maturity in one year. Curiously, the snow gentian, which is now only found in Britain on or near Ben Lawers, is an exception. For those plants which manage to flower, pollination remains a problem because of the shortage of insects. Bumble-bees, contrary to the summery associations we have of them, are well adapted to arctic conditions because of their furry bodies. Species such as the bearberry rely on them to transfer pollen from one plant to another, but other species such as alpine hawkweed and dandelion need no pollination or, as with grasses and sedges, are pollinated by the wind. Some grasses start their lives as offshoots of the parent plant or as bulbils, which are supplied with nutrients

Left Many plants that became established on the tundra that spread over Britain behind the retreating ice-sheet had to grow in shapes which protected them from the drying effects of the glacial winds and the extreme cold. Today on the flat, exposed plateau of the Cairngorms, the moss campion grows in compact tussocks that hug the ground.
Right Ben Lawers which rises behind Loch Tay is home to a variety of relic ice-age plants – notably the alpine gentian with its tiny star-shaped electric-blue flowers.

before dropping off to start their pioneering lives. One way or another such hardy plants as these gained a foothold at the edge of the ice.

Today we can still find pockets of these glacial plant communities high in the mountains of Scotland and Wales, where in many respects the Ice Age has never really ended. What all these places have in common is that since the Ice Age they have not been forested or disturbed to any great extent, and the flora that developed in the wake of the ice has retained an arctic character. Such modern-day sites range from the mountains of Snowdonia where there are many calcareous rocks high up near the summits, to the limestone of the coastal Burren in west Ireland where the strange rock formations have probably never supported dense woodland of any great size. Other strange relic sites include the steep sides of inland gorges and the windswept edges of sea cliffs — many of which still harbour elements of an arctic or alpine flora that once was typical of the British Isles immediately after the ice.

If you visit the Upper Teesdale National Nature Reserve in the early summer, you would not think of it as a relic from the last Ice Age. Yet this small area has one of the most fascinating plant communities in the whole of the British Isles. The reason, it is thought, is that it has survived almost intact since the ice

On the west coast of Ireland, in County Clare, is the Burren – one of the most extraordinary landscapes in the British Isles. The extensive limestone pavement is littered with large boulders left by the retreating glaciers. In early summer the ground between these 'glacial erratics' is carpeted with mountain avens. So characteristic was this plant of the time just after the ice that botanists refer to this period as the 'Dryas' – the scientific name for this spectacular flower.

retreated from the Pennines. Much of the area is made up of an unusual rock called 'sugar limestone', because of its granulated texture. The instability and chemical properties of the soil it forms have prevented the successful colonisation by woodland. Here you will find spring gentians and mountain avens, lady's-mantle and alpine bartsia, sea thrift, saxifrages, the rare alpine meadow-rue and surprisingly the dwarf birch, a great rarity south of Scotland. Altogether there are some seventy-five rare and beautiful flowers which between 15,000 and 10,000 years ago were widespread over the British Isles, in the lowlands of the south as well as the uplands of the north and west. Teesdale today is a microcosm of that varied and colourful late-glacial flora – a 'time-capsule' preserved for us in the twentieth century to cherish as a celebration of wild Britain just after the ice.

Further south in Europe, the forests were slowly advancing in the wake of the warmer climate that was gradually becoming a permanent feature of the continent. It is difficult to visualise forests on the move, but over the hundreds of years that followed the end of the Ice Age, that is just what they did. Each autumn, trees and other plants in the warm south released their millions of seeds which either, as with oaks, fell to the ground close to their parent tree or, like those of the birch, were carried by the wind to more distant parts. For thousands of years the ice-sheet had imposed an invisible but real barrier for each species of plant, north of which not even the hardiest of individuals could survive. As the climate of Europe became progressively moister and warmer, that frontier shifted northwards opening up new lands. Here, on virgin territory, a few seeds took root and gave rise to saplings that grew into mature trees and in turn produced seeds of their own. These pioneers, notably the birch, were the vanguard of the main army of forest that advanced across the continent and so over the land-bridge that still linked this land with the body of Europe.

The history of the British flora at this time is still being unravelled but we have already gleaned much information from pollen analysis. The technique, developed in the 1910s by the Swedish geologists von Post and Lagerheim, relies on the discovery that most species of flowering plant, including trees, produce pollen grains of a unique shape – each species, or at least each closely related group of species, having its own characteristic shape of pollen grain that can be readily recognised under a microscope. Luckily for botanists, these pollen grains can survive intact for hundreds, even thousands of years, if buried in an inert medium such as peat. As, year by year, new layers of peat are formed, each embodying samples of different pollen grains, a chronological record is built up of the plants that have lived in that area. Of course, the technique presupposes that the peat has remained undisturbed since it was formed, and also requires a sophisticated method of radio-carbon analysis to date accurately each layer of peat.

Left In spring birches produce huge clouds of pollen from their catkins, and in autumn release vast quantities of seeds. Borne by the wind, these seeds were swept northwards to colonise the tundra which already clothed the bare landscape left by the retreating ice.

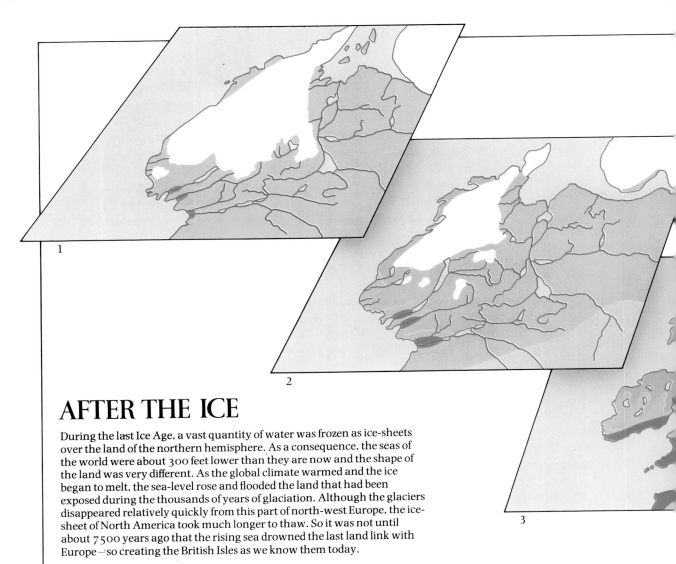

AFTER THE ICE

During the last Ice Age, a vast quantity of water was frozen as ice-sheets over the land of the northern hemisphere. As a consequence, the seas of the world were about 300 feet lower than they are now and the shape of the land was very different. As the global climate warmed and the ice began to melt, the sea-level rose and flooded the land that had been exposed during the thousands of years of glaciation. Although the glaciers disappeared relatively quickly from this part of north-west Europe, the ice-sheet of North America took much longer to thaw. So it was not until about 7500 years ago that the rising sea drowned the last land link with Europe – so creating the British Isles as we know them today.

1   Around 18,000 years ago, at the peak of the last Ice Age, a vast ice-sheet covered Scotland and northern England, Wales and most of Ireland. To the west of the ice-sheet, beyond the Hebrides, there was probably a narrow, low area of land – as bleak and inhospitable as the land to the south of the glaciers. To the east was the depleted North Sea bounded to the south by an extensive low-lying area of frozen tundra and marshy land that linked Britain with mainland Europe. This was 'Doggerland'. To the far south was a wide valley with rivers flowing west towards the Atlantic; this is now the English Channel. At its most westerly end there were probably pockets of birch and pine forest, perhaps even oak, ash and other broadleaved trees; from these 'refuges' some plant and animal species spread back into western Britain and Ireland, as the climate improved.

2   About 14,000 years ago the ice-sheets had melted over much of southern Ireland and the inundating sea had begun to isolate it from Britain. The ice-free land in the south of England was still mainly tundra, but birches and pine were rapidly spreading from the mainland of Europe.

3 By 11,000 years ago only the Scottish Highlands still had glaciers. Ireland had become an island and the English Channel was nearly formed. The rising sea had flooded Doggerland as far south as East Anglia. The seeds of oaks and other broadleaved trees were carried northwards by the rivers that flowed from mainland Europe. As the climate became more temperate, other plant and animal species colonised Britain.

4 By 8000 years ago, Britain had almost become an island. Broadleaved trees covered much of southern England, lowland Wales and southern Ireland, whereas the north was still forested by birches and pines.

5 Around 6000 years ago, the familiar shape of the British Isles had been finally formed. During the warm 'Atlantic' period that followed, the sea-level rose a further six feet, drowning many river estuaries and coastal plains, but by 5000 years ago, it had settled back to its present level. It was at this time that the people of the New Stone Age came from mainland Europe in increasing numbers, to make this land their home and to begin its transformation into the landscapes and habitats that we know today.

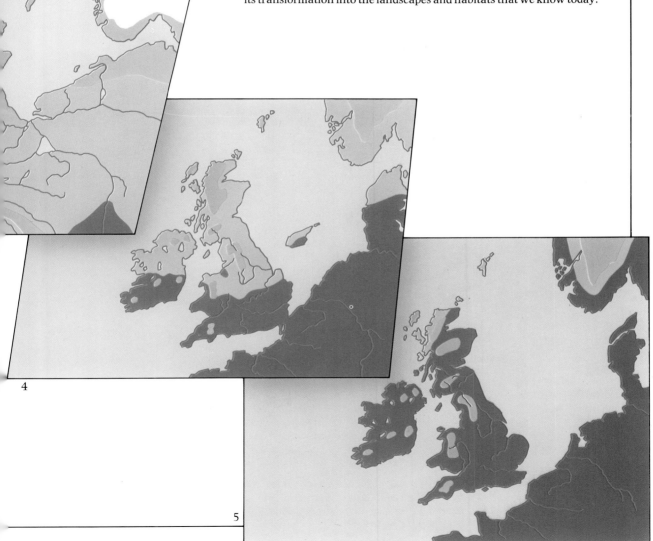

4

5

What of the animals that moved into Britain behind the ice? The picture we can conjure of their icy world is more scant than the one we have of the plants. For animals there is no such simple evidence as a pollen record. Fossilisation is really quite a rare event – the animal must perish in almost ideal conditions for the process to happen at all. In the long-term story of the history of the Earth, fossilisation has been frequent enough for us to decipher the most basic chapters of animal evolution, but fossils are too rare to be of real help in the very recent story of the natural history of the British Isles. There have, however, been findings of bones and teeth in caves or petrified remains of feathers and scales – even whole animals preserved in the inert depths of mires and bogs, after dying from some sudden, probably dramatic event. In the Welsh cave called Ogof-yr-Ychen, which means 'Cave of Oxen', there are piles of bones including those of woolly rhinoceros, wolverines, wolves and cave bears, which perished by falling through a hole in the roof. It is from such evidence that we have pieced together the story of one of the most mysterious and romantic inhabitants of late ice-age times – the so-called 'Irish giant elk'.

Throughout the Ice Age herds of reindeer migrated across the bleak tundra of southern England. They became extinct in the British Isles at the end of the last Ice Age – but were introduced from Lapland to the Cairngorms in the 1950s.

About 13,000 years ago, the climate of Ireland, particularly in its low-lying central plain, had become so markedly warmer that a wave of green spread over the countryside; grassland rich in docks and other pioneering herbs replaced the open vegetation of the early tundra. Ireland must have looked a treeless, emerald land – if not yet quite an isle. It was at this time that its famed 'elk' reached the zenith of its success. This magnificent creature was not in fact an elk – it was more closely related to the red deer – but it was certainly of giant proportions. Standing more than six feet at the shoulders, the male carried a handsome set of antlers that spanned almost ten feet from tip to tip. These antlers, like those of its surviving relatives, were shed each year and were grown the following spring to an even more impressive size. Though very heavy, the antlers were feeble in strength and would have been ineffective in combat; their purpose was clearly to impress. You can imagine the spectacle of one such mature male, the current monarch of the herd, standing proudly in full view of the younger stags and the females of his harem – slowly raising and lowering his magnificent headpiece as a sign of dominance. The need to produce so much bony tissue every year must have put great strain on the physiological system of the beast; he would have been compelled to consume vast quantities of vegetation in order to absorb the calcium and other minerals needed to form the new antlers. The virgin soils of Ireland were rich in calcium carbonate and other essential ingredients that as yet had not been leached out from the surface. Consequently, plant life must have flourished in this relatively warm early period after the ice-sheet disappeared from the Irish lowlands. The giant deer had been quite common during the early part of the Pleistocene right across Europe and western Asia. Later on, it was to be found as far south as north Africa – presumably when conditions there were also favourable for this giant vegetarian. A great obstacle to its success was forest. Wherever there was dense woodland, the giant deer was excluded by the impediment of its massive antlers. Its insatiable appetite for calcium-rich vegetation, and the restrictions imposed by its antlers, forced the giant deer to stay with the new prairies of open grassland. Over the ages, as the climate changed, so these bands of grassland moved like waves up and down the continents. As these prairies were displaced either by encroaching ice or trees, so the giant deer was obliged to follow.

The giant deer is known to have lived in England, where the climate often matched that of Ireland, but it was never as numerous as in the land with which we associate its success and its extinction. It had lived in Ireland 30,000 years ago, before the last Ice Age and then returned 13,000 years ago, for the last time, to share in the fresh green abundance of that time. Interestingly, the preserved remains of those individuals which have been found in lakes and caves are notably more numerous in the area around Limerick, which today is renowned for the richness of its grasslands and is the centre of the Irish dairy industry. In the north of Ireland, remains of the giant deer have been unearthed in County Down, where the equally verdant modern grasslands are the source of Belfast's milk. With so few trees in Ireland today, there is every reason to

The golden eagle – majestic symbol
of the Highlands of Scotland and
northern England.

assume that the giant deer would have fared well alongside our contemporary grassland fauna. Predators were never a real threat to the creature. Even wolves and arctic foxes would have avoided all but the old and sickly individuals, and at that time man had not yet arrived. Life in Ireland just after the ice must have been ideal for this wandering prairie giant. Then the Ice Age loomed large again and claimed another victim. It seems that the Scottish ice-mass retained some of its vigour after the Irish one had waned. About 10,500 years ago, the climate of Britain took a brief turn for the worse and the ice-sheet which had disappeared from so many parts of our land made one final advance. Although not nearly as extensive as the previous ice-sheet, this last thrust of glaciation had a marked effect on the fauna and flora of Ireland. The vegetation of this cold snap reverted to the more arctic-like tundra that had preceded it. The grasslands broke up and disappeared as the summers became too cold and dry to support them. Unlike the Irish elk, reindeer were able to adapt to different conditions and continued to do well on the tundra, feeding on the traditional diet of 'reindeer moss' which is high in carbohydrate. The giant elk was not suited to this way of life and when its grassy plains were displaced by the cold, it was forced to move on. With the land-bridge to Britain either drowned or frozen over, there was, this time, no retreat. Ireland's 'giant elk' was cut off and the species perished in the land which had become its adopted home.

Not all plants and animals are bound by the land. Many seeds and spores of plants can be carried great distances by the wind and over all kinds of natural obstacles. Most birds and a great many insects can fly and their mobility has given them great independence from the comings and goings of the ice-sheet and the sea. Southern England would have soon been extensively colonised by arctic mammals – including the lemming and the arctic fox. From the warmer south came the first mountain hares and water voles – and, in time, red deer, brown bears, lynx and wolves. The smaller mammals, such as voles and lemmings that bred prolifically whenever climate and vegetation became more temperate, would have attracted many birds of prey. Their powers of flight and endurance gave them superiority over many less mobile creatures. This must have been the heyday of the golden eagle, the peregrine and the snowy owl, the piratical long-tailed skua and the opportunist raven. Today, our highest uplands are a refuge for many of the bird species which once quartered lowland Britain and Ireland. Here, too, were the plant- and seed-eaters that we think of as upland rarities – the ptarmigan, black grouse and snow bunting. Feeding in the icy waters that had become a widespread feature of post-glacial Britain were the geese and swans: species such as greylags, whoopers and Bewick's, and the waders and waterfowl such as knot and sanderling, long-tailed duck and red-breasted merganser – all of which are more common now in winter than in summer. Think of the wetlands of upland Britain and Ireland in winter today and you have an impression of our wilderness and its wildlife after the ice had gone. Such species were the first in the race to colonise the emergent landscape and most of them have a distribution today that extends as far north as the tundra of the Arctic Circle. It is an interesting thought that the Bewick's swans

that now come to Slimbridge in winter, may have once nested there rather than in Siberia as they do today.

There were, of course, many other animals that moved in to colonise the new terrain. Many of our contemporary insects may date from that period – the mountain ringlet butterfly, the northern dart moth and the craneflies, familiar to us as daddy-long-legs and which now number some 300 species in the British Isles. In the fresh waters were arctic species of fish such as charr and grayling, together with the familiar frog, and many species of shrimp and other crustaceans that still thrive today. It is to the watery world of these freshwater creatures that we turn in the next chapter – the stage in the natural history of these islands when the last melt-waters of the Ice Age joined the rivers to flow away towards the sea.

There is, though, one species that returned to brave the cold of wilderness Britain that has not yet featured in our story. *Homo sapiens* came back to this

Above The dotterell nests on the high plateaux of Scotland and north Wales where snow lies almost until summer; in winter it migrates south to North Africa.
Previous page In some severe winters, even the Highland waterfalls freeze; our islands are only just beyond the grip of the Ice Age.

land long before the ice had gone. Some experts believe such people never left the tundra of the south but braved the bleakest winters of the Ice Age in caves, protecting themselves as best they could. In summer, these hunters of the Old Stone Age ventured out on to the tundra in pursuit of reindeer and wild horse, elk and deer. Like such peoples today, they moved with the fortunes of their quarry, living in the summer in temporary dwellings which were probably made of animal skins. Such ancient Britons were close relatives of those men and women who created the works of art found in the caves of warmer southern Europe. The cave-dwellers of Britain ventured as far as Wales and Cumbria late in the Ice Age, but they never reached Scotland or Ireland. Like the plant and animal species which colonised this new wilderness, these humans were a hardy race. The entire population of Britain 10,000 years ago was possibly no more than a few hundred people. They used fire, probably wore skin jackets and trousers, and fashioned sophisticated tools and weapons from flint, bone and antler. To survive here at all, such people had to be ingenious, technical, robust and opportunist. Always conscious of the cold, they had little time or inclination to celebrate the wildlife they hunted by painting on the walls of their winter caves. They were constantly on the margins of survival. For them and the other pioneering species of arctic Britain, living in the wake of an Ice Age had become a normal way of life.

CHAPTER TWO

STREAMS OF LIFE

There is nowhere more expectant, more full of promise, than the birthplace of a river. From its source – a spring gently trickling from a rockface, or a slight ribbon of water forming on the surface of a mountainside – will flow a new life force. First a stream, then gathering the support of other tributaries, it matures into a vibrant, restless waterway that courses through the landscape until, generous and spent, it floods into the sea to merge anonymously with the other waters of the world. Sadly, such is the destiny of every river.

The story of our rivers and lakes and of our fens and boglands is one in which the main ingredient is fresh water – once the frozen fabric of the Ice Age, but now the very lifeblood of a reawakened landscape. At their richest, the wetlands of Britain and Ireland support a greater quantity as well as diversity of plants and animals than any habitat on dry land; paradoxically, some fresh-water places are so sterile that they resemble deserts. The extremes of this natural productivity are to be found in our rivers but are most obvious in the lakes of the British Isles. Compare any lake or pond in the south of England with a loch in the Highlands of Scotland and you will see just how different fresh water can be. A typical lake in lowland Britain will be fringed with beds of vegetation, on which crawl a multitude of snails, leeches and insects – many of which are food for the moorhens and dabbling ducks that pick their way over the shallow water at the edge. On the open water is an armada of pond-skaters and other water-bugs, sculling between the grebes and diving ducks that disappear beneath the surface in search of the water-weed and small creatures that flourish in the rich water of the lake. Here, too, are tadpoles of frogs and newts, prey for the great diving beetle and its equally predatory larvae. On the bottom of the lake, the mud is alive with the larvae of other beetles, caddis-flies and dragonflies which, after their growing stages here in the rich, murky water, will emerge as handsome adult insects to grace the lake in summer. Down to the last microscopic drop, the water of a lowland lake teems with life. In contrast, the clear, cold water of a Scottish loch hides little plant and animal life – its very clarity is a sure sign of the scarcity of the microscopic plankton that is the basic diet for so many freshwater creatures. Where the water is stained brown by peat, there is very little life – the basic chemistry is wrong.

For healthy plants, as every gardener knows, the most essential nutrients are potassium, phosphorus and nitrogen – and water-plants are no exception. Without these basic ingredients in the water, very little plant life will grow and in turn animal life would have nothing to eat. Water that springs from or flows over the newer, softer chalk and limestone rocks picks up a much higher proportion of these nutrients – together with calcium – than water which comes from older, harder rocks. It is this basic distinction that makes all the difference to the life that water can support. Hard, ancient rocks are predominantly a feature of our mountain areas while the chalk and limestones of the British Isles are mostly found in the lowlands. Hence the contrast between our impoverished Scottish loch and that vibrant southern lake – both are a reflection of the underlying geology of their local landscapes.

Although the lakes of northern Britain support a smaller variety of plant and animal species, they do have one or two fascinating specialities which are not to be found in the south. Loch Ness, for example, may never reveal its monster but it can boast an ancient fish whose story baffled biologists for many years. Here, if you spend a night fishing in the middle of the loch, you may catch a glimpse of the mysterious freshwater charr.

Upland lakes are poor in nutrients and support little plant life. Characteristic species are the primitive horsetails which, rooted in the sediment, grow up through the crystal-clear water to form a miniature freshwater forest.

This beautifully coloured and elegant fish is a member of the salmon family but unlike its more common cousin prefers cold, almost arctic waters. Elsewhere in the arctic seas of the northern hemisphere they are migratory, ascending rivers to spawn like the salmon. But in the British Isles the charr is exclusively freshwater – spending the whole of its life in cold, upland lakes in Scotland, Cumbria and North Wales and in several lowland lakes in Ireland. Closely related species can be found in lakes high in the Alps and elsewhere in Europe. They all live deep in cold water, coming to the surface only at night to feed. Like the mountain avens of Upper Teesdale, the charr is clearly an ice-age relic. As the ice-sheet moved north, so did the migratory charr. At that time the salmon was at home in the Mediterranean but the charr, preferring colder waters, lived in the Atlantic. From here it swam up the rivers of Europe to spawn where, as the general climate warmed, isolated populations were cut off in deep lakes that were cool enough for them. It is thought that, as the glaciers

In contrast, down to the last microscopic drop, a lowland lake or pond teems with life – often so prolific that the water in spring and summer becomes opaque. On the surface grows a luxuriant variety of vegetation.

35

melted from Britain, a large lake formed between Britain and Ireland where today is the deepest part of the Irish Sea. This 'Lake Hibernia' was probably slightly salty from contact with the Atlantic. Into it began to flow the rivers of eastern Ireland and western Britain that still flow there today. The charr migrated up these rivers and as the climate of northern Europe continued to improve, several different populations of the fish were stranded in the cool lakes near their headwaters. These relic communities of charr have been genetically isolated for ten thousand years and have evolved their own slightly different forms. Windermere in the English Lake District has two varieties, distinguished by the fact that one population spawns in spring and the other in summer, which suggests that the lake adopted two quite distinct charr populations at two different stages in its history. Those in Loch Ness also comprise two separate communities but these contrasting forms have possibly developed from the same ice-age ancestors. There was once a separate race in Lough Neagh in Ireland, but it became extinct in the early nineteenth century – probably because the lake became too shallow for the comfort of the arctic charr.

The mysterious charr – isolated relic of the Ice Age.

After the last trace of the ice-sheet had melted and flowed away down towards the sea, the lakes and rivers of our land were replenished by the rain and snow that fell, season by season, year by year, on the new landscape. In carving their path to the sea, these rivers and their tributaries have moulded the surface of the land, creating the contours and textures that we see today. The process still goes on. For plants and animals this ever-changing pattern of waterways has brought a succession of different freshwater habitats – each in its own way a new opportunity for a different freshwater community. When people first returned to the wilderness left after the ice, they also capitalised on the river system – both as highways for reaching remote parts and as natural barriers for defending their settlements. Today, our great rivers still serve as boundaries between counties and nations, and their water and wildlife provide us with a constant source of many of the basic ingredients for our way of life. Rivers are not only essential as a natural drainage system for the landscape but also give it a relief which we see as pleasing to the eye. Some still follow the broad pattern set for them millions of years ago; others have been created in the last ten thousand years since the ice-sheet melted. It is thought that a few rivers emerged from the Ice Age with a completely different course. For example, the direction of the River Severn changed dramatically. We know that prior to the glaciation, it flowed northwards from near to where Shrewsbury is today, and probably joined the River Dee, emptying into the Irish Sea more or less where the Dee estuary is now. During the glaciation, this river system was prevented from reaching the Irish Sea by the advancing glaciers and was ponded up to form a great lake, which geologists have named Lake Lapworth in honour of one of their most eminent professors. Eventually this lake overflowed to the south, to form the route of the Severn as we know it today, cutting the famous gorge at Ironbridge in the process.

Anglers have noted that there is a great contrast between the rivers like the Thames, which flow east towards the North Sea, and those on the other side of the country, which flow west towards the Atlantic, which without exception have a noticeably poorer assortment of fish. Over in Ireland, the rivers are even less endowed with variety, although clearly blessed with quantity. The distribution of fish in the British Isles is a puzzle; speculation about it is fascinating for both the angler and the naturalist. One species of fish that is found in almost every river in both Britain and Ireland is the brown trout. Although it comes in many sizes and colours, all its forms are easily distinguished from its close relative the sea trout. This sea-going member of the salmon family migrates into many of our rivers to spawn and must have soon found its way up almost every river after they began to flow. As the climate warmed, some of these trout lost their migratory habit and remained in our rivers and lakes all year round. In time, their freshwater way of life gave them an appearance that was quite distinct from their sea-going ancestors, and they became the various forms of brown trout so prized by anglers today.

Our rivers are home to other species of fish that spend some or most of their lives at sea. The most obvious of these are the eel and salmon, whose remarkable

migrations are well known – the salmon leaving the sea to spawn in the upper reaches of our rivers, and the eel doing the reverse by traversing the Atlantic to spawn in its salty birthplace. Clearly, both fish can tolerate the extremes of fresh water and salt water. There are also a few species of fish which, although essentially marine, will happily wander into fresh or brackish waters. The bass is well known to some river anglers, as is the grey mullet. Even the flounder seems to have developed a liking for fresh water, particularly in the colder north, where it is often discovered in the estuaries and lochs of the northern mainland of Scotland and on Shetland. Conversely, the three-spined stickle-back, the champion of the schoolboy's jam-jar, seems at home in the shorepools of our northern coasts. For all these fish, the sea does not act as a barrier to their natural passage between one river system and another. It comes as no surprise that, along with the brown trout and the sea trout, the eel, salmon and the diminutive stickleback are the most widely distributed of our freshwater fishes; in the absence of man-made barriers, such as dams and weirs and chemical pollution, they would inhabit all suitable fresh water in the British Isles that has access from the sea.

Left Born of the melting ice, this infant river sets out on a journey that retraces the story of our fresh waters – one which started with the great thaw that marked the end of the Ice Age. *Above* The predatory pike lurks in the shallows. With hardly a movement of its fins, it slowly rises towards its prey and with a sudden flick of its powerful tail seizes its victim in jaws armed with rows of backward curved teeth.

It is the origins of those species of fish which are exclusively freshwater that is the real puzzle. Maybe they never really left during the Ice Age, and remained in the south of England and Ireland where there was no ice-sheet. For much of the year the air temperature would have been below freezing and the fish would have had to endure long periods in ice-covered water. Most native fish can survive harsh winters when lakes and ponds freeze over, but none of the strictly freshwater species, except the pike, is adapted to spawning in winter. They all wait for spring or summer before they breed. Even if an adult fish could spend the whole winter under the ice, it could not breed successfully in such cold water. Even in the ice-age summers, our lakes and rivers must have been near freezing. The chances of our fish surviving in freshwater refuges here at home are extremely slim. How then did they get here without swimming through the sea with its intolerable salt? Clearly, they must have made the crossing after the ice retreated but before the seas rose, cutting off the British Isles from the freshwater rivers of Europe.

It is fascinating to visualise how the area we know as the North Sea might have been in those centuries soon after the ice retreated from England. At its lowest, the sea-level had been perhaps 300 feet below that of today – so great was the quantity of sea-water locked up as ice at the poles. With the melting of the ice-sheets, the seas began to rise; but it did not happen overnight, or all at the same time. The glaciers had formed over land and in the northern hemisphere the great bulk of the ice had accumulated over the land mass of North America and Greenland. In Europe the ice-sheet was neither so large in area nor so thick in depth, because this continent has far less land in arctic latitudes. Consequently, the ice-sheet here melted away sooner than that on the other side of the Atlantic. This explains why most of Britain and Ireland were completely free of ice long before the world sea-level rose to its present height. Today, there is no part of the North Sea floor, in the area south of Flamborough Head in Yorkshire and the mouths of the rivers Thames and Rhine, which is more than 120 feet deep. It is quite conceivable that for long periods both before and after the peak of the glaciation the river systems of the Humber, Thames and Rhine might have been linked as one. The trawlers that now fish over the Dogger Bank occasionally bring up antlers and bones and roots of trees from the bottom of this shallow sea. Here was a land-bridge over which much of our wildlife migrated from mainland Europe to colonise Britain. This vital link, now lost beneath the waves of the North Sea, has been given the name 'Doggerland'.

Long before many of the terrestrial animal and plant species made the crossing, a host of freshwater plants and animals probably made their way through the river systems and marshes of Doggerland. There was a substantial land-bridge until about 3000 years after the glaciation ended in Britain – ample time for our climate to have favoured their return. Even if those rivers were never completely joined, it is very likely that their winter floodwaters overflowed into a common flood-plain. One way or another, most of our freshwater plants and animals could have become established long before the sea cut off our lakes and rivers from the freshwater systems of continental Europe.

By the time the New Stone Age man arrived by boat from Europe across the North Sea and the Channel, the freshwater lakes and rivers of the newly formed British Isles were well-established features of the landscape. All traces of the ice-sheet had long since gone, but in the spring of each year the rivers of the mountainous regions re-enacted the drama of that first long thaw. Today, if you go to the Highlands at the end of the winter, you can witness the same rush of melt-waters from the glacial corrie lakes on their urgent course down towards the sea: first a persistent, bubbling burn, and then, as it gathers the momentum of early spring, a foaming torrent. The River Spey is such a river. It has the second largest catchment in Scotland, carrying the winter's accumulation of snow down from much of the Grampian and Cairngorm mountains where, most years, snow will lie in gullies all year round. The Spey is renowned for its salmon which, because of the copious melt-waters, are able to 'run' unheeded into the river throughout the year. As they ascend to spawn, there are no natural barriers to impede their passage, nor any man-made obstacles to hinder them until they reach the very headwaters. The waters are almost as pure as the time when they first cut the course of the river to the sea. For the salmon that battle against the flow, the River Spey retains its pristine character.

As it descends to the valleys, the river slows its pace – giving freshwater life a chance to gain a foothold. In the winter the River Feshie, a tributary of the Spey, abounds in the larval stages of many insects, which in spring and early summer will emerge as winged adults.

In the steep headwaters of the Spey's Highland birthplace, only tenacious creatures such as the larvae of stoneflies and mayflies can survive. As the river drops into Strath Spey, its current slows and more animals can get a foothold. Other insect larvae appear, together with small crustaceans and molluscs – all of which are food for the dipper, that denizen of the mountain stream. This short-tailed, chunky little bird is ideally shaped to walk under the clear water in search of mayfly nymphs and other creatures that cling to the stones on the bed of the river. If you watch a dipper at work, you will not fail to be entertained and impressed by the industrious way it flies to the downstream limit of its long, narrow territory to work its way up against the current, pausing and bobbing on the rocks before fearlessly plunging into the icy water to walk upstream, turning over pebbles in search of its next meal for itself or its young. Here, in the fast-moving upland stream, the dipper is in its element.

Three hundred and fifty miles to the south, another stream, the Little Avon, starts its brief journey to the sea by way of the River Severn. Like the headstream of the Spey, it too abounds with dippers, but the two streams have little else in common. The Little Avon not only runs over soft, calcareous rocks that are rich in nutrients, but it flows through a landscape which is wooded by deciduous trees. Not only does the water itself generate plant life but it also receives regular enrichment by way of leaves which fall into the stream. Such leaves are not particularly nutritious to animals, because of their high cellulose content; but once decomposed in these warmer, southern waters by the hordes of bacteria and fungi that abound throughout the year, they release nutrients that turn the clear spring waters of this lowland stream into a bustling waterway that teems with plant and animal life. Such is the contrast between north and south, between the streams that flow from the time-worn Highlands

The flattened body and legs of the mayfly larva enable it to hug the surface of the stones on the river bed, avoiding the full force of the current. Scuttling crab-like across the stones, they rasp off algae and plant fragments until the spring, when the adults emerge above the water to lead their ephemeral lives – often as brief as a few hours.

and those that spring from the newer, unscathed chalklands of the south.

The headwaters of the Little Avon start as a number of almost imperceptible trickles that need to unite before you can detect that there is a river in the making. Even the schoolboy with his jam-jar would pass them over as an unpromising hunting ground. But hiding in the tufts of moss and under the algae-covered stones is a profusion of small freshwater creatures – not only many of those which are typical of the upland Spey but also many others which find life attractive in this rich, shallow water. Many of the insect larvae which overwinter here take advantage of the fresh fall of leaves which, each autumn, add to the detritus trapped by the mud and stones. The larvae of caddis-flies are masters in the art of shredding leaves – both as food and as material for making the tubular cases in which many of them spend their juvenile lives. When they emerge as winged adults in the summer, the caddis-flies are rather moth-like in appearance and are known to anglers as 'sedges'. Like moths, they are mostly nocturnal and sustain their brief adult lives by drinking nectar and other plant fluids. Their aquatic larval stages are, on the other hand, voracious eaters and go to great lengths to capture their food. Those that do not spend their time dragging their cases over the bed of the stream in search of leaves and other rotting vegetation, spin silken nets to catch passing morsels. Many caddis species have evolved ingenious devices for filtering out their food from the running fresh water. To prevent themselves from being swept along by the current, many of the species build their cases of small stones and sand grains which, like ballast, help to keep their station. With their cases adorned with fragments of the river-bed and sporting strange contraptions to trap their passing meals, the caddis larvae constitute a bizarre assortment of creatures. Their name comes from the 'caddis man', the traditional pedlar who wandered the countryside with his clothes decorated with samples of his wares.

For the caddis larva, the ornate case is not intended as an advertisement – it is essential for protection and disguise. Patrolling these shallow waters are small fish with an appetite for the larvae of caddis-flies and mayflies. The stone loach and bullhead are typical of stony streams and are found in both upland and lowland streams. The smallest of our freshwater fish is the three-spined stickleback, a hardy little creature which is found in almost every type of stream and ditch – even those too polluted for other species. Together with the minnow, the stickleback is a favourite prey for the kingfisher, whose flashing beauty you might be lucky enough to see on most unpolluted streams in England, Wales and Ireland – rarely, though, in Scotland. Darting a few feet above the surface of the stream, the kingfisher patrols its patch. From a favoured perch it plunges headlong into the water in pursuit of bullheads and minnows that venture into view. The large, dagger-shaped bill of the bird grasps its victim which it carries, with powerful underwater beating of its wings, back to its perch. There, it stuns it and swallows it head first, to smooth the passage of the scales. In a few brief moments the last link is completed in a natural chain that converts the productivity of the leaf-litter and algal growth on the bed of the stream into the savage beauty of this spectacular bird of our lowland rivers.

Left Lowland streams support a wide range of caddisfly larvae, many of which construct protective cases of stones, shells or plant fragments – as armour and camouflage.
Above The kingfisher – jewelled fisherman of the stream – emerges with its catch.

The River Spey runs for much of its length over a wide, flat bed of shingle. It is here that the introduced blue lupin has become one of the famous sights of Speyside. Here as the river becomes broader and shallower, its current slows down. Much of the silt carried down from the mountain course is deposited on its bed. Now for the first time, plants can take root. Sedges are the most common but occasionally, where more nutrients are trapped, you will find phragmites reed beginning to form beds of taller vegetation. In more marshy areas are water avens, marsh cinquefoil and the northern marsh-orchid – a splash of colour creeping into the clear waters of the Spey. The river now meanders sluggishly over a wide, marshy flood-plain of the Insh marshes until, just after it is joined by the River Tromie, it reaches Loch Insh – an area which abounds in wildfowl and pike-infested pools. This large, shallow lake was once deeper and much more extensive. Like most of the lochs of Scotland, it was shaped by the Ice Age but during the subsequent 10,000 years the silt and vegetation have accumulated around its margins and gradually encroached towards the deeper water. Loch Insh and the Insh marshes are classic examples of the natural, pernicious process of 'succession' which eventually transforms all open fresh water to dry land. It is in this respect that so many of our lakes, borne of the Ice Age, are merely temporary features of our landscape – doomed to be taken over by the plant life they support.

THE DOOMED LAKE

All lakes are doomed to become dry land. Silt washed into the lake basin is trapped by the vegetation. As sediment accumulates, the water becomes shallower and different sets of plants move in, taking advantage of the new conditions. Each in turn will be ousted by another wave of vegetation adapted to even shallower water.

A lake such as this one in East Anglia can be seen as a series of different types of vegetation that advance across the open water until the edges meet and the lake finally disappears. Left to itself, the reed swamp will eventually become woodland; managed by man it can however be sustained as fen.

From the edge of any lowland lake you can see the various stages in the natural succession from open water to dry land.

In deeper water, where light cannot penetrate and where plants are therefore not able to grow rooted in the bottom of the lake, the characteristic plant species are those which float. Frogbit (1) has curious three-petalled flowers and small, lily-like leaves connected by floating stems to the roots. The water-soldier has similar three-petalled flowers but has leaves which for part of the year protrude from the surface of the water. In winter this plant sinks beneath the surface, where it is protected from the cold.

In shallower water, plants can root themselves in the rich sediment at the bottom of the lake but can still reach up through the murky water to the light at the surface. The yellow water-lily (2) has creeping stems which spread rapidly through the mud and at intervals send up long stalks with floating leaves and flowers. These leaves may cover large areas of the lake and are favoured as sites for resting or egg-laying by dragonflies and damselflies.

In even shallower areas, light can penetrate almost to the bed of the lake. Here you will find plants with submerged leaves. Many of these – such as the water-violet (3) – are pollinated by insects, so their flowers must break through the surface before opening. The mass of leaves beneath the surface traps sediment and accelerates the build-up of the bed of the lake.

In the very shallow water at the edge of the lake grow plants which are rooted in the sediment but which have leaves in the air. There are many species of this kind, but the two which usually appear first are the true bulrush (4) and the reed-mace. Accumulation of more sediment and dead leaves in this narrow zone soon raises the bed of the lake above the water to form the first land – albeit marshy in character.

Once the accumulating sediment almost reaches the surface of the water, the common reed (5) takes over. This plant can form huge areas of reed swamp – home to a unique community of animals such as bitterns, bearded tits and reed warblers. Regular cutting of the reed for thatching stops the build-up of plant remains – so preventing other plants from becoming established on the edge of the lake. In this way man has often interrupted the natural succession to dry land.

Left to itself the reed swamp dries out and sedges (6) begin to take a hold. The reeds are ousted and the mat of tough sedge leaves raises the ground-level until it becomes dry land.

Either on the tops of the sedge tussocks or on the dry ground behind them, seeds of trees can germinate. Alder (7) and willow are invariably the first to become established, soon forming the very characteristic woodland called 'alder-carr'. In time this, too, will be replaced by other species of tree, creating a woodland landscape that completely disguises its origin as a lake.

The variety of plants in northern marshes such as those at Loch Insh is restricted by the low nutrient content of the water. Just as most northern lakes have a character quite distinct from those of the south, so a northern fen can be distinguished from its southern counterpart by the nature of the vegetation that is found there. What they have in common is peat. In southern Britain, ground-water is rich in minerals and slightly alkaline. Characteristically, fens and swamps are dominated by sedges and reeds. Those in East Anglia form a very distinctive region over much of Lincolnshire and Cambridgeshire, which neighbours the Wash. Here the ice-sheet left a great area of tills and gravels which are still the major source of building ballast for Peterborough and other towns and cities of East Anglia. The four great rivers Witham, Welland, Nene and Ouse all once drained the basin left after the Ice Age to the east of the present-day Wash. They were tributaries of the Rhine, which, as we have seen, flowed northwards towards the depleted North Sea of that time. It is thought that in the immediate period after the Ice Age, the fenlands were created as a series of peat-forming marshes – probably very like today's northern marshes such as those at Loch Insh. As the North Sea rose towards its present level, the four great East Anglian rivers were separated from the Rhine – their own freshwater fauna intact. Their flow then slowed down even more, creating great inland areas of swamp and fen.

Except for a few fragments – preserved by design or accident – the natural fenlands of England have ceased to exist. What was once wet wilderness has, over the years, been drained to create the most extensive and fertile area of arable land in Britain. Starting with the Romans but gaining momentum through the Middle Ages, this ambitious plan for the Fens culminated in the great schemes of the eighteenth and nineteenth centuries. There are, however, relics of the natural fen preserved like oases of wetland in the desert of our modern agricultural landscape. Wicken and Woodwalton Fens are two such places – tiny remnants of the watery wilderness that once characterised this region – refuges for the freshwater plants and animals that once abounded in the vast wilderness. Here was an almost impenetrable jungle of reeds and sedges which provided a perfect refuge and feeding ground for marshland birds such as the elusive bittern and water-rail. Today there are places in East Anglia where you can still hear the booming cry of the bittern as it calls across the fen. In the phragmites reed-beds the great crested grebe moors its floating nest of water-weeds and on the stems above, the reed warbler weaves its intricate nest, often the unwitting host to the cuckoo's egg. Flitting among the reed heads are the secretive bearded tits, their long tails streaming out behind, giving them the appearance of miniature pheasants. Above the reed-beds, the marsh harrier quarters the fen in search of frogs and the other small creatures that make their home in this watery jungle. The marsh harrier is now one of our rarest birds but there was a time when its leisurely flight across the vast stretches of fenland must have been a common sight for our ancestors. So, too, were the colourful and often large butterflies and dragonflies that cruise among the reeds – species such as the swallowtail, our largest butterfly, and the British

Dragonfly adults live through the summer for several weeks. The males establish territories where they mate with passing females which they may defend until egg-laying is complete.

49

race of the large copper, now extinct. The big hawker dragonflies often have a wingspan of four inches, of which the emperor dragonfly is rightly king of the fenland, patrolling over the water at speeds of nearly twenty miles an hour. Even the biggest British spider makes its home here: poised watchfully on a floating leaf is the great raft spider, the female of which has a body nearly an inch long. Here, in the pockets of fenland that remain at Wicken and Woodwalton and in the reed-beds of broads and meres such as Hickling and Leighton Moss, you can discover a watery world of plants and animals that was once common over the eastern lowlands of England – a true paradise lost. But left to itself in a stable climate a fen is naturally doomed. In time the reed-beds become clogged by the luxurious vegetation and, as the peat accumulates, the open fen is colonised by shrubs and trees – a process that must have happened over

Above The water-rail is a secretive bird of the reed beds; often the only clue to its presence is its pig-like squealing.
Right Great crested grebes favour open stretches of water to perform their spring ritual courtship. The surrounding reed beds often offer seclusion in which to raise their young.

much of this part of England before man started draining the fens to make a different kind of dry land. Whether of its own making or at the hand of man, the freshwater paradise of our southern fenland, created after the ice, was always destined to vanish into history.

If you walk along the banks of the Tees downstream towards the market town of Croft, you will leave behind the ebullience of the young river. From this point, as it flows towards the sea, the Tees adopts the more mature character of a lowland river. It meanders across wider valleys and lingers in generous curves and ox-bow bends. For many rivers, this process of slowing down has been accentuated by the rising sea-level, which has progressively reduced the fall from source to mouth. The River Tees rises at Cross Fell, high up in the Pennines, and flows to the North Sea over a varied course of about 100 miles. At the Yorkshire town of Croft, some 100 feet above sea-level but still forty-five miles from its mouth, the river changes its character. It flows over a great clay plain laid down during the Ice Age and, although still fairly rapid because of the heavy rainfall on the Pennines, follows a meandering course. The nature of the river is also influenced by the addition of its large tributary, the River Skerne, which flows over more calcareous soils and is more heavily polluted than the upper Tees. Not only is the water enriched by the fertilisers from the farmland but also by the sewage from towns that have developed over the centuries along its banks. It has not been just a recent effect; ever since people first built settlements on the Tees, the river has been profoundly changed by their activities – whether simply by the lime spread on the fields which leached into the rivers, or by the more complicated chemical effect of urban and agricultural effluent. Although, compared with the Spey, the water of the Tees contains much more of the nutrients required for plant growth, there are very few species which can take advantage of it – notably blanket weed and 'sewage fungus'. The latter is a reddish-brown bacteria and its rapid growth in the waters of sewage outfalls drastically reduces the oxygen content of the waters downstream, to such a degree that only a few invertebrate creatures can survive. In more recent years, far less untreated sewage has escaped into the river and anglers report that the brown trout as well as coarse fish such as chub, dace and perch are flourishing. As the Tees approaches Middlesbrough, the effects of industrial pollution become more intense and, one by one, the plant and animal species disappear from the river scene. In a pristine river, the unpolluted fresh water would mingle with the salt of the sea to create the estuary conditions which we will explore in a later chapter. Many estuaries and river mouths have been radically changed by the hand of man – and for wildlife the effects have been catastrophic. The Tees is now typical of most of the larger rivers in Britain, in that its final stretch is effectively devoid of wildlife and acts as a barrier that cuts off the life of the upper reaches from the sea. The Tees, like the majority of rivers in Britain, once spawned its own salmon – but no longer.

It is left to Ireland to recall how the larger of our southern rivers once naturally ended their journey. Not only is the Shannon the longest river in the

TALES OF THE RIVERBANK

A quiet tributary of the Thames in early summer provides a sample of the delightful wildlife of the riverbank.

One of our most charming aquatic mammals, the water vole dives and swims as effectively as any otter. You may see it plunging underwater in slow-moving streams (the rat, for which it is often mistaken, swims at the surface).

Lurking on the flower of the yellow flag, a large orb web spider may capture damselflies as they alight briefly in their own search for insect prey. The very beautiful *Calopteryx splendens* males have metallic-blue colours vividly displayed during courtship flights around their breeding territories.

Some of the water vole's tunnel entrances are close to or below the waterline, among the sedges, pond-weeds and roots of river-bank willow trees.

The water vole feeds on grass and weeds, often closely 'mowing' vegetation around the entrance holes to its tunnels in the banks.

As the water voles emerge from the streams they may pause to wash their faces or disappear into one of their narrow burrow entrances. As they struggle through the restricted opening they squeeze surplus water from their fur to help keep them dry in their sleeping and breeding chambers. Two to four litters of up to six young are produced each year in a nest lined with grasses.

The mute swan, romantic symbol of fresh water, has recently suffered the rigours of man's disturbance and pollution: but the clock can be turned back and the river once more allowed to run sweetly to the sea.

British Isles but it is also one of the least polluted – possibly the longest unpolluted river in Europe. Because of its extreme westerly situation, the Shannon does not have the diversity of freshwater life that is found in many other European rivers but its inhabitants enjoy almost pristine conditions. After leaving the Leitrim hills, the river flows lazily southwards across the great central plain of Ireland. In winter it frequently floods out over the surrounding countryside that backs on to the vast boglands to the south of the river – a reminder of the extent of the freshwater lakes that must have been left after the Ice Age. Then, after passing through Lough Derg, the Shannon drops rapidly to sea-level at Limerick and swings westwards into its fifty-mile-long estuary – its final link with the Atlantic Ocean. It is here that, each summer, the salmon gather to start their run up the river – a pilgrimage to their place of birth, to spawn another generation. This annual event must have taken place ever since the Shannon re-emerged from the grip of the ice and took on the course it now follows to the sea. Over those 10,000 years the river has shaped much of Ireland's landscape and has been the main highway for many of the plants and animals – including man – which colonised it. Like an artery, the river brought back the lifeblood of the land. Throughout the British Isles, from the south where life first returned, to the Highlands of Scotland where the Ice Age has still not completely disappeared, our rivers tell a story which spans the whole of that natural history. As the salmon sets off on its course upstream against the current, it is retracing the story of our landscape and its wildlife from the seas that have given our islands their special character, back to the ancient mountains that give birth to the rivers themselves.

CHAPTER THREE
BENEATH THE GREENWOOD

Everyone has a favourite piece of woodland. It may be a whole forest or just a single tree but to each of us these wooded corners of the countryside have an attraction that appeals to our inner being. There is a compulsion to return, if only once a year; it is almost a ritual visit, for reassurance. In late autumn these feelings are enhanced by the smell of damp earth and the warm colours of the leaves that cling on as vestiges of summer. There is a stillness which prompts reverence and a timelessness that underlines the antiquity of the landscape.

Such instinctive feelings belie the real nature of our forests and woodlands. Far from being remnants of wilderness, the tree-scapes of the British Isles are for the most part man-made. Their story is, however, one that spans not only the 5000 years of human history on these islands, but also the previous 5000 years, before the men of the New Stone Age first took a hand in the making of the greenwood of Britain.

Woodland is the natural vegetation of the British Isles; left to itself, most of our countryside would be covered in it, almost to the top of every mountain. Yet today, Britain and Ireland, together with Holland, are the least wooded countries in Europe, and have been so for hundreds of years. The history of our woodlands is a complex story in which the main influences have been climate, the soil and the shape of the land but, above all, it has been a story of the relationship between trees and ourselves. It touches on all the phases in our social history – it is inextricably bound up with the fortunes of the hundred or so generations of people that came before us. In our woodlands can be charted the progress of civilisation in this corner of Europe: the coming of the New Stone Age to Britain, the flooding of the dry channel between here and the Continent, the Bronze Age, the iron-age Celts, the Roman invasion and then the Anglo-Saxons, the Normans and the Royal Forests, the Middle Ages, the Tudors and royal patronage, the Enclosures, the Industrial Revolution and two world wars. These are all familiar landmarks in our own history; they are also the turning points in the natural history of our woodlands. The story of woodland is essentially about the fabric of the forest – the trees themselves.

After a hesitant start, the climate of post-glacial Britain improved quite rapidly; over a few hundred years average temperatures rose several degrees and temperate conditions had returned to southern England by 9500 years ago. The native species of trees returned across the land-bridge in a series of waves of colonisation – usually starting, as you would expect, in the east and south-east. The first to arrive were those most cold-tolerant of trees, the birches, whose windblown seeds accelerated the colonisation of the tundra-like land which may well have looked similar to parts of Greenland today. It is possible that birches, certainly the hardy dwarf birch, had survived in the far south of England throughout the last glaciation, together with dwarf willow and perhaps even juniper. You can still find relic pockets of these species growing around the high moorland bogs of Scotland, a scene very similar to that which would have prevailed over much of the south of Britain 10,000 years ago. Of our other two native birches, the downy birch still favours the damp conditions of the Scottish Highlands and some of our southern heaths, suggesting that it was also one of the early colonisers.

It was probably a mix of birches and Scots pine that soon characterised much of lowland Britain and Ireland. Nine and a half thousand years ago there was a dramatic expansion of Scots pine from Europe that soon swept north. Aspen and rowan had by now joined the birches; these are all relatively short-lived species needing light and do not survive well under the shade of taller trees. Except in the far north of the advancing forest, these pioneer species gave way to the invading pines. Hazel was also becoming widespread and it is thought that it grew then in a tall tree-form, rather than the short, multi-stemmed

The short life and the prolific seed production of birches make them ideal colonisers of open ground. Their winged seeds were borne on the wind as the forests moved northwards across the tundra. The birches were the pioneer trees.

shrub that is common in today's broad-leaved woodlands. You can still find traces of these tree-style hazels in woods in Essex as well as on the other side of the North Sea in Denmark – from where the hazel presumably came. But it was the pine that dominated the landscape. From pollen analysis, we know that it reached East Anglia 9000 years ago and that it had invaded most of England 500 years later. By 8000 years ago, it had covered most of Wales and was well established in Ireland. Between eight and seven thousand years ago, the pine reached the Highlands of Scotland, which has today become its stronghold in Britain, where it is at the most westerly limit of its European range. Although it thrives all over England, often as an introduced feature of the landscape, it is in the Scottish Highlands that it is seen in its true glory. Here, the craggy qualities of this noble tree match the wildness of the northern land. Beneath the Cairngorms, at Beinn Eighe on the west coast and in such romantic outposts as Glen Strathfarrar, the Black Wood of Rannoch and Glen Affric, you can explore the last relics of the Great Wood of Caledon. This vast, natural forest once covered 3 million acres of Scotland – the most impressive tract of primeval pine forest that the British Isles have known.

As climatic conditions improved, the Scots pine joined the birches to create the first wildwood – remnants of which survive today in the Highlands of Scotland – such as here at the Black Wood of Rannoch.

PINEWOOD PIONEERS

The majestic Scots pine was the dominant tree of the first wildwood to appear in the British Isles after the ice retreated. The tough, leathery needles and woody cones of this tree would seem unattractive to woodland creatures. However, a specialised community of animals has moved northwards with the pioneering pine trees.

Crossbills are almost totally dependent on the Scots pine. Their crossed bill is an adaptation for twisting open the scales of its cones to extract the nutritious seeds. The red squirrel's gnawed pine cones can be commonly found on the forest floor and look quite distinct from those discarded by crossbills.

The caterpillars of the pine beauty moth feed on pine needles. The three creamy-white stripes which run along their green bodies help camouflage them in the long, thin pine needles.

The crested tit's thin bills allow them to reach into the needles to feed on insects such as pine beauty caterpillars.

Pine martens, originally widespread in various types of woodland, are now restricted to inaccessible parts of Scotland. Their diet seems to be mainly ground-living creatures such as short-tailed voles.

A large relative of the grouse, the capercaillie became extinct throughout the British Isles in the mid-eighteenth century. The present population in Scotland are the descendants of birds which were reintroduced from Sweden in 1837.

Although the terrain of the Highlands is quite different from that in the south of Britain, we can form an impression of that early pioneering pinewood. As in Glen Affric, there would have been a mixture of pine and birch, with the pine taking over in places with less favourable conditions. In Scotland today, the pure pinewoods are found principally in Deeside and Speyside, and in valleys of the Great Glen where the climate is less influenced by the Atlantic and is more continental in character. Elsewhere, particularly on better soils, the pine shares the tree-scape with birch and oaks. Sometimes you will find an occasional ash tree but it is the alder which more frequently replaces the pine on moist ground such as river-banks, where it grows alongside willow and rowan. It is the delicate rowan tree which, more than any other species, is the characteristic companion tree to the pine and birch of these ancient pinewoods. It graces the forest as individual trees or as groups in clearings. In the underwood it grows as shrubs alongside the juniper and sometimes the holly and hazel. But where the pine dominates the woodland, its needles form a thick carpet on the forest floor, stifling the establishment of all but a very specialised selection of ground plants. Heather, cowberry and bilberry manage to gain a foothold but these pine forests are not noted for a large number of herbaceous flowering plants. A few orchids are exceptions, of which the creeping lady's-tresses is a fine example of the special nature of pinewood flora. It grows among the deep layers of rotting pine needles and moss, and spreads by underground rhizomes which creep through the soil. Its pale spike of flowers is pollinated by bumble-bees – also pioneers of cold terrain. Other inhabitants of the needle-litter include the wintergreens and the lesser twayblade, but perhaps the most striking is the plant that even Linnaeus called his favourite – the twinflower. It is a small evergreen shrub that forms dense patches in the pinewood. In June and July, pink, bell-shaped flowers hang from the plants, bringing splashes of delicate colour to the sombre forest floor.

The first forest of majestic Scots pines and birches would have been home to woodland mammals such as red and roe deer, wolves and brown bears, lynx and wild cat, pine martens and red squirrels, and to predatory birds such as buzzard, goshawk, sparrowhawk and the long-eared owl. As well as the capercaillie, there would have been smaller seed- and insect-eating birds such as crossbills, crested tits and coal tits, and the ubiquitous chaffinch. But compared with the fruits and seeds of other trees, the cones of the pine provide food for only a handful of specialist forest dwellers, and the needles themselves are about the least succulent of nature's inventions. For most other woodland birds and mammals, for the herbs and grasses of the woodland floor and, of course, for the mighty world of insects, the arrival of the oaks and our other native broad-leaved trees must have been of paramount importance. Interestingly, a few high, cold corners of the Scottish Highlands and much of the fiord-like west coastline of Scotland were not colonised by Scots pine until the time when the Romans landed in the south. But in most of lowland Britain and Ireland, the once widespread pine forests had long since given way to the new wave of tree invaders.

Once a common predator of the wildwood, the native wild cat, *Felis sylvestris*, has been banished by persecution to remote corners of the Highlands.

Jays are notorious for carrying acorns far afield and obligingly burying them in the soil, far away from the parent tree. Many of these oak seeds are rediscovered as they sprout and are eagerly eaten by the jays; but many others survive to form a nursery of infant oaks. Other species of tree have seeds which are carried by the wind or by birds and mammals in their stomachs or on their feet, and in their feathers and fur. The earliest arrivals of our broad-leaved deciduous forest probably grew from seeds transported in this way, forming outposts of the forests in the warmer south. Because of their different methods of dispersal, the tree species returned to Britain at different times and at different rates of progress. It is considered that an average migration rate of fifty to a hundred yards a year is fast work for a tree, so we can guess how long some species took to establish themselves as residents. The various parts of Britain and Ireland were colonised at different times and by a different mix of tree species. This must have given a very varied character to the developing 'wildwood' of the British Isles – much of which would have been quite unlike any ancient woodland that survives today. It was later, as the climate changed again, that a more familiar forest pattern was created – one that has analogies in our contemporary tree-scape. Sadly, in a way, there are very few of our present tree-scapes which we can look at with confidence to discover the nature

Acorns and other seeds are buried by jays as a cache to supplement their winter diet. Many remain undiscovered and germinate the following spring to start another generation of oak trees.

of the wildwood of our land at a time before 5000 years ago. From the pollen profile, we can make a hazy map of where and when the main tree invasions occurred. From our knowledge of how they grow today, we can perhaps conjure some impression of how the wildwood might have looked.

Hazel, wych-elm, oak and alder all spread quite quickly throughout Britain, except for the very north of Scotland. They probably arrived in most parts in that order and all of them seem to have reached Ireland just before it was cut off from Britain. The earliest pollen datings establish the oak back in Britain 9500 years ago. Five hundred years later it had spread to a line running from the mouth of the River Shannon in Ireland to the Wash. Considering that an oak spreads itself by the heavy acorn – helped admittedly by the hungry jay or squirrel – such a rapid spread northwards is extraordinary. Five hundred years later, the oak was north of the Pennines and in a further 500 years, that is by 8000 years ago, it had begun to establish itself in the Scottish Highlands.

Following the oak, most of the other broad-leaved trees familiar to us today as 'native' species arrived in Britain. Notable was the lime which, although it scarcely reached north beyond the Lake District and never into Ireland, was an important member of the wildwood. Though comparatively rare now, it can still be found over much of its earlier range, particularly in parts of Essex and

East Anglia, in the north in Derbyshire and in the south in Hampshire and Wiltshire – all places with woods which are almost certainly fragmented relics of the wildwood. Mixed with oak, elm and hazel, the lime had become well established by 7000 years ago and would have been a conspicuous tree in much of the lowlands of the south and east. It was at about this time that our climate entered a new phase of weather – perhaps prompted by the final flooding of the land-bridge. From the dry and warm climate that had developed since the Ice Age, these newly isolated islands entered a warm but wetter phase, with average temperatures two to three degrees Celsius warmer than now, which lasted for over 2000 years. Birds like the nightingale, which today are at the most northern limit of their European range, must have been common in the broad-leaved wildwood of Britain, their spring song bubbling from the lush foliage that now dominated all but the highest and wettest parts of the British Isles. This appropriately named 'Atlantic Period' brought a long era of stability to our forests and their wildlife.

The very term 'wildwood' conjures up primeval images of giant trees with long, unbranching trunks that support a massive leaf canopy towering towards the sky. On the forest floor lie large, rotting trunks where they have long since fallen through old age, creating sunlit glades in which woodland herbs and grasses bloom alongside the seedlings of another generation of majestic trees. Sadly, the evidence is so incomplete that we must question this romantic notion, but recently there have been tantalising clues that it may be very near the truth. Grass pollen, for example, is frequently found in ancient woodland samples, confirming that there were frequent semi-permanent glades which would have attracted deer, wild oxen and other herbivores to graze there. These would have offered a sunlit habitat to the flowers, like willowherb, that we associate today with forest paths and clearings; you can still see this ancient pattern in the mosaic of woodland and glades in the New Forest at places such as Bramshaw Wood. Certainly, the massive 'bog oaks' dug up from the peat of Fen country, with their trunks measuring nearly seventy feet to the first branches, suggest that giant forests did exist here at that time. Of one fact we can be certain: the primeval wildwood covered two-thirds of the British Isles – which made our land one of the most wooded in Europe. Such is the contrast with today.

While we now have very little forest, that which remains is extremely varied and constantly changing. Nearly all of our surviving areas of woodland have been managed by man at some time, but many of these are certainly modified relics of the ancient forest. The list of relic woods is as varied in its geographical spread as it is in the differing character of the woodlands it includes. There are the pinewoods of the central Highlands of Scotland, the hazel woods of the Burren in County Clare, and the oak and birchwoods by Loch Maree in the north-western Highlands and around the Killarney Lakes in south-west Ireland. These are all examples of quite large tracts of forest that may be directly descended from the ancient wildwood. The dwarfed oaks of Dizzard Point in

The oak woods of south-west England and Ireland are a reminder of the warm, wet Atlantic period during which our deciduous woodlands flourished.

In the wildwood there were natural clearings grazed by red deer and other herbivores. Today's New Forest has glades which echo this ancient mosaic of dense woodland and grassy clearings.

Cornwall and those of Tycanol Wood near the exposed Atlantic coast of Dyfed are probably two smaller vestiges of that mixed wildwood that stretched almost unbroken across the breadth of Britain. There must be many others disguised in the tapestry of our varied modern tree-scape.

Today, if you travel up the Wye Valley towards Tintern Abbey and look across the deep gorge cut over the millennia by the flow of the river, you will see on its steep slopes an ancient woodland that in general tree composition, if not in structure, is perhaps close to the wildwood. It contains more than sixty species of tree and shrub – all in natural groupings. There are stands of the rare native large-leaved lime and, beside them, you will discover wych-elm, field maple and even the wild service-tree – a sure indicator of ancient forest. Although they have been managed as coppice for centuries and contain few really large trees, these woods have a continuous link with the wildwood. If you glance further up the valley beyond Tintern, you will see the uniformity of modern conifer plantations, growing side by side with these relics of the prehistoric forest. In one sweep, your eyes take in 5000 years of woodland history.

Most plants of the forest floor such as dog's mercury grow and flower early in the spring to avoid being shaded by the dense canopy of leaves that shuts out the light later in the season

It is difficult to tell when stone-age people made any real impact on the wildwood – or even when they first arrived from the Continent. There had been previous wandering tribes of hunters ever since the ice had released its grip on the land but perhaps most of these nomadic people moved on when the great pine forest made its way north. It was not until the arrival of the people of the New Stone Age five or six thousand years ago that the native forests of Britain began to be transformed by any influence other than time and climate. These neolithic people from Europe were small in stature – no more than five and a half feet tall. Theirs was a culture that had spilled over from the Mediterranean and the Nile valley, where for thousands of years civilised people had intelligently exploited the natural riches of the world. The new tribes who came to land on our shores were no longer mere hunters of game and gatherers of fruits of the forest; they were farmers to whom the trees of the wildwood were not only building material for their homes and fuel for their fires but, more importantly, obstacles that had to be removed to create more grazing for their cattle and tillage for their crops. As the pioneering population established a more settled way of life, the wildwood of the British Isles came increasingly under the axe.

The felling of trees by axes of flint or sharpened stone must also have been aided by burning and by the stripping of bark from around the tree – and the clearings enlarged and maintained by the browsing and rooting about of cattle and pigs. For the cattle, the foliage of trees such as elm was a source of food as important as the grass. The so-called Bronze Age with its new technology of metal took some time to reach Britain but when it did, around 4000 years ago, the use of bronze for tools and weapons flourished for about 1500 years. The Atlantic Period in our climate had come to an end and had been replaced by warm but drier conditions, rather more continental in character. It was after this dry spell that the beech which flourishes in more humid conditions expanded its range throughout southern Britain. It spread rapidly into south-west England and even into Wales, where today there is a relic beechwood surviving at Cwm Clydach in the Brecon Beacons National Park. In other places in southern England the beech continues to thrive, particularly on the drier chalky or gravelly uplands, where it has often become the dominant tree; but many of the majestic beechwoods we see today have been planted on chalkland in very recent times and are not descendants of those established here naturally in the Bronze Age and early Iron Age.

It was the Celts who introduced iron to Britain. Arriving about 2500 years ago, these practical farmers brought with them the iron tools and heavy ploughs which were able to tackle dense forest and heavy clay soils. During the Iron Age, huge areas of southern England were cultivated by these industrious people. The population of Britain rose dramatically as communities, such as many crannog lake-dwellings in Scottish lochs, sprang up in hitherto virgin corners of the British Isles. When the Romans arrived, Britain was no longer a wilderness land. During the next 400 years the Romans, with their wheeled furrow-turning ploughs, transformed the existing arable land into highly productive fields of corn and other crops reminiscent of the Romans' more southern homelands. Their impact on the face of the countryside was not restricted to the light soils around their great villas and camps but extended

Above Millipedes abound on the forest floor and play an important part in the process of returning the nutrients in leaf litter to the soil – thereby sustaining the growth of the forest.
Right The enlarged jaws of our largest beetle, the stag beetle, are used like the antlers of deer to wrestle with rival males. Its larvae live inconspicuously burrowed in rotting wood.

into the heavy soils of Essex and Suffolk and into the difficult terrain of the Fens. Even the heavily wooded areas to the north and west of London came under their expansionist policies. The timber was needed for their ambitious civil and military building and as fuel for working metals and firing pottery and bricks.

The Romans withdrew to their more southern territory just as the British weather became less hospitable – perhaps our climate became too much for them! After the legions finally left, the pace of woodland clearance may have slackened for a while but there was probably not the widespread return to scrub and secondary woodland as was once supposed. The Anglo-Saxons were essentially carpenters; they preferred to work with wood rather than stone – their ships and timber-framed buildings are witness to their skills. They, and then the Danes, systematically cleared more and more of the wildwood as they spread northwards, creating tracts of 'woodland pasture' – areas of grazing around tall, mature trees, rather like today's parkland. There would also have been plots of arable crops, but the cooler, wetter climate would have favoured grass more than corn. It was during the Dark Ages – that little-chronicled 500 years after the Romans left – that much of our landscape developed into a changing mosaic of grass and woodlands. The villages that sprang up throughout the country with their Christian churches and parochial economies still have the same names today, many of which give us clues about the woodland around them. Gradually, the grassland expanded at the expense of the forest and by the time William had arrived in 1066, England had become a pastoral land.

The Normans came over from a mainland that was still heavily forested. William's Domesday survey of 1086 revealed the stark reality of the shortage of trees for timber and game. His concept of Royal 'forests' was an attempt to redress the balance but was motivated more by his passion for hunting than his

Left Many of the beeches – which Gilbert White described as 'the loveliest of trees' – were planted for their timber. Nevertheless they now form distinctive woodlands which are an attractive feature of the Chilterns and the Cotswolds.
Above Few animals find the leaves of beech palatable; one of the more bizarre is the larva of the lobster moth.

concern for the lack of trees. It was the Normans who introduced the fallow deer which became the most important beast of the Medieval Chase. The New Forest in Hampshire was a royal preserve of unenclosed country including much woodland, over which the king and his entourage had exclusive rights. Throughout the Middle Ages, many Royal Forests and Chases were established – mainly as a source of winter meat for the wealthy. It is probable that many of these parks enclosed, and thereby protected, some remaining fragments of the wildwood. Slowly, the ravaged woodland began to recover, if only because the strict laws deterred traditional practices. Forest animal life fared less well. Many of our woodland species were already on the brink of extinction, hunted or persecuted by generations of country people for whom the forest had long since been an alien world. To the primeval fear of the darkness beneath the trees had been added centuries of folklore. The land abounded with tales of Little Red Riding Hoods and big bad wolves. Of all our woodland creatures, it was the wolf that suffered most. Old English literature is full of tales of awesome wolves and their fearless hunters; even their month of January, the wolves' vulnerable cubbing time, was called 'Wolfmonat' – the wolf month. From her lair deep in the dark wildwood, the she-wolf would emerge in search of food for her offspring – a winter threat to all who ventured into the forest, or so it seemed. In the north of England and in Scotland, where forests and wolves persisted longer, many place-names still include the word 'spittal' which was traditionally a strongly constructed forest refuge, secure from wolf attack. Even our modern term 'loop-hole' may be linked to the chinks through which the petrified travellers could glimpse the approaching wolf – the 'lupus-hole'. So deeply entrenched was our fear of the wolf, that this magnificent beast of the forest was doomed to perish.

In 1486, a year after the Tudors began their reign, the *Book of St Albans* was published, and in it were given details of a close season for wolf hunting, whereby it was restricted to the winter months of January to March. This suggests that persecution of the wolf was no longer an urgent necessity – simply a popular sport. But this attempt at conservation came too late – and in any case the animal's native home, the forest, had all but disappeared under the woodsman's axe. Here was a classic case of a principle that is still often ignored in today's conservation strategies: conservation of a species is meaningless without conservation of its habitat. There are, however, few people today who would really relish the return of the wolf to our local woodlands and there would have been even fewer devotees in medieval England. Interestingly, the expansion of the monasteries at that time was based on an economy that depended on sheep. Such flocks needed more grazing land and fewer wolves. Paradoxically it may well have been the sheep that finally banished the wolf, as its forest refuge was felled to make way for grass.

Left The greater spotted woodpecker. Trees provide the entire livelihood for this forest bird – it nests in holes excavated in the trunks, it finds its insect food in the bark and it even uses resonant trees to amplify its drumming call in the breeding season.

SEASONS OF
THE WILDWOOD

By the time the flush of new leaves emerges on the elm in spring, the male great tits have moved to the tree-tops to establish song-posts. From here they will spend many hours of each day proclaiming their breeding territory. The nest is built in an existing hole usually high up in the tree trunk, where the birds tend to concentrate their search for insect larvae, especially caterpillars.

The winter woods are relatively quiet with only the resident birds and a few hardy visitors from the north. The great tit acrobatically forages in flocks for insects in the cracks and crevices of the bare branches. It is a day-long search to find enough food to sustain it through long, cold, winter months.

The luxurious growth of lichens and mosses is typical of the wet sessile oakwoods of the west. The great tits work incessantly during the summer months to feed up to a dozen or more young. Their diet is mainly caterpillars, spiders and aphids, plucked from any part of the tree. The abundant insect life is shared by the pied flycatchers, summer visitors to these remote upland woods.

In autumn, as the leaf litter increases beneath the massive beeches of the chalky soils of southern England, the great tit will pick and dab at the decaying vegetation of the woodland floor. There are rich pickings of centipedes, wood-lice, small slugs and insect larvae as well as nutritious beechmast. Beautiful fungi emerge from the autumn debris.

Such was the fate of the ancient wildwood – a gradual but perhaps inevitable loss of identity, a surrendering of its wildness to the might of axe and plough and the grazing of livestock. Where it was clear-felled, arable land or grassland, moor or heathland took its place. Alternatively it was allowed to regenerate either by design or by neglect. Such infant forest would take the form of rambling scrub. In time, since it still had its roots in untilled soil, mature forest would emerge with a character akin to the original wildwood. But once ploughed, such land would seldom revert to woodland with the same rich variety of trees, shrubs, ground vegetation and lichens that was once the hallmark of the original forests. However, our ancestors were not as relentless in their attack on the trees around them as the overall picture might suggest. They depended on the forest for their basic way of life, and were far from witless. They had always left areas of forest around their settlements, to meet their day to day needs for shelter, fuel and wild food. As the shape of our modern countryside and villages emerged during Saxon and Norman times, so these tracts of woodland became incorporated into the more formal pattern of the lowlands.

It is unlikely, though, that such village communities had great need of massive trunks of timber. Once the houses were built, their daily demands would be for thinner poles for making fences and hurdles, handles for tools, spokes for wheels and wattle for walls. Such timber was also ideal for fuelling domestic fires and the charcoal-burner's kiln. Mature trees were reserved for the sweat of the saw-pit, where they were fashioned into structural planks and beams. What was needed was an ever-youthful woodland that would be the inexhaustible provider of domestic-sized timber. The answer was the 'coppice'. All woodsmen knew that most of our broad-leaved trees, when they were cut down near to the ground, would quite naturally regenerate healthy shoots from their stumps. These 'stools' would live almost indefinitely if the wood was regularly harvested; in the formal coppice, this was done in strict rotation – perhaps every ten years or so. Each type of tree in the coppice had its different uses – very little went to waste. It was a very simple but effective way of adapting and modifying the natural cycle of the woodland to provide just what the woodsman wanted – and the trees themselves were endowed with virtual eternity. Each stage of the coppice, from the open ground created by the initial cutting through to the dense shade that developed towards the end of the cycle, encouraged a different set of plant and animal species to flourish – each adapted to the prevailing condition of the coppice habitat. The ground flora, for example, flowers more profusely after the understorey has been cut back, while a few years later, when the stools have regrown to form a dense thicket, song-birds such as the garden warbler, whitethroat and blackcap find the seclusion attractive for building their nests and rearing their young. Such intimate diversity of habitat was probably not a feature of the wildwood; in this respect at least, the woodsman had improved on nature.

In a corner of west Suffolk are the Bradfield Woods – perhaps the most telling examples of how management by man over the centuries has enriched the woodlands of Britain. One of these, Felsham Hall Wood, has an unbroken record of coppicing that goes back to the middle of the thirteenth century and it probably looked very much the same then as it does today. In Bradfield Woods, botanists have recorded more than 350 species of flowering plants, including forty-two native trees and shrubs. Many of these species are indicators of antiquity. As you walk through this ancient coppice, between the standards which are mainly oak, you will find a rich underwood of hazel, ash, birch, lime, maple, crab apple and willow – all of which have a use in the coppice economy. On the floor of the wood, at the feet of the strangely gnarled stools, is a brilliant carpet of flowers and grasses, ferns and fungi, which unfolds its ever-changing splendour as the seasons progress and as the coppice rotation takes its man-made course. Each stage in the cycle has its highlights as different species, both plant and animal, play out the natural rhythms of their woodland way of life. At all times of year the Bradfield Woods are full of wildlife interest and delight; they celebrate a woodland history which, if not strictly 'natural', reaches back 700 years unchanged and, before that, to the wildwood. The traditional coppice may be a far cry from our ancient forest and its wolves, but measured in terms of the variety of wildlife it supports, it is a worthy substitute.

In Tudor England, timber was at a premium – especially the solid English oak. The nefarious civil and military schemes of the Crown created an insatiable demand for woodland products, particularly for iron smelting and for making gunpowder, let alone for Tudor homes and ships. By the time the Stuarts had

Left Primroses flower profusely in woodland that has been recently coppiced.
Right Bluebells thrive in the warm, damp climate of the British Isles. The English bluebell wood is a very characteristic feature of our countryside.

continued the trend into the middle of the seventeenth century, the shortage had become embarrassingly acute. Charles II instigated a survey of the wood-lands of his realm. It fell to John Evelyn to write this forest report, which he titled *Sylva*. In it he pointed to iron smelting as the most extravagant use of forest timber. In 1664, Charles introduced laws which rationed timber, pro-hibiting the use of newly felled trees for domestic buildings. The common man was required to re-use old timber salvaged from shipwrecks or demolished houses. Hence, cottages dating from that time are often found to be supported by beams and lintels that are perhaps 100 or so years older. For the first time in Britain, tree plantations were deliberately established to meet growing demands for timber but it was not enough to slow down the consumption of the more natural woodland. Even the forests of the Lake District fell under the axe; it is said that this part of England is more wooded today than it was in Shakespeare's time – a measure of the success of nineteenth- and twentieth-century replanting schemes.

But the publication of *Sylva* had fired the imagination of major landowners. They began to realise that timber was a renewable resource and, if only motivated by the thought of profits, they intensified their woodland manage-ment and set about planting trees for their heirs to fell. Alongside this woodland renaissance grew the English landscape movement which was, over the next two centuries, to shape much of the countryside, particularly its tree-scapes. William Kent, 'Capability' Brown and, later on, Humphrey Repton were not only good gardeners but wise botanists. In their hands, trees and some other woodland plants and animals had a respite from the general decline that continued to erode the valuable natural forest resources of Britain. It was not until Georgian and Victorian times that the new sources of fuel and building materials took the pressure off timber. If timber was needed in a hurry, it was now cheaper to venture overseas in iron boats and plunder the wildwoods of other people's lands.

During the twentieth century it has been economics rather than our national conscience that has created the new conifer plantations here at home. The First World War hindered imports and in 1919 the Forestry Commission was set up to make Britain more self-sufficient in trees. The fertile land fashioned over the centuries from the ancient broad-leaved forest was, for the most part, left to the farmers; the new woodland plantations were sited on the poorer soils of the uplands – which although once covered with natural forest were by now reduced to moor and heathland. In such places oak, ash, beech and the other traditional broad-leaved trees make slow progress; the favoured trees have been conifers introduced from Europe and North America, mostly spruces which are ideal for pulp. In the British Isles there are now great tracts of conifer forest which, although far from natural, have in their own way restored some woodland cover to our landscape. Today's forester has a different view of the forest than yesterday's woodsman – his job is to grow timber, not wood.

What about the woodland we have now? Can we recognise in the man-made mosaic of our modern countryside any surviving fragments of that ancient wildwood? The experts do not agree with each other and the honest answer is probably 'no'. But this does not acknowledge that all history involves change, and that the natural history of our woodlands has always had its own momentum. Left to itself, the wildwood of 5000 years ago would not have looked the same now – there would simply have been much more of it.

Our land today is admittedly one of the least wooded areas of Europe, but what our woodlands have is variety. From the Highland beauty of Glen Affric and Strathfarrar to the damp oak forests of Killarney, from the classic English oaks of Sherwood, Savernake and Bramshaw to the fine beechwoods of the Chilterns, the Cotswolds and the New Forest, the British Isles are known for their majestic woodlands – each of which has its own special character. So, too, have the countless smaller woods, copses and spinneys, which you can find in every county. Together they add up to an immense diversity – perhaps acre for acre of woodland, these islands now have the greatest variety of trees and forest plants in Europe. For 5000 years our predecessors have consumed, managed and created woodlands in such a way that we have inherited a more varied mix of woodland life than nature might have produced on her own.

No matter how often man has cut down, replanted or otherwise changed the nature of woodlands, he has never really lived in them. We have an inborn fear and respect for the forest world. John Evelyn in his timely book, *Sylva*, observed, 'It is natural for a man to feel an aweful and religious terror when placed in the centre of a thick wood.' Even in today's depleted woodland there is a feeling of ancient wildness. There may no longer be a fear of bears and wolves, but there is still a primeval atmosphere that we revere as wilderness.

CHAPTER FOUR
ISLAND WATERS

Exactly how long ago our land became the Isles of Britain, no one really knows – but had it been too soon after the great thaw, many species of plants and animals might never have reached our shores. As it is, Britain was denied some of the flora and fauna of mainland Europe, and Ireland suffered even greater deprivation. Compared with Britain, the 'Emerald Isle' has only two-thirds the number of species of flowering plants, ferns and mosses, and its fauna has a hundred fewer species of bird, no moles or weasels and only one reptile – the common lizard. That Ireland has no snakes is attributable to the rising sea, rather than St Patrick. The nature of our islands has been governed by the fact that we are surrounded by salt water – without it we would be just another corner of the vast Eurasian land mass. We may lament the absence of some species that failed to become established before we were cut off, but there is one fundamental feature of the British Isles that distinguishes our wildlife from that of the rest of Europe – one that brings to our islands a natural richness and diversity that is the envy of the world. It is the sea itself.

The seas of the world fell some 300 feet as the great polar ice-caps grew during the last glaciation – much of the seabed around Europe was left high and dry. Land-bridges joined north Wales to the east of Ireland, and south-west Scotland to northern Ireland. England was linked to the low countries of Europe by way of Doggerland and to France across the more shallow parts of what is now the English Channel. It would have been very difficult to distinguish the now familiar outline of our land. Gradually, as the seas rose, the British Isles took shape. First Ireland was cut off, perhaps eight or nine thousand years ago as the Irish Sea was created in the place of the great melt-water lake we know as Lake Hibernia. With the final flooding of the last narrow link, probably between Scotland and County Derry, Ireland was cut off from Britain.

To the east of Britain, the North Sea invaded the broad land-bridge that linked England with Holland and Denmark. Year by year it moved further south, drowning more and more of Doggerland. From the south, the salt water of the Atlantic Ocean reached out to form the arm of the English Channel, completely cutting off England from France when the sea had risen less than half-way to its present level. The effects of the rising oceans were felt worldwide; every coastal plain would have been flooded. Though it escaped the rigours of the ice, the Mediterranean also rose. Perhaps at its eastern end, along the 'fertile crescent', the flooding sea devastated the land and forced the cradle of civilisation to take to higher ground. It is not hard to imagine how the biblical story of the Great Flood could have been based on legends passed down from ancestors who had witnessed the slow but persistent rising of the sea.

This gas platform off Grimsby, with its feet resting on the sea-bed a hundred feet below the surface of the North Sea, stands where, 7000 years ago, there was still dry land. This was part of the land-bridge that connected East Anglia with the mainland of Europe; across it came the waves of plant and animal colonisers, including man.

Seven thousand years ago, or thereabouts, the last dry link across Doggerland succumbed to the sea. Rather like the fragile spit of land at Spurn Head on the Yorkshire coast, it was inevitably fated to give way. One day it was still intact, and then, probably after a winter storm, it disappeared almost overnight. Once the North Sea and the English Channel became united, there was no return. Rapidly, the currents would have swept aside the last traces of the land-bridge and the severance of Britain was complete. It had begun its island history.

Compared with the depths of the open ocean, the waters around the British Isles are relatively shallow. Beyond our present coastline, the continental shelf slopes gently to the edge of the Atlantic and Arctic ocean basins, where the seabed falls away steeply to the dark, cold abyss. The English Channel, the Irish Sea and most of the North Sea lie on the continental shelf – much of which would have been exposed or glaciated in the Ice Age. Today, the nearest edges of the shelf are some thirty miles west of Ireland and about seventy-five miles north of the Scottish mainland. The seabed of the continental shelf is largely made up of the vast quantities of finely ground rocks and sediments that over the millennia have been carried out to sea. This process still continues and the waters above the continental shelf are constantly replenished with minerals and other nutrients. It is this combination of shallowness and replenishment that makes the seas around the British Isles some of the richest in the world.

We are in an enviable position. To the north lies the great expanse of cold arctic waters, to the east the temperate waters of the North Sea and to the south and west the warm waters of the Atlantic. From north to south our islands span more than ten degrees of latitude – and at no other point between the equator and the North Pole could we come under the influence of a greater range of maritime conditions; the British Isles lie on the great divide between the arctic and temperate provinces. If we were a few degrees further south or a few degrees to the north, the seas around us would support a much less varied collection of plants and animals.

But we have not always been so well placed. At the peak of the last glacial period, icebergs floated south past Land's End in the chilly waters of the Atlantic. The Gulf Stream came nowhere near our shores – having crossed from the Caribbean, it veered south to moderate the ice-age chill along the coasts of north-west Africa. Even 12,000 years ago, when the ice had gone from most of Britain, the Gulf Stream hardly brushed the coast of Portugal. As the influence of the ice receded north, the Gulf Stream changed its course until it reached the western seaboard of the British Isles. Its effect was very dramatic. The warming effect of water from the tropics not only changed the nature of our western seas but also the climate on land. Much of the British Isles became temperate – wetter and warmer in winter – which was ideal for many of the plants and animal colonists which had arrived from the south. It is thought that this change was quite abrupt and that the breaking of our links with Europe may even have hastened the amelioration of the climate.

The pattern of the currents around our coasts governs the basic nature of the sea, from the minutest plants to the massive shoals of fish which are the basis of the commercial fishing industry. It is surprising how distinct the oceanic water remains from the coastal water of the Channel and the North Sea. They seem hardly to mix at all. Each has its own character, even its own colour: the waters of the Atlantic being deep blue in comparison with the green coastal waters in the Channel and North Sea. Certain species of animal are found to be restricted to one type of water. There are, for example, two main species of the arrow-worm *Sagitta* around our islands. These slender, transparent creatures are about an inch long when adult and are an important part of the diet of many fish. One species is more typical of oceanic water from the Atlantic, while the other is found only in the eastern half of the Channel and the southern part of the North Sea. The divide between the two waters is sometimes so pronounced that a fisheries research vessel out from Plymouth can net one species on the port side of the boat and the other on the starboard. It is by charting the movements of such indicator species as *Sagitta* that marine biologists have built up a picture of how the sea and its wealth of wildlife move around these islands.

Sagitta is a member of the plankton – that all-embracing term adopted by biologists to describe those countless plants and animals which drift through the water at the mercy of the current. The Greek roots of the word literally mean 'that which is made to wander'. Some animal species are only members of the plankton during their larval stages; as adults they live on the bed of the sea if they are, for instance, whelks or crabs, or swim freely in the current if they

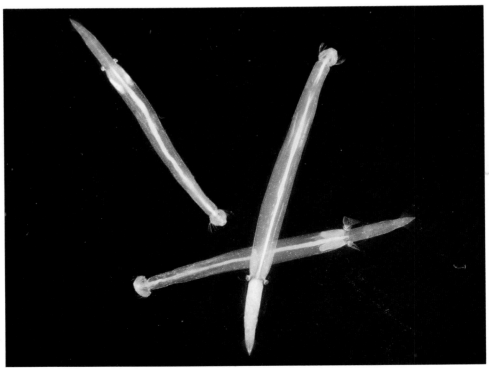

Sagitta – the arrow worm – is a conspicuous member of the marine plankton. These tiny transparent creatures are voracious predators of young herring and other fry.

are destined to be fish. Whatever the species, every animal member of the plankton is dependent, directly or indirectly, on the plant members of this drifting community. As on land, all flesh is indeed grass, and the plant plankton are the pastures of the sea. Just as in our freshwater lakes and rivers, the plant plankton is dependent on a supply of nitrogen, phosphorus and potassium – the basic nutrients for healthy growth. In the seas around the British Isles, the plant plankton is composed mainly of single-celled organisms invisible to the naked eye and a host of free-floating algae called diatoms, each no bigger than a grain of sand. Some species of diatom unite in chains that drift through the sea as green threads. Like freshwater plants, they utilise the energy of sunlight to convert the inorganic nutrients dissolved in the water into the living chemistry of the plant. Here is the beginning of the food and energy web that supports all animal life in the sea, and provides more oxygen to the atmosphere than the vegetation on the land.

The animal plankton of the sea contains representatives of a wider range of creatures than you could find in almost any habitat on land or in fresh water. Only the insects are conspicuously missing, but in the sea their place is taken by crustaceans which swarm in our coastal waters like gnats above a summer pond. The most plentiful and prominent are the copepods – crustaceans with oar-like feet. There are innumerable species, many probably waiting recognition. The sea contains vast quantities of them; it is claimed that there are more

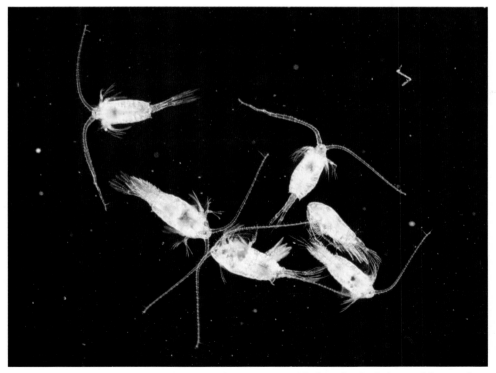

Calanus – a crustacean the size of a grain of rice – is a vital link in the food chain of the North Sea, sustaining the huge shoals of herring.

individual copepods in the oceans of the world than all the other multi-celled animals put together. Some are no bigger than a pin-head but the most common genus, *Calanus*, is about the size of a grain of rice. *Calanus* is beautifully transparent except for a few spots of scarlet on its long, segmented body. It has a single eye, like Cyclops, in the middle of its head, and a pair of long antennae which help keep the creature poised in the water. It usually hangs head upwards with these antennae stretched out sideways, except when the five pairs of oar-like limbs on the side of the body propel it jerkily through the water. Altogether, *Calanus* looks more like an alien from space than the most common inhabitant of the sea. Vast swarms of *Calanus* in our coastal waters provide the staple diet for one of the most abundant fish of the North Sea, the herring.

More familiar on the fishmonger's slab, the herring is seldom seen at its best. Swimming in the sea it has a beauty of its own. It is perfectly adapted for living in the upper layers of the water, its blue-green back matching the deep colours of the ocean when seen from above, and with silver flanks which mirror the dancing light and shade of the water when approached from the side. Few fishermen have seen the herring in its true light; their first sight of these fish is when they are hauled aboard – probably in the early hours of the morning – as their nets are winched up over the side of the vessel. If the catch is good, its arrival on deck is spectacular – a shimmering mass of silver.

Herring were once the most important commercial harvest of the North Sea, until over-exploitation drastically reduced their numbers. Now the stocks are recovering and may again provide an ample regular harvest for both man and sea-birds.

The sea is still a vast, unexplored wilderness and the men who fish in it are still hunters and not farmers. Man is now a major predator of the sea and therefore forms part of its natural history. Although the recent expansion of the fisheries industry has had a profound effect on the general balance and ecology of the seas around the British Isles, it is through the business of fishing and the study of its biology that we have come to know about the private lives of the fish themselves. Each fishing technique relies for its success on an understanding of the secret ways of the quarry; each net and line has been devised over the centuries to intercept a different species of fish according to its seasonal and daily habits. To their knowledge, passed down over generations, we can now add the scientific discoveries of marine biologists and piece together a natural history of the herring.

There are records of herring being caught off East Anglia long before the Norman Conquest and it was probably a popular catch back in Saxon times. It was not, though, until the middle of the twelfth century that herring became big business. The Danes built up the great Baltic fishing fleet operating mainly off the south coast of Sweden, which was then a part of Denmark. This was the era of the Hanseatic League whose great merchant fleets carried herrings from the Baltic ports to trade around the coasts of northern Europe, returning with wool from Britain and wine from France. Then an extraordinary event challenged the supremacy of the Danish fleet. According to their historians, some time between 1416 and 1425 their herring 'suddenly migrated from the Baltic to the North Sea'. Their fishing industry collapsed and the Dutch took over the role as the herring catchers of Europe. We now know that the Baltic herring was, and still is, a different race from the North Sea stock: it is smaller, with fewer vertebrae and not so long-lived. Quite clearly there was some kind of natural catastrophe affecting the herring stocks off Sweden – from which the Baltic herring never really recovered. For nearly 400 years Europe depended on Holland for its favoured fish and the foundations of Amsterdam were said to be built on herring bones!

Gradually, Britain took a greater initiative in the international herring trade. It was Oliver Cromwell who, in 1652, finally seized supremacy over the North Sea fishing grounds in the war with the Dutch. From that time, the herring became the symbol of the British fishing industry. By the beginning of the nineteenth century, great fleets of luggers – often a thousand strong and accompanied by a shore-based army of wives and daughters with their gutting knives and barrels of salt – would work their way down the coast from fishing towns in north-east Scotland during the season in pursuit, they thought, of the migrating shoals of herring. In summer, the fleet sailed off Scotland, by autumn it had reached the seas off the Yorkshire coast, and by October and November they were drifting off East Anglia – the climax to the herring season. There was at that time even a herring fishery which worked in the Channel off Plymouth during December and January. It was quite understandable that everyone assumed that the herring had also worked its way around the entire eastern coastline of Britain.

From the tagging studies started in the 1950s, the fisheries people have discovered much about the annual movements of the herring. They do in fact migrate, but the shoals that are pursued off the east coast of Scotland in midsummer are not those found off Lowestoft a little later on, and are quite different from the herring caught at the eastern approaches to the Channel at the turn of the year. Just like the Baltic stock that dwindled, there are around Britain several distinct races of herring – each with their own breeding season and migratory route.

Each female herring lays between 10,000 and 120,000 eggs which, unlike those of many other species of fish, are actually laid on gravel banks on the seabed, where they remain for two or three weeks. Here is a bonanza for the fish living on the sea-floor, particularly the predatory haddock which grows fat on the herring eggs. They are known as 'spawny haddocks' by the fishermen who net them in their trawls. As soon as the young herring larva hatches, it must fend for itself. It swims up into the upper layers of the sea to feed on diatoms and other minute plants of the plankton. As it grows, its diet graduates to small copepods and other tiny creatures that drift alongside. But the young herring larvae are themselves prey to other animals of the open sea. The spherical comb-jellies, 'sea gooseberries' as the fishermen call them, can devour several young herring larvae at a time, and the voracious arrow-worm Sagitta can engulf one almost its own size. Here is the classic food-chain of the sea, portrayed in cartoons where every fish is pursued by one of even larger size.

The young herrings that survive the dangers of the open sea gather together in shoals and seek shelter in shallow waters and estuaries. Here, along with the young of their close relative the sprat, many are caught and sold as whitebait. The survivors stay in coastal waters for six months or more before leaving for the open expanse of the sea to grow to sexual maturity – a process that in some races takes up to five years. The nursery grounds of the immature herring were exploited by fast-moving trawlers in the 1950s. It is, without doubt, the harvesting of these young herrings for fishmeal that depleted the North Sea stocks. Today, following an international agreement to conserve the species, the prized herring of our island waters is starting to regain its former status. We are, of course, not the only predator of the adult herring. Around the north of Scotland, schools of fin whales, piked whales, porpoises and even killer whales have been seen to follow shoals of herring into the North Sea. When the shoals are near the surface they also attract flocks of gannets. Circling perhaps 100 feet above the sea, these spectacular sea-birds wait for the right moment to fold their massive wing-spread and plummet into the water in pursuit of the fish. But one of the most effective predators of the herring is another fish – the cod. Fishermen, when gutting their catches of cod, frequently find the remains of several herring in the stomach of a medium-sized cod.

Left Comb-jellies drift through the layers of the sea, their beating combs creating spectacular waves of iridescent colour around their transparent bodies. Behind them trails a web of stinging tentacles to ensnare other members of the plankton, including herring fry.

Adult cod are aggressive carnivores, patrolling the seabed and lower layers of water in search of herring and other fish that spend much of the daytime avoiding the well-lit surface of the sea. They eat crabs and other crustaceans as well as bivalve molluscs and occasionally even sea-urchins – altogether a catholic diet. Of the fish which now live in the seas around the British Isles, the cod was probably one of the first to re-establish its breeding haunts here after the Ice Age. It is a highly adaptable creature and will migrate over great distances of the ocean. The North Sea has several different stocks of cod which together represent one of the world's largest populations of this economically important fish. Together with its close relatives the haddock, whiting, bib, pout and pollack, the cod is the most characteristic fish of our northern waters.

Wheeling above the trawlers off Shetland and the other Northern Isles are fulmars – true oceanic birds that glide effortlessly through the air on their long, narrow wings. They spend nearly all their life at sea, travelling vast distances across the North Atlantic towards Newfoundland and Greenland to feed on fish and crustaceans from the ocean. The fulmar is now the most widespread of the petrels that return to breed on our coasts but just over a hundred years ago the only colony in the British Isles was at St Kilda in the Outer Hebrides. Since then, the expansion of deep-sea trawling has produced an abundance of fish offal for which the fulmars patiently track the fishing fleets. In 1878, a few pairs nested in Shetland, since when the fulmar has established nest sites all around our coasts. It is only when the fulmars and all the other species of sea-bird come back to rear their young each spring that we can get an impression of the abundance of the marine birds that flourish on the seas around the British Isles. For many species our island waters are their international headquarters.

The small island of Noss in the Shetlands is one of Europe's largest sea-bird colonies. It has towering sandstone cliffs along its southern and eastern shores which, during the breeding season, clamour to the cries of thousands of birds nesting on the narrow cliff ledges. If you take a boat from Lerwick and on via Bressay to Noss at the height of the summer breeding season, you will witness one of the most dramatic wildlife spectacles of Britain. It is the sheer number of birds in such a small place that is so impressive. The fulmars, now looking ungainly on land, have been joined by other birds of the open sea – kittiwakes and guillemots, gannets and puffins. The air above you, the cliffs under your feet and the sea to the horizon seem filled with the urgency of rearing another generation. In the centre of the island, the eider ducks have laid their eggs in nests of grass and seaweed, lined with their own down. These, the largest and most robust of our sea-ducks, spend most of their lives bobbing on the surface of the sea, occasionally diving for molluscs and crustaceans. They seem at home in the worst of storms, and as soon as their offspring can walk, the females lead their ducklings back down to the sea. On the rough moorland of this tiny island, the skuas – both great and arctic species – make their nests. At sea, they win their living by robbing other sea-birds of their catch and here on the cliffs of Noss they prey on young puffins and kittiwakes and frequently raid the colony of arctic terns. But the vast majority of young birds reared on Noss are being supported by the sea. Their parents repeatedly set off on fishing trips over the rich seas around Shetland. While the gannets plunge for herring and other smaller fish, the puffins dive in the shallower water using their wings like underwater flippers and often return to the surface with their multicoloured beaks crammed with a neat line of silvery sand-eels. From the cliff tops of Noss the sea seems to be inexhaustible.

Every spring and summer this frenzied scene is enacted on many offshore islands and sea-stacks around the coasts of Britain and Ireland. Here the birds find sanctuary from many of the predators such as foxes which, on the mainland, would be a threat to rearing young. Bass Rock, St Kilda and Ailsa Craig off Scotland; Skokholm, Skomer and Grassholm off Wales; the Scillies off south-west England and the Skelligs off south-west Ireland are all well within the continental shelf. Of our islands, only Rockall lies beyond it. Most of these island sanctuaries, so prized by the sea-birds and valued by the naturalist, were created when the seas rose seven or eight thousand years ago. The Farne Islands just off the coast of Northumberland are the most easterly point on the outcrop of the Great Whin Sill, an ancient sheet of hard dolerite rock that runs for some seventy-five miles across the north of England. After the ice-sheet had retreated from Northumberland, dry land would have extended much further out to the North Sea of those days; only when the rising water reached within fifty feet of its present level would the rocks of the Farnes have become islands. It is a very graphic reminder of how the archipelago of Britain and Ireland was created by the sea.

The Farne Islands off the Northumbrian coast were cut off from the mainland as the sea-level rose. For millennia they have provided a sanctuary for colonies of breeding sea-birds and seals.

From the wedge-shaped, grass-topped Inner Farne, the largest of the islands, out to the bare rocks of Longstone with its lighthouse made famous by Grace Darling, the Farnes have a wide range of sites that attract the nesting sea-birds to these islands. As if by some assignation made the previous year, the birds flock in from the North Sea and far beyond. Often first to set up home are the shags, which can be seen building their ornate nests as early as March – by the end of the month some have eggs. Early in April, the eider duck arrive and the drakes with their striking black and white plumage encourage the females to leave the water and build their nests in safe places on dry land. Out to sea, rafts of puffins begin to congregate, while above the main islands sandwich terns and kittiwakes wheel and tumble before settling on their chosen site. By the middle of April, the puffins have cleaned out their burrows on the cliff tops and the first cormorants, guillemots and eiders have laid eggs. Everywhere there is a clamour for space – a cacophony of different calls as each species stakes its claim on sites and mates. Usually last to arrive are the arctic terns – those graceful, long-distance travellers of the bird world. Though called 'arctic', their yearly trail spans both the northern and southern polar seas. Those that breed on the Farnes form the most southerly permanent colony on our North Sea coast; the species breeds as far north as there is land in the Arctic. At the end of the northern summer, it migrates as far south as there is open water in the Antarctic – taking advantage of the long hours of daylight and rich polar seas. When the British Isles emerged from the ice, these polar travellers must have been one of the first birds to skim across our chilly coastal waters in search of food. Today, on the Farnes, they are almost at the southerly limit of their breeding range and their arrival each year is an attractive reminder of the earliest post-glacial natural history of the North Sea.

Left Kittiwakes are the most oceanic of our gulls: they spend most of the year at sea, returning in spring to breed on our sea-cliffs.

Above and overleaf The arctic tern – the world's greatest ocean traveller – returns to our northern waters to raise its young. Sometimes called the 'sea swallow' it would have been one of the first birds to grace these shores after the long winter of the Ice Age.

93

The shallow waters around our islands, rich in fish, support an immense population of sea-birds, of which the most spectacular and characteristic is the gannet. The British Isles are now their international headquarters.

Round most of Britain and Ireland, shags usually nest in sheltered crevices in the cliff face; on the Farnes they choose exposed sites and are a very conspicuous and amusing feature of these islands in summer.

Top The short wings of the puffin are a compromise to serve both flight in the air and movement in the water, through which they twist and turn, penguin-like in pursuit of sand-eels with which to feed their young.

Below While puffins nest in the relative safety of burrows on the cliff tops, guillemots rear their young precariously perched on the narrow cliff edges high above the sea.

Early in May, the first eider ducklings emerge and wander round the islands in groups attended by several females. On the ledges, the eggs of cormorants, shags and guillemots hatch into youngsters that clamour for fish, and by the end of the month the first puffin chicks wait patiently in the dark security of their burrows for their parents to return with sand-eels. On the two main puffin islands of the Farnes, there can be as many as 15,000 pairs of these spectacular birds, each busily catching food for the hungry offspring underground. It seems that the breeding season of the puffin and several other sea-birds is linked to the greatest profusion of sand-eels in the sea. That in turn is dependent on the blooming of the plankton. By mid-June, when the sun is at its highest and the days are longest, the nursery slopes of the Farnes are at their peak. The cliff-edge colonies of kittiwakes have nests which bulge with downy youngsters and the turf of the nest sites of the arctic terns is alive with tiny mottled chicks that are galvanised into frantic begging antics by every passing shadow of the returning adults screaming to one another overhead.

By mid-August, the stacks and cliff tops of the Farnes have been deserted. You might see the occasional cormorant drying its wings, or gulls squabbling over the carcase of a young puffin that died in its burrow. The whiteness of the ledges bears witness to the vast quantities of sand-eels and fish that were plucked from the sea to satisfy the appetites of a new generation of sea-birds. Soon the winter storms and rain will wash the lime back into the sea returning nutrients for the plankton. After the frenzy of the breeding season in this sea-bird city, the quietness of autumn on the Farnes is almost eerie. On the outer islands and particularly on the North and South Wamses, a new, quite different sound can be heard above the surge of the waves. The seals of the Farnes have returned to give birth to their calves. Here on one of the few groups of islands off the east coast of England is one of the main centres of the grey seal – or Atlantic seal as it is sometimes called. In October, these bulky marine mammals haul themselves up on to secluded rocky shores mainly on the west coasts of Britain and Ireland to prepare for this important annual event. The cows are heavily pregnant from the previous year's gathering, and the birth of their offspring has been postponed until now by a process of delayed implantation whereby the development of the egg is suspended for two or three months after fertilisation. Within a few weeks of giving birth, the females mate again and so leave the traditional breeding ground, assured of a reason to return next year. This is clearly an adaptation to life in the vastness of the sea. Now, for a brief period, they have returned to their birthplace – some of them for the first season in four or five years, which is the time a female takes to reach breeding maturity. For the bulls it is even longer, and many will not be strong enough to challenge for harems until they are nine or ten years old, nearly half-way through their lives. When the young bulls eventually haul themselves out of the sea, they are met by fierce opposition from the established bulls. Fighting and ritual challenges reaffirm or redistribute male supremacy. It is a noisy business and, to us, rather comical. Fast and graceful underwater, the seals seem hopelessly clumsy on land as they try to restore to their front flippers the forgotten dignity of legs.

Grey seals have dramatically increased their numbers in the waters around Britain and Ireland since the late 1950s. More than seventy-five per cent of Europe's population live here. It is not really understood why they are so successful; many inshore fishermen claim that the seal has learnt to steal his catch. Certainly those fishermen involved in the commercial salmon fisheries on the coast and in river estuaries voice concern about their livelihood. The seal is very partial to mature salmon and as many as fifteen per cent of the fish caught in Scottish waters bear the tell-tale teethmarks of the agile seal. One of the seal's other favourite delicacies is the squid, of which our seas have plenty. Other than the errant killer whale, seals have no natural predators and their numbers are governed by the basic productivity of the sea. Just across the North Sea in Danish waters, the grey seal has become extinct as a breeding species. For whatever reason, our island waters are now the main sanctuary for this marine creature – the largest of our wild mammals.

After they are born in late autumn, grey seal pups grow rapidly on their mother's rich milk; soon they must face the severe cold of winter in our northern seas.

A similar story surrounds the gannet and its recent history. In the early part of the last century there were probably a third of a million of these handsome sea-birds breeding in the North Atlantic; by the end of the century the number had been reduced to about 100,000 – mostly due to their persecution by fishermen who visited the massive colony at Bird Rocks in the Gulf of St Lawrence. They used the gannet flesh as bait for their cod lines. Similar fates befell colonies on this side of the Atlantic, notably on Lundy in the Bristol Channel and Gannet Rock at Yarmouth. But other British and Irish colonies flourished unmolested and, during this century, have grown to such strength that they now carry more than 140,000 pairs, which is over seventy per cent of the world's total gannet population. The largest is at St Kilda off west Scotland but those on Little Skellig off south-west Ireland and on Grassholm in south Wales are impressive for their settings. The only mainland gannet colony is at Bempton Cliffs in Yorkshire. To visit these or any of the other gannetries around our coasts is one of the obligatory pilgrimages for every ornithologist. To all but Bempton, you must journey by boat – an opportunity to reflect on the generous but powerful nature of the sea. The crossing from Valentia to view Little Skellig is seldom calm but the wildness of the Atlantic adds to the spectacle of the gannets. They wheel around this jagged island with a breathtaking mastery of the air. With a wingspan of almost six feet, they confidently ride the air currents that rise up the sheer rockface of this barren outpost of Europe, as if this were the centre of the world.

Beyond the Skelligs there is open ocean – no more land until America. From there in the tropical Gulf of Mexico, the Atlantic Drift starts its flow eastwards towards Europe. At the peak of the warm 'Atlantic' period in our climate, 6000 years or so ago, the warm Gulf waters brushed the craggy coastline of Norway, but now its influence just reaches our western shores. It not only moderates our weather but it brings to our shore a variety of sea creatures that would otherwise be restricted to more southern seas. Stranded on the south-west coasts of England and Ireland you may find turtles from the Caribbean, violet sea-snails, carried north on their bubble-rafts, the strange by-the-wind-sailor from the tropics with its transparent plastic-like sail, or even the very beautiful but dangerous Portuguese man-of-war. At sea you might be lucky enough to glimpse the waving dorsal fin of the sunfish, a mysterious disc-like fish that can sometimes measure ten feet in diameter. In some years great plagues of the Mediterranean octopus invade our waters from the south and here, too, fishermen catch pilchard, anchovy, red mullet and tunny – all more reminiscent of Mediterranean summers than home waters. Some of the larger fish migrate here in a warm summer but the smaller creatures and those that drift like plankton at the mercy of the currents have been brought here by a remarkable accident of nature. A surface stream of Atlantic water enters the Mediterranean through the Strait of Gibraltar and, at the same time, very salty water from the Mediterranean pours out at a deeper level. Carried out by this lower current are the eggs and larvae of many animals from that sea. This current then spreads out underneath the Atlantic water and some is carried northwards along the edge of the continental shelf off Portugal. This 'Lusitanian' plankton eventually surfaces north of the Bay of Biscay and drifts along the western coastline of Brittany and Cornwall, often reaching southern Ireland and beyond. In some years it has been known to reach the northern isles of Scotland. Wherever they settle, if the sea is warm enough, these planktonic travellers establish colonies on the seabed. It is only in the last decade or two, since scuba diving has become a practical tool for the marine biologist, that the extent of this Lusitanian fauna has been appreciated. Places such as Lough Ine at the most southern tip of County Cork in Ireland and Lundy Island off the North Devon coast have become Meccas for the marine naturalist equipped with mask and aqualung.

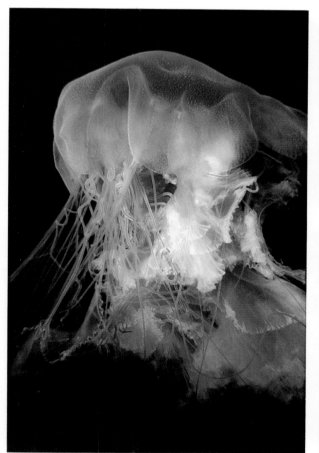

Left This jellyfish, *Cyanea lamarckii*, is a northern species: in the Arctic Ocean it reaches six feet in diameter – in our waters it rarely exceeds two and a half feet but is an effective predator of small fish which it entangles in its veil of tentacles.

Top right *Facelina coronaria* is a sea-slug typical of our warmer south-west coastal waters. Less than an inch in length, it browses on colonies of hydroids, the stinging cells of which pass intact into the coloured fronds of the sea-slug to provide for its own protection.

Bottom right The brilliantly-coloured anemone, *Leptosamnia*, is of Mediterranean origin and in our waters is found only in the south-west in such localities as Lundy Island.

THE UNDERWATER WORLD OF LUNDY

Scuba-diving has brought a new perspective to our understanding of the sea. Around the coasts of the British Isles, divers with masks and aqualungs have discovered many sites of great beauty. Some of them are now designated as nature reserves because of their rich diversity of wildlife and their spectacular underwater scenery. Lundy, a small island off the coast of North Devon, is regarded by divers and marine biologists as the finest.

 1 Kelp forest
 2 Red and brown seaweeds
 3 Colonies of sea-firs
 4 Jewel anemones
 5 Sea-slug   6 Sea-fan
 7 Red sea fingers
 8 Dead man's fingers
 9 Sea-squirts
10 *Zoanthid* anemones
11 Branching sponges
12 Yellow sponge
13 Yellow cup coral
14 Devonshire cup coral
15 Ross coral

As you sink beneath the surface of the sea, you enter a completely new world. Above the water, the cliffs of Lundy are home to a mass of sea-birds and brightly-coloured flowers; beneath the waves, the cliff plunges downwards to form an underwater wall that is adorned with a completely different community of plants and animals.

The water filters and absorbs the sunlight, each wavelength disappearing at a different depth. The red colours are the first to go and very soon the whole scene has a blue-grey hue. The diver's torch bathes the cliff face in white light and restores the full spectrum of colour to this twilight world.

The underwater wall plunges more than 100 feet to the sea-bed. To its cracks and crevices clings a carpet of miniature animals.

It is its underwater world which earns Lundy the distinction of being one of our finest nature reserves. To leave the surface and sink towards the seabed, more than 100 feet below, is perhaps the only real way of appreciating the natural wilderness of our island waters. Here, on their own terms, we come face to face with the creatures of the sea. Weightless, we drift with the currents in wafting forests of kelp and other seaweeds that flourish in the upper sunlit waters. As we sink deeper, hugging the underwater cliff face, the darkness creeps towards us and the familiar bright colours of the terrestrial world pale into the deep inkiness of the sea. Twenty-five feet down, under the canopy of kelp, it is so dark that few plants can grow. Here, the animal species begin to dominate the scene. What at first look and feel like a turf of vegetation covering the rocks and boulders, turn out to be dense mats of bryozoans – microscopic animals linked together in branching colonies. Some of these colonies appear as encrusting, chalky layers on seaweeds and boulders, while others form bushy growths resembling a miniature forest of ferns. They feed by filtering out plankton and other minute particles of food from the water. Among their fronds lives an array of other unfamiliar animals, whose exquisite beauty is revealed by the beam of an underwater torch. Sponges and sea-squirts, anemones and corals, starfishes and sea-urchins all compete for space in this twilight world of the seabed. Strange segmented worms, adorned with bristles, crawl over the surface, while others emerge from their protective tubes, waving an elaborate crown of tentacles. Five-armed brittle-stars pick their elegant way over the seabed, while above them the fronds of elaborate sea-fans seem to defy the constant surging of the current as they filter out the endless supply of food suspended in the turbid waters of the Bristol Channel. Perhaps the most colourful inhabitants of Lundy's seabed fauna, however, are the sea-slugs – and those with Lusitanian origins are often the most spectacular. These exotic creatures have no shells but sport feathery gills which absorb oxygen from the water; they feed by rasping away the soft parts of the bryozoans, sea-firs and sponges in this miniature jungle. Most of these animals, which have their origins in more southern seas, are outstandingly colourful, with vivid shades of yellow, orange and pink which, when illuminated by the torch, stand out like jewels on the seabed. Most exquisite of all is the jewel anemone itself. Dense colonies of this iridescent sea anemone carpet the vertical faces and overhanging ledges of Lundy's underwater cliffs, transforming them into a magical grotto. It is easy to imagine the breathtaking excitement experienced by the scuba divers who first beamed their torches on this marine wilderness.

Cruising into the waters of Lundy may come one of the largest fishes known to our waters – the basking shark. The first sight of it is usually its great tri-angular dorsal fin, a menacing image which belies the gentle nature of the beast below. Although often thirty feet in length and weighing three or four tons, this shark is harmless to all but the plankton. Its enormous gill-clefts are equipped with countless rows of gill-rakers which, like combs, sieve copepods and other tiny animals from the water. The shark cruises through the sea with its vast mouth gaping wide – the water streaming through the expanded gill

Jewel anemones reproduce by budding, creating a colony of identical offspring which colour the face of the rock.

slits. At only two knots, more than 2000 tons of water are filtered every hour – its rich haul of plankton being converted into the bulk and energy that fuels this giant of the sea. In winter, the basking shark loses its gill-rakers, which have become frayed with constant use. The animal sinks into the deep trenches somewhere on the edge of our continental shelf, stops feeding and grows a new set in preparation for the next bloom of plankton in our coastal waters. Although it has been sighted off the entire length of our west coast and sometimes cruises into the North Sea, the basking shark's favoured waters are those off the west coast of Ireland and Scotland. Here, it encounters the great swarms of *Calanus*. As soon as these copepods become abundant in April and May, the basking sharks mysteriously appear off our coasts, particularly in sheltered areas such as the Clyde sea. Here, from Girvan and other ports, a few fishermen set off in pursuit of the 'sail fish' whose dorsal fin gives away its presence. Captured by harpoons, the basking shark is slaughtered for its gigantic liver, which yields vast quantities of oil. The precise effect on their population is unknown, but the great majority survive the summer in our waters and then return to the depths of the ocean beyond the reach of man.

The sea around our islands is indeed the last great wilderness we have. From the cold seas of the north, with their great shoals of whitefish, to the warm southern seas, tempered by the Gulf Stream and home to an array of tropically-coloured creatures, our island waters embrace 10,000 years of marine natural history. Yet it is only recently that we have become a significant part of that story. Man the hunter is now also man the conservationist – it is clearly in his interests to take stock of the natural assets of the sea. Compared with many other waters of the world, we still have something left to celebrate. Much will depend on how we treat the shallow waters that fringe our coastline. Here, we enter an ever-changing world where the richness of the sea meets the new opportunities of the land.

CHAPTER FIVE

TIME AND TIDE

During the night of Saturday, 31 January 1953, the sea changed the shape of Britain. A depression passing from the Atlantic into the North Sea created hurricane-force winds, which urged more water along the route of the advancing tide around the north of Scotland. On the mainland, wind speeds reached 175 mph, flattening the forests. Along the east coast, the storm caused havoc. Where the cliffs were made of clay or sand, the erosion could be measured in yards; whole beaches and sand dunes were swept away. Sea walls were breached and reclaimed lands flooded with salt water. In the Thames estuary, water-levels rose an extra eight feet above high tide. There had been a full moon on the previous Thursday but the spring tides were not normally the highest of the year. Nor were the rivers in flood. Even so, the storm that night killed 307 people and drowned much of the east coast of England. It was for the whole nation a harsh reminder of the restless nature of the sea.

Compared with the overall changes in the sea-level since the Ice Age, that tidal surge of 1953 was a ripple in the history of our coastline. Not only has the entire body of the ocean risen some 300 feet but in some parts of Britain and Ireland the land itself has either sunk or risen in relation to the sea. Geologists regard the crust of the Earth as being made up of a series of ever smaller shells of increasing density. These layers are not molten, but under the great stress to which they are subjected they undoubtedly yield, changing the height and shape of the crust at the surface. The formation of the ice-cap over northern Britain – sometimes more than a mile thick – added an immense weight to underlying rocks. As it grew in size, the land beneath yielded to this colossal downward pressure. Such movements within the Earth's crust are slow – and they are also reversible. Ever since the peak of the last glaciation, there has been a slow rebound as the land shrugged off the burden of the ice. The effect has, of course, been more marked in the north, which bore the full weight of the ice-cap; in the south, which escaped the impact of the glaciers, the land has, if anything, sunk from its ice-age level. The whole of the British Isles has tilted. In Scotland and Ireland, the land has risen, whereas in counteraction the south and east of England has sunk. The pivot seems to be on a line that runs through Morecambe Bay. The best evidence of this remodelling of our coastline can be seen in Scotland, where there are many coastal areas noted for their 'raised beaches'. They were created by marine erosion and then, from about 6700 years ago, when the rising sea-levels no longer kept pace with the recoiling of the land, these platforms were gradually lifted above the level of the sea. Today, around the north-west of Scotland and Ireland, you can see distinct 'raised beaches', which are some twenty-five feet higher than the sea.

About 1000 years before, there had been a rapid rise in sea-levels, probably due to the sudden melting of the North American ice-cap. Here in Britain, the sea rose more than thirty feet – at a far greater rate than the uplift of the land. Great areas of low-lying land and river valleys were flooded with salt water, bringing with it deposits of marine sediments. The famous Carse Clays in the Midland Valley of Scotland were deposited in this way in a belt right across the country between the Firths of Forth and Clyde. In southern Britain, where the land was not rising, the sea invaded many low-lying parts of the country, much of which was densely forested. All around our coasts are the remains of these drowned forests. In Somerset, clay was deposited in the area between the Mendip, Polden and Wedmore hills, on which the raised bogs of the Somerset levels later developed.

In Wales, Cornwall, Ireland and nearby Brittany, there are many legends about overflowing lakes or the drowning of low-lying areas by the sea. In the Isles of Scilly and neighbouring parts of Cornwall, there is the legend of Lyonnesse – a fertile land that is believed to have extended beyond Land's End. There are indeed rocks called the Seven Stones, midway between Cornwall and the Scillies but, sadly, no evidence that this marks the site of a sunken bronze-age city. Perhaps the most interesting area for speculation about sunken settlements is Cardigan Bay in West Wales. Here, there are several sarns, or causeways, running out to sea from the present coastline. The longest is Sarn Badrig, or St Patrick's Causeway, as it is sometimes called, which runs for about twenty miles south-west from Mochras Island. Like the others, it is formed of

The rapid rise in sea-levels 8000 to 7000 years ago would have led to increasing erosion of the coastline – particularly in areas of softer rocks. Here at Flamborough Head in Yorkshire the steep chalk cliffs and stacks are reminiscent of that rapidly-changing frontier with the sea.

loose, rounded boulders and is quite narrow. Here is the basis for the legend of Cantref y Gwaelod, a lost land which folklore claims was drowned some time in Wales's Celtic history. The so-called Black Book of Carmarthen even ascribes the tragic event to a specific year – AD 520. While there is no factual support for this dating, there may well be a more ancient foundation for the legend. Although the sarns are probably natural features left by the glaciers that flowed westwards from the Cambrian Mountains, and not the remains of masonry, they could well have once been part of a low-lying plain which was submerged in the Bronze Age. That such an event could be passed into folk memory is made even more plausible in the light of the belief that many of today's inhabitants of Wales are direct descendants of neolithic man. Their ancestors may actually have witnessed the drowning of this coastal land.

In time, the sea stopped rising in relation to the land. Today, it is in fact six feet lower in some places than it was at the end of the warm Atlantic period, some four or five thousand years ago. Since then, the flooded lands have been reclaimed by nature. The slow springing back of the crust in the north has almost restored the land to its equilibrium. Even so, much of Scotland is rising by about two inches every century, and London is still sinking even faster. The upheaval of the land in the north and the sinking of the south, and the overall rise in the sea has created the basic shape of the British Isles as we see them today. It has left us with a coastline of 7000 miles, which is more varied than any other in Europe. From towering cliffs to flat expanses of estuarine mud nearly a mile wide, from moving sand dunes and shingle spits to rocky bays and

As a more temperate climate returned to the British Isles, much of the land became covered with woodland; the exposed coasts were among the few areas to remain treeless. Here plants such as thrift form close swards of vegetation which bring a blaze of colour to our cliff-tops.

golden sands, we have a coastal landscape that rivals the beauty of many more exotic seaboards of the world. Although the sea and land have come to terms over the new frontiers between them they continue to dispute the details.

On the west coast of Ireland and the south-western peninsula of England, the margins of our land face the full force of the Atlantic. Here is a very transient world where the annual rhythm of the sea reclaims its riches and keeps the land-based life at bay. This is one of the most harsh environments colonised by plants and animals and those that have managed to stake a claim on this ever-changing frontier-land are the hardiest of pioneers. Not only do they face the twice-daily impact of the tide but also the extremes of wetting and drying, and fluctuations of temperature that come with such frequent exposure to the air. Each species of shore plant and animal thrives best in a particular part of the beach, according to its ability to survive the rigours of this daily rhythm of the sea. When the tide retreats, the anemone withdraws its tentacles, the limpet clamps fast to its favoured contour of the rock and the periwinkle closes its shell with an operculum that keeps the snail moist until the sea returns. Only in the rockpools can truly marine creatures keep their heads below water, but these natural aquaria have a very different character from the open sea. On hot days, the water evaporates and becomes warmer and saltier; on rainy days, it is diluted. Isolated from their parent sea, the inhabitants of the rockpool must cope with these extremes. It is now, while the beach is exposed to the air, that

Left Despite harsh extremes created by the tides, the rockpool is a rich and varied world in which a specialist community of plants and animals flourishes where the land meets the sea.
Above left Barnacles are crustaceans which, when covered by the tide, sieve plankton from the sea with their feathery limbs. By withdrawing into its shell, the barnacle can survive long periods exposed to the air, high on the beach.
Above right The snakelocks anemone cannot withdraw its tentacles and is restricted to the lower shore which for most of the day is covered by sea water. It feeds on shrimps and other small marine creatures which become ensnared in its stinging tentacles.

land creatures can venture below the reach of the tide. Springtails scavenge among the decaying debris at the top of the beach – sometimes forming a black patch on the rocks as a great herd of these primitive insects cluster round dead barnacles. One of the most adventurous land-based invertebrates is a centipede which, following the retreating tide, raids the beach in search of periwinkles and barnacles.

Of all the different coastal habitats, it is the river estuaries that best illustrate the richness of this tidal zone. Most estuaries in Britain and Ireland were formed by the drowning of a river valley, by the long-term rising of the sea or sometimes, as at the mouth of the Thames, by the sinking of the land. The river carries with it from the land great quantities of sediment and nutrients; the sea carries with it the sands and clays scoured from the coast itself. At this meeting place is the best of both worlds but also, for the wildlife inhabitants, is the problem of coping with the extremes created by the tides. Here is a rich and constantly renewed source of nutrients but also some of the worst physical contrasts that aquatic plants and animals are designed to endure. As on the rocky shore, it is not the easiest of environments for life. But in spite of its seemingly inhospitable character, the estuarine habitat is attractive to a great variety and quantity of wildlife.

On the south side of the wide estuary of the River Ribble is the famed Crossens roost – probably the largest known roosting site for wading birds in the British Isles. The entire west coast of industrial Lancashire is renowned for the birdlife of its estuaries. Here, within a short stretch of coastline, is Morecambe Bay, the mouth of the Ribble, and the Wirral, flanked by the Mersey and the Dee. Together they make up a vast area of tidal mud and marsh, which is a magnet for hundreds of thousands of waders and wildfowl and for an ever-growing number of appreciative birdwatchers. What is it that attracts them all to this apparently barren, muddy waste? The attraction is, of course, the mud itself – or rather, the invertebrate life that lives in it. In the mud and silt of estuaries are small creatures in enormous density – all thriving on the algae and other plants of the mud, constantly enriched by the outflow of the river, or on the plankton swept in by the sea with every tide. Ragworms, lugworms, cockles and other small molluscs – together with immense concentrations of tiny crustaceans, sometimes 50,000 beneath every square yard – all contributing to the glorious generosity of mud!

Around the coasts of the British Isles are more than 300 estuaries, over which the tide races and retreats twice a day. Keeping pace with this rhythm are vast flocks of waders and wildfowl that seek the shelter of this no-man's-land and the bounty revealed by the tide. In winter, our estuaries and wetlands play host to more than half the total number of waders in Europe. Three estuary complexes are the most significant – the Wash, the Solway and the vast mudflats that link Morecambe Bay, the Ribble and the Dee. Together, these three areas often harbour more birds than the Waddenzee in Holland, which is the most important wader refuge on the mainland of Europe. The vastness and diversity of the estuaries of Britain and Ireland are legacies of the Ice Age

Where the wind drives sand to the head of the beach, constantly shifting ridges of sand provide a foothold for marram grass. The rapid growth and extensive root-system of this plant help trap more sand and stabilise the developing dunes.

and products of the continuing seasonal and daily movements of the sea that surrounds these islands. Under the gravitational pull of the sun and the moon, the oceans of the world swell twice a day, creating tides. Islands, such as Tahiti, in the centre of their tidal basins, experience tides of little more than a foot from low to high; here in the British Isles, on the rim of the Atlantic basin, we have one of the most extreme tidal ranges in the world. The funnel shape of the Bristol Channel gives it the largest in Europe; at Chepstow it can be as much as forty feet at spring tides, when the sun and moon pull in unison. The complexities of the sea currents and the shape of the British Isles govern the different timing of the tides around the coast and, in turn, they govern the rhythms of the birds. They can only feed when the tide is out; when it returns they seek refuge in communal roosts, waiting until the mudflats are exposed again. On the Wash, the highest spring tides happen in the early morning and in the evening. This leaves the birds the best of the daylight to search for food and the night-time to roost. For the waders of Morecambe Bay and the Wirral estuaries, life is not so simple. The spring tides tend to occur two hours before and after midday and midnight, so compelling the flocks to spend much of the brief winter daylight roosting beyond the reach of the tide. This is one of the reasons why this area of the east coast makes such fine birdwatching. The waders are forced close to dry land when the light is best for binoculars and cameras. Most favoured by photographers is Hilbre Island, one of three small islands in the mouth of the Dee. Fortunately for the birds, the long trek out from West Kirby over the sands and mud at low tide deters all but the hardiest of

ornithologists. The canvas of his hide gives the photographer precious protection from the January winds that cut across the flatness of the estuary. In the distance, the tide is on the turn; by midday it will be lapping within yards of his shelter. With luck the waders will roost within reach of his lens. The spring tide moves in at walking pace and the oystercatchers side-step to avoid the water. The flocks of different species still feeding on their favoured stretches of the mud rise into the air as collectively they decide to make for slightly higher ground. As their food is submerged out of reach of their bills, each species gives up feeding and takes to roosting, only to be forced further towards the high-water mark. The leap-frogging flocks wheel above the estuary, their piping calls announcing their imminent arrival to the silent watcher in his hide. In the distance, a patch of sand is still visible, crowded with oystercatchers; soon even this refuge will be submerged.

The flats that surround Hilbre Island support vast flocks of oystercatchers; in all, there are some 20,000 of these piebald birds in the Dee estuary. At roosting time, their aerial manoeuvres make a striking spectacle as they gather their forces before settling on their favourite ground. On the rocky islet of Hilbre a flock of more than a thousand gathers to roost. Here they stand in characteristic wader pose, facing the wind, often on one leg, with the other tucked up for warmth under the feathers of a wing. Each species tends to keep to itself, forming distinct roosts. Like the oystercatcher, the knots spend most of the high-tide period at rest. After noisy communal greetings and some preening, they sleep. This routine is typical of the larger waders such as the godwits, the

Left As the tide advances across the Dee Estuary, oystercatchers and other waders are driven off their muddy feeding grounds to roost on the rocky islets of Hilbre.
Above The oystercatcher – one of the most numerous and visually striking inhabitants of our mudflats. An oystercatcher can find and devour as many as fifty cockles an hour; allowing for the limitations of the tide, that could amount to over 300 every day.

curlews, the redshanks and the grey plovers. The smaller waders continue to feed whenever possible, so demanding is their need for energy to keep their bodies warm. While the larger birds sleep through the high tide, the tiny dunlins, sanderlings and ringed plovers dart like clockwork toys along the tideline in search of morsels uncovered by each lap of the water. As, eventually, the tide ebbs, it is these miniature waders that are first to leave the roosting sites, following the waterline out over the mudflats, constantly probing and picking. Next to leave are the bar-tailed godwits, which quickly make for the water's edge as soon as fresh mud is revealed. The curlews wait patiently until the bars and mudflats are exposed again out in the estuary. As if prompted by their wisest member, the flock lifts off from the roost and heads purposefully towards the chosen feeding ground. The redshanks disperse, each in search of a favoured gully or corner of the salt-marsh, to spend the next five or six hours searching for the tell-tale signs of food. Last to leave are the oystercatchers. They often wait at the roost for nearly an hour after all the other species have departed, waiting for the ebbing tide to reveal their feeding ground with its feast of cockles. There are only a couple of hours left of winter light and this time is precious. As the birdwatcher packs up his gear and sets off across the glistening mud and sand of the Dee estuary, the distant air is alive with the sights and sounds of tens of thousands of birds as they move between their familiar haunts. Like winter smoke, the dense flocks lift and fall against the evening sky as they disperse over the vastness of this fertile wilderness between the tides.

Year by year, each of our estuaries changes its shape. As more mud and silt is deposited at the mouth of the river, new land emerges from the sea. In time, it is colonised by plants and converted to permanent dry land. This natural process of succession is rather like that of the doomed lake. If you follow the ebbing tide out to the point where the marsh meets the sea, and then retrace your steps back towards dry ground, you will see how land is naturally reclaimed from the sea. From the green algae and the eelgrass of the mudflats, through to the swards of sea aster and sea lavender of the salt-marsh, the plants of the estuary re-enact a saga of succession that builds up land above the reaches of the tide. Such places are at their most colourful in the late summer when the sea lavender forms a blue haze at the head of the salt-marsh. Here, at low tide, it is brimming with greenfinches and yellowhammers, linnets and meadow pipits, all fattening up on the harvest of seeds. Beyond this zone, at the very limit of the highest tides, you will find the first signs of natural turf that can be grazed by rabbits and sheep. Here, among the fescues and rushes are the compact rosettes of thrift and sea plantain – both tolerant of the close-cropping effects of grazing by wild and domestic animals. It is to such saltings that huge numbers of barnacle geese and white-fronted geese are attracted in winter. All around the

Left Typical of the low-lying parts of the east coast of England are extensive tracts of saltmarsh – built of sediments left by the rivers and the sea. Such places have a distinctive plant community which changes in colour as the seasons pass – until in late summer it is a purple haze of sea lavender.

British Isles there are examples of such reclamation by nature. This natural process is slow but, aided by drainage and sea walls and by the introduction of pioneer plants, salt-marsh can be rapidly converted into productive farmland. In 1870, a hybrid of the cord-grass *Spartina* was discovered in Southampton Water. So vigorous was its growth that it almost choked the waterway. Elsewhere, this accidental hybrid has been introduced to speed up reclamation. On the Dee estuary, the seaside town of Parkgate, with its Victorian promenade, is now cut off from the water by a vast salt-marsh of this freak *Spartina* grass. Walking along the esplanade, out of sight of the sea, you cannot fail to be impressed with the way nature can so rapidly reshape the coastline.

On the opposite east coast of England, salt-marshes have a very different character. Along the northern coast of Norfolk, the passage of sediments carried southwards by the sea is checked and much of the sand and shingle accumulates in formations such as those at Scolt Head and Blakeney Point. Long sand or shingle ridges can build up, which become partly covered by dunes. Here, sea couch grass and marram grass can become established, so adding to the permanency of the land. Some dunes, in their infancy, are swept away by storms and strong tides, but others survive to form the foundations of

Above Striking emblem of bird conservation in Britain, the avocet has been encouraged to return to breed on specially created coastal reserves in Suffolk. Even greater numbers over-winter on estuaries in the south-west of England.
Right The knot breeds on the tundra beyond the Arctic Circle; in winter huge flocks return to our ice-free estuaries to feed on the rich life in the mud.

dry land. Blakeney Point is joined to the mainland at its eastern end and, in the sheltered lee of the spit where there is shallow water, a salt-marsh has evolved which is bounded on the seaward side by sand dunes and shingle and to the south by permanent dry land. This sheltered tidal area, like so much of this coastline, is rich in coastal plants, wildfowl and wading birds. Further down the coast of East Anglia, another shingle spit at Orford has created a haven for wildlife, the pride of place being given to the famed Havergate Island and its avocets.

We usually think of 'waders' as estuary birds; their long legs and bills seem perfectly designed for finding food in that kind of muddy, watery world. But for a few months of the year these same birds lead a quite different way of life. Most of the waders that spend winter here migrate north to breed on the grassy tundra of the Arctic. There, during that brief summer, they change to another diet. In place of the worms, crustaceans and molluscs of the mud, most waders turn to insects – mainly the adults and larvae of craneflies and midges. As the season progresses, each species moves on to a different food source and towards the end of the breeding season waders such as curlew and whimbrel frequently feed on beetles and berries. It seems that 'waders' are just as well adapted to

their brief season on the arctic grasslands as to their long months spent on the estuaries here in Europe and the south.

The waders that return to us in autumn come from three quite distinct parts of the northern hemisphere. There are those including knot, sanderling, turnstone and the pale-bellied brent geese which breed in the north-west of the American continent – in places such as Ellesmere Island, the Baffin Islands and northern Greenland. Second, there are those from north-western Europe, including much of Scandinavia, Iceland and western Greenland. These bird populations include oystercatchers, ringed plover, dunlin, redshank and geese such as the pink-footed and white-fronted species. Third, there are those that come from Siberia, which include some knot and sanderling but mainly bar-tailed godwit, grey plover, the dark-bellied brent geese and Bewick's swans. Predictably, each year these populations turn up at their favoured estuaries. In the late winter, they set off once more, religiously honouring their birthplace by returning there to raise their families. Why should some species go one way while others choose a totally different destination? Why do some members of one species, such as the knot, set a course for Greenland, while birds that look identical to us turn eastwards for distant Siberia? The answer had its origins back in the last Ice Age and neatly accounts for the apparently random and inordinately long migrations of these birds.

At the peak of the last Ice Age, 18,000 years ago, the ice-sheets covered much of north America and northern Europe – including many parts of those continents which are today the summer breeding ground for wildfowl and waders. But the two great ice-sheets did not overwhelm the whole of the far north. The Arctic Ocean was free of ice and helped moderate the climate of adjacent land. There were several large areas of land in the Arctic which remained free of glaciers throughout the Ice Age and which, in summer, would be revealed as tundra. It was to these refuges that the waders migrated to breed. From east to west these refuges formed three distinct regions. In northern Russia there was a wide band of ice-free land in summer, particularly around the mouth of the River Ob. In northern Europe, just south of the present position of the North Sea, the tundra offered an ideal breeding ground for the birds – and this narrow belt included the south of England. Surprisingly, there was also a large ice-free region at the most northerly tip of Greenland and many waders migrated there for the arctic summers of the long Ice Age. Such birds probably included the knot and pale-bellied brent geese – species which still make that long trek every year. As the glaciers retreated, the breeding ranges of these groups of birds extended further afield but their migration routes remained traditional. The birds from northern Greenland still cross the Atlantic in search of their familiar wintering grounds in Europe, rather than join the much larger, and more straightforward movement of birds southwards over the Canadian archipelago. Old habits die hard, and in the collective memory of each species and even in each geographical grouping of birds, there is a natural resistance to change. The Ice Age has long since gone, but the patterns of migration and distribution which it fashioned have lived on.

Today, free of ice, our estuaries and other coastal areas are vitally important for much of the wildlife of Europe – either as wintering grounds, breeding grounds or simply as secluded staging posts. Waders and wildfowl come here in winter from all points north, to share in the mildness of our climate and the natural richness of the margins of our land. In summer, sea-birds flock in from the ocean to rear their young on the cliffs and stacks around our coast. From the southern hemisphere come the terns to take up residence on the dunes and shingle spits so characteristic of our eastern seaboard. Down on the beach itself, the ebbing tide reveals the crevices and gulleys, rockpools and shifting sands that offer an endlessly changing variety of habitats to the less conspicuous but equally diverse plants and animals of the shore. Here is a world between the tides that is neither open ocean nor permanent dry land. Life here is in a continual state of flux – changing with the daily rhythms of the tides, the seasons of the year and the slow but dramatic movements in the surface of the Earth. During the few thousand years since the beginning of this story of our islands, our coastline has always had a dynamic nature and that continual process of change has given us the immense variety of coastal habitat and wildlife that we have today. This precious diversity has been created by the forces and rhythms of the sea and by the passage of time.

CHAPTER SIX

OUT OF THE FLAMES

A strange area of gently undulating landscape lies on the border between Norfolk and Suffolk; it is called the Breckland. Here, in this open part of East Anglia, the summers are hot and dry and the winters often bitingly cold. The look and feel of the place is more like central, continental Europe than the temperate countryside of island Britain. The mosaic of wind-blown sandy heath interspersed with pockets of chalky grassland gives this unique terrain a distinctly different, prehistoric, atmosphere. It is as if, in the story of the making of the British Isles, this corner of England has been overlooked.

In reality, the Breckland reveals a long and fascinating natural history – one in which our early ancestors played a major role which changed the course of nature. For many years naturalists thought that this exposed part of East Anglia had always been treeless – ever since the sands so characteristic of this region were formed during the last Ice Age. Historical records dating back seven centuries show it to have been open grassland – sheep walks and rabbit warrens – and what mature trees exist today are known to have been planted recently as shelter belts. Perhaps because of its dry soils and its remoteness from the temperate influence of the Atlantic, the Breckland had never been invaded by the wildwood that had once been a feature of most of wilderness Britain. Then at Hockham Mere, one of the few permanent pools on the northern margin of the Breckland, pollen studies showed conclusively that there had been extensive forests here until the early neolithic times and that their disappearance began with the arrival of the peoples of the New Stone Age with their flint axes and fire. Between five and four thousand years ago, this had probably been one of the most populated parts of Britain.

About ten miles from Hockham Mere is the famous archaeological site with the intriguing name of 'Grimes Graves'. These workings in the chalky soil are not ancient burial grounds but the largest group of neolithic flint mines ever discovered in Britain. Here, on the gentle slopes of a dry valley, the entrances to the mine shafts are now almost entirely surrounded by Forestry Commission plantations, but if you visit them you will gain a good impression of the industrious lives led by the East Anglian flint miners in neolithic times. There are several vertical shafts descending some forty feet below today's surface. From the bottom of the main pit, no fewer than twenty-seven galleries have been discovered during excavations this century. These run horizontally to connect with other shafts, forming a maze of tunnels at the level of the 'floorstone' – the top-quality flint that was the basis of the stone-age technology. The main galleries were up to seven feet wide and five feet high – just large enough for two miners to pass with bent backs to carry out chalk and flints. In

the smaller galleries, the miners lay prostrate, prising the flints from the seam with polished flint axes and the antlers of red deer. It was obviously skilled work and the miners were probably professionals who laboured in the bowels of these wooded slopes while their contemporaries cultivated crops and grazed their livestock in the clearings below. The flints were knapped to fashion sharp axes with which these ancient pioneers cut down the wildwood. To the might of the axe, they added the consuming force of fire. The forest succumbed to the flames to reveal a light sandy soil that was relatively easy to till. From the ashes of the wildwood, a new, open landscape emerged. Its fertility was short-lived and when these farmers moved on to clear more virgin woodland, the exhausted soils were left, once more, to nature.

Grimes Graves and the surrounding woodlands were perhaps the first of Britain's industrial landscapes. Here, a natural resource was hewn from the earth which then, stripped of its spoils, was left to be reclaimed by a new invasion of plants and animals. The process was to happen time and again throughout the natural history of these islands – creating an ever-changing patchwork of landscapes and habitats for wildlife. What happened in the Breckland was mirrored throughout the south of England, then further north, as the population of ancient Britain spread through the wildwood with its 'slash and burn' style of agriculture. Whenever these tribes moved on to create new forest clearings, the open areas of grassland and heathland left behind would be quickly reinvaded by the shrubs and trees of the adjacent forest. But in the Breckland and some other heathland parts of Britain the wildwood never returned. Today, it is the rabbits and sheep that keep the shrubs at bay but in neolithic times, once the people and their domestic stock had moved on, the man-made heathland was probably perpetuated by the dry continental climate of that region and by the red deer and other herbivores that emerged from the forest. The flora of the Breckland still reflects its unique combination of soils and climate. In the sandy areas the nutrients have been leached away, leaving an impoverished acid soil which will only support plants such as heath bedstraw, wavy hair-grass and lichens, together with some coastal species such as sand sedge and buck's-horn plantain. In contrast, the chalky areas have shallow soils rich in plants normally associated with downland – species such as fescues and bent grasses, meadow oat-grass, knotted pearlwort and wild thyme. It is here on the calcareous soils that you may find the beautiful spiked speedwell, with its tall heads of deep blue flowers. The fauna of this eastern heathland is also continental in character. In addition to the grayling, its butterflies include the green hairstreak and the silver-studded blue and several moths more typical of coastal sand dunes. The ringed plover takes advantage of the open sandy ground for nesting and on the more chalky patches the rare stone curlew can be glimpsed among the grass and bracken. Perhaps the most characteristic creature of these heaths is the adder. In early summer, the pregnant females laze in the open, soaking in the warmth of the Breckland sand.

Left The green colour on the underside of its wings, unique among British butterflies, makes the green hairstreak difficult to see on gorse – the favoured foodplant of its caterpillar

The adder, the only poisonous snake in Britain, is absent from Ireland. The females retain their eggs within their bodies until hatching – an adaptation which has allowed this reptile to extend its range to our northerly climate.

In time, throughout the length of Britain and Ireland, the devastating mix of flint and fire cleared away vast tracts of forest. Just as we can see today in the tropical forests of South-East Asia and elsewhere, such unsophisticated 'slash and burn' techniques of agriculture soon deplete the soil of its nutrients. The disappearance of the trees with their extensive root systems changes the structure and chemistry of the soil; burning removes much of the plant material which might otherwise bind it together. Rain leaches the minerals down through the soil, often forming a podsol – a dense pan of iron salts and other crystals which permanently restricts the growth of most trees. Without these minerals, the soil becomes acid, changing the nature of the land. While forest can seldom return without help from man, conditions are then perfect for the development of heath, moor and, in the wettest areas, the peaty 'blanket bog' that is now so characteristic of much of upland Britain and Ireland. What all these places have in common is the acidic and peaty nature of their soils – the differences between them are simply ones of degree. The peat of heathland, such as that in the south of England, is shallow and relatively dry, whereas the moorland peat of the south-west and northern uplands is deeper and has less sand, which gives it a greater capacity for holding water. The wettest parts of moorlands are the blanket bogs themselves and it is here that thick mats of sphagnum moss become the characteristic vegetation. But such boggy areas are not confined to the high moorlands; you will find them in the valleys of lowland heaths where the rain collects, helping to create the damp conditions of bogland. These seemingly wild, untouched places were originally forest and their present nature is a result of man's management of the landscape over the millennia.

The large conspicuous yellow eyes of the stone curlew are indicative of the nocturnal habits of this bird of dry open spaces in southern and eastern England. Its name derives from its shrill curlew-like call that pierces the Breckland dusk.

Some of the familiar lowland heaths of southern England on the light, sandy soils that stretch across from Hampshire to the London basin and down through Surrey and Sussex were probably initiated even before the Breckland of East Anglia. Pollen evidence suggests that parts were created from pine forest and some heaths may be as old as 6000 years. Today, because of their soils and climate, they have a distinctly different character from the Breckland. In some places, where there is no longer grazing or burning, woodland has managed to re-establish itself. Birch is now common on the heaths of Surrey and north Hampshire, while in the New Forest and Dorset it is the Scots pine which has once more become established on the impoverished soils – though probably by planting in historic times. The most characteristic plant of the southern heathlands is of course heather – sometimes called ling. It is perfectly adapted to colonising new open ground and has a prolific capacity for reproducing itself. Each heather plant produces a vast number of minute seeds which need light to germinate. If shed on the open soil surface, they develop rapidly; if the seeds are buried, they can remain viable for many years. Fire actually encourages their germination by removing the other vegetation.

Controlled burning is an effective way of heathland management, discouraging the growth of plants which might otherwise dominate the grasses and heathers that provide the main diet of domestic stock and wild game. Gorse, that thorny beauty of late winter, is very characteristic of heathland. It seems that before the creation of heaths, this hardy bush was common on treeless, windswept hilltops, rather as it is on the Lizard peninsula today. It may have been planted by neolithic farmers as a source of winter fodder for their livestock, being rich in protein. Like other members of the pea family, gorse helps to enrich the soil but, if allowed to grow too large, its bushes form dense thickets inhibiting the growth of other, less tenacious plant species. Throughout history, fire has controlled the natural tendency for the fragile character of heathland to be overwhelmed by a new regime of shrubs and trees. Whether by accident or design, it has often enhanced the habitat in the interests of man and his domestic stock and also to the benefit of a small but fascinating variety of wild plant and animal species which have colonised heathland and made it their special home.

Paradoxically, it is the impoverished nature of the soil and limited variety of species that can thrive on it which give heathland its unique character and attraction. Not only are there fewer kinds of plants and animals but fewer numbers. For naturalists, the principal interest of heathland species is their ability to survive under difficult conditions; it is their highly adapted way of life that makes them scarce elsewhere and this rarity value enhances their appeal to us. It is the insect fauna of these heather-covered tracts of Britain that excels in rare and dramatic creatures. Many of them are predatory – as anyone knows who has been pursued and bitten by the myriad biting insects of a Scottish moorland summer – including dragonflies, flying beetles, ants, gnats and many kinds of solitary wasps. Dragonflies are often the most conspicuous, hunting for

Above Sand lizards bask on the open sandy patches between heather clumps; in England this colourful reptile is on the edge of its European range and is restricted to a few southern heaths.
Right Ling is the most characteristic heather of dry heathlands. Its small, leathery, overlapping leaves help cut down water loss – but surprisingly still provide food for a host of heathland animals, from emperor moths to grouse.

128

food over the heath, and some of our rarest species are found only on a few southern heaths – dragonflies such as the emerald hawker, which frequents the heaths of the Ashdown Forest, and the white-faced dragonfly, which darts across remnants of heathland left in Surrey. The New Forest, which still has great tracts of heath, has ideal conditions for dragonflies and other insects which lay their eggs in unpolluted water – a vital feature which is disappearing from many otherwise perfect sites. The tiger beetle is a strong flying insect with large eyes and immense jaws. In sunshine it chases over the heath in pursuit of all kinds of insects – flying very rapidly with a tell-tale and menacing buzzing sound. Its larvae are also highly predatory, living in burrows in the sand, from which they emerge to seize passing prey in their huge jaws. Food is scarce and many heathland creatures must actively pursue each meal. The hunting wasps are especially characteristic of these southern heaths where you can come across a female dragging large caterpillars, which she has paralysed with her sting, into nest holes in the ground. Here, she lays an egg on her prey and seals up the hole. Later when her offspring hatches, there is a living larder waiting to be devoured. Even the spiders of the heath can be preyed on by these wasps. The relatively common wolf-spider catches its own prey by building a silken tunnel from which it pounces on smaller creatures; it, too, must watch out for the marauding wasp. Below the heather, armies of ants search the sandy soil for prey, and in the autumn collect stores of grass and heather seeds. Just above the heather, the long-bodied robber flies patrol the heath, catching other insects in mid-air and sucking out their nutritious juices.

It is an uncompromising world of prey and predator. Even plants feed on plants. The parasitic dodder entwines the stems of gorse and heather and absorbs their sap through penetrating roots. Of the insects, it is really only the moths and butterflies and the bees and beetles of the heather which are conspicuously dependent on the vegetation. Of these, the large emperor moth is the most distinctive. Its caterpillars feed on the leaves of heather and bramble, and the moths emerge on the wing in April. They have four large eye-spots on their wings, which seem to deter attack by the many predators which scan the heath. Equally spectacular is the pine hawk-moth, which is often found where heathland has been invaded by conifers. As on the Breckland, the characteristic butterflies of heath are the grayling and the silver-studded blue. Although the so-called heath fritillary is really a butterfly of scrub and woodland edge, it has recently taken to more open heathland, especially where its main foodplant, the common cow-wheat, has been encouraged by controlled burning. Although there are few grasses and herbs for the other herbivorous insects of the heath, there are several species which consume the heather itself. Insects such as small black thrips or thunderbugs have mouth parts which can pierce its tough cellulose. Other insects that tap the sap of the heather include some psyllid bugs and leaf-hoppers. However, most of the vegetation of heathland goes to form

Left The caterpillars of the emperor moth are entirely black when they hatch on the stems of heather; it is only later in the season that they acquire their vivid green coloration which gives them superb camouflage.

litter and eventually humus or peat. This in turn forms the staple diet of soil animals such as pot-worms and cranefly larvae, but each year as much as ten per cent of the plant production remains unconsumed and adds to the accumulating humus or peat.

The dry, warm habitat of a southern heath with its strange array of large insects makes it a perfect setting for reptiles and all six British species are found on our lowland heathland. The adder and the grass snake both need to be within reach of water but the rare smooth snake and sand lizard are both able to occupy dry, open heathland throughout the year. The smooth snake is now confined to the extreme south of England and the sand lizard, although found as far north as Ainsdale on the Lancashire coast, is limited to a handful of heathland sites. Likewise, the slow-worm is more common in the warmer south but can be found in Scotland and Wales. Only the common lizard reached Ireland and in summer it can be seen basking in the drier heather-covered fringes of the west coast bogs. But it is the southern heaths of Dorset, Hampshire and Surrey that are the best haunts of reptiles in the British Isles; there are even some sites where all six species are found together. Such places are treasured as prime examples of ancient English heathland.

For ornithologists, heaths epitomise rare birds. Not only is this special habitat becoming a scarce, fragmented commodity but several of the bird species that live in it are at the northern limit of their natural range. The much cherished Dartford warbler has suffered dramatic rises and falls in its numbers in the last century and above all other birds has been adopted as an indicator of the success of heathland conservation in southern England. It is one of our few resident

Left The undersides of a resting grayling butterfly's wings allow it to blend with the mottled colours of its heathland habitat.
Above It is not just the birds of heathland that are threatened by the fragmentation of their habitat, but also many of the heathland insects. The reeling song of the heath grasshopper is now as rare on southern heaths as the scolding call of the Dartford warbler.

133

passerine birds that feeds on insects throughout the year. For this reason its population is greatly affected by cold winters, such as those of 1961–2 and 1962–3, following which only ten pairs could be found throughout all the lowland heaths. The two most important factors determining the distribution of the species on our southern heaths are the presence of mature heather plants for nesting sites and a generous mixture of medium-sized gorse bushes to provide the insect life on which the birds depend. Modern management of heathland is often unfavourable to these warblers because the burning intended to improve the grazing has encouraged grass and bracken but stunted the growth of the heather and the gorse. The survival of the Dartford warbler in Britain may now be totally dependent on the management of heathland reserves aimed exclusively at its welfare.

Another heathland bird at the northern extremity of its climatic range is the woodlark, the bird that many people claim has the most superb song of our islands. Its clear fluty notes are interspersed with an enchanting warble that is pure music to the human ear. Like the Dartford warbler, this bird is also very selective about its diet and its terrain but its specific requirements are different. It prefers heather that is short and also needs a few tall trees from which it can broadcast its song. The conflicting needs of these two birds must pose problems for conservationists concerned with heathland management! But there is now a real urgency to study the detailed ecological requirements of the creatures that live on the heath. What was once created by our ancestors for rough grazing has been reclaimed by later generations to meet more pressing human needs. Most of it has given way to our twentieth-century demands for more land on which to build houses, grow food, extract sand and oil or plant a new generation of forests. When Thomas Hardy immortalised the heathland of his native Dorset at the end of the last century, there were more than 50,000 acres of heather-covered countryside in that county. Now there is little more than a fifth of that figure and the remnants are fragmented far and wide. The story is the same on the Continent, where only small pockets survive from the once extensive heathlands that stretched from Jutland down to the maritime heaths of Spain; there is precious little left of this colourful habitat that exists nowhere else outside western Europe. Like the characters in Hardy's novels, the heathland of Wessex has become part of a tableau that is truly English.

Nothing captures the spirit of such ancient heathlands better than the sight and sound of that nocturnal bird, the nightjar, stirring in the embers of a summer's day. As dusk falls over the heath at the end of June, the air is full of the heavy scent of gorse and the hum of insects on the wing. Grey against the fading sky, the male nightjar arrives back at the nest from his secret daytime roosting site on the heath. A flash of white on his wings announces his approach to his mate who, brooding her chicks, crouches motionless in the nest on the ground like a lichen-covered log. Swooping over her, the male utters a soft, croaking call of greeting and then drifts away into the gloom. From a songpost in the heather he starts his churring song – like a distant motor bike it quickens the pulse of the heathland night.

In response to her mate's soft calling, the female nightjar leaves her well-hidden nest to join him in a dusk hunt for moths over the midsummer heath.

WESSEX HEATH AT NIGHT

In a pool of moonlight we can hear, see and smell how many plants and animals use the darkness of the night on a Wessex heath. Night-scented plants attract moths for pollination, glow-worms display for mates and grasshopper warblers sing their reeling territorial songs. To experience a southern heath at night is to be transported back to the wilderness of Thomas Hardy's corner of England.

In the dim light you may see the spectacular aerobatics of the nightjar as it chases moths or indulges in wing-clapping breeding display flights. Its churring song carries in the still air, a mysterious, eerie sound of the heathland night.

Many small mammals, especially mice, and reptiles are active during the night, foraging for their food in the undergrowth. Toads, too, usually emerge under the cover of darkness, and predators such as the silent-flying, sharp-eyed owls roost during the day and emerge at dusk to hunt these night creatures.

Emperor, lover's-knot and knot-grass moths are three of dozens of species of moths which fly after dusk across the heath. Many will be caught in the webs of hammock spiders stretched out across the ling.

Araneus quadratus is another spider spinning a web in the spikes of the gorse bushes. *Armillaria*, the honey fungus, is a fascinating luminous fungus, once used to mark paths across heaths and open land.

137

The heathland of ling and bell heather is essentially a place of dry, peaty soils; wherever water saturates the ground, the vegetation takes on a different character. In place of the familiar heather, the cross-leaved heath takes over, together with heath-rush, cottongrass, sundew and purple moor-grass. In the damp valleys of our southern heathland there are pockets of waterlogged bogland where sphagnum mosses and other damp-loving plants come into their element. Because of the nutrients in the water, such 'valley bogs', whether in the lowlands of southern England or more northern upland regions, can be appreciably richer in plant life than the drier heather-covered land around them. Sure signs of that fertility are the conspicuously dark heads of the black bog-rush which stand proud of the surface of the moss. In the cooler north, valley bogs are poor in animal life but in the warm south such soggy places are the haunts of the large marsh grasshopper – the largest species of grasshopper in the British Isles. On Hartland Moor, in the New Forest and in western Ireland, this impressive insect clings to the stems of bog myrtle and bog asphodel in the wettest parts of these bogs. Equally at home in the damp valley bogs of our southern heaths is the bog bush cricket with its continuous chirping song which, in late summer and autumn, is a characteristic sound of so many English heaths.

In other, damper, parts of the British Isles, bogland extends over great tracts of the open countryside. On the high moorlands of the north, this takes the form of rolling expanses of blanket bog but in central Ireland and the rain-lashed west of Britain, you may come across one of the most extraordinary bog features of these islands – the 'raised bog'. Often with their origins in low-lying, well-watered, fertile ground, these boggy mires formed successive layers of peat which, in time, raised the whole surface of the bog above the water-table, away from the influence of the underlying bedrock and drainage water. What had started perhaps as a lime-rich fen was transformed into an acid bog in which only heathers and bog-moss and other plants tolerant of such impoverished conditions could continue to thrive. These communities totally depend on rain-water for an input of nutrients. One of the fascinations of such bogs is that their centres are often twenty or thirty feet higher than their edges. You can stand on the rim of one of these raised bogs and see a gentle dome of heather rising into the distance. If you venture cautiously out on to the bog, stepping from one dry tussock to another, you will be rewarded by discovering a secret delicate community of plants that over thousands of years has developed a character quite unlike any other habitat in the British Isles. Here is the world of the cottongrass and bogbean, bog myrtle and the stunningly beautiful sundew. The further you go towards the centre of the bog, the more acid is the water in the pools. Year by year there is an increasingly fragile balance between the slender supply of nutrients in the water and the growth of the bog vegetation that lifts the terrain further from the water-table of the surrounding landscape. The sundew, with its ability to trap and digest insects which land on its sticky spoon-shaped leaves, has evolved a way of supplementing its mineral diet. In a very similar way, the butterwort catches insects in a sticky secretion on its fleshy leaves, which then curl inwards along their edges trapping the prey and absorbing its nutrients. By turning carnivorous, these species escape the tyranny of the frail bog regime; but if the bog dries out they, too, are doomed.

Bogs are indeed ancient and mysterious places. Many of them are surrounded by superstition and folklore. Even the beautiful bog asphodel, a small lily with a spike of yellow flowers, is accused of causing brittle bones in sheep and cattle that are allowed to graze on it. Like all plants of this bogland deprived of lime, the 'bone-breaker', as the asphodel is sometimes called, is blameless. From time immemorial, you let your livestock graze there at your peril. Instead, over the centuries, farmers have drained most of the raised bogs of Britain and Ireland and created more fertile grassland in their place. Conservationists are understandably alarmed by how little of this delicate and internationally important habitat survives to help tell the tale of our natural history.

From a distance, the fluffy white seedheads of the cottongrass are one of the most conspicuous features of bogs. This sedge is common from the lowland bogs of the New Forest to the bleak blanket bogs of Ireland.

Left Although uncomfortable to explore, all bogs reward the intrepid naturalist with a colourful but delicate world of plants and insects – fragile communities that, in different forms, have developed in many poorly-drained areas.
Above In summer the yellow spikes of the bog asphodel bring a splash of colour to many bogs in the British Isles.

About 7000 years ago – at the time when the British Isles were cut off by the sea – the climate became much wetter. This warm but wet Atlantic period lasted for 2000 years or so. During this damp era there was a resurgence in the formation of bogland – particularly in the Pennines and Scotland. It seems that on this higher ground the tree cover was gradually overwhelmed by the spread of peaty bogs from the bottoms of the valleys or on gentle damp slopes. Then, in time, the flat plateaus higher up became blanketed in the encroaching bogland. Deep in the peat of these blanket bogs are the remains of the ancient forest that it submerged – often pine, birch and oak – which were rooted in the underlying mineral soil. Sometimes there are bands of charcoal indicative of extensive forest fires. Such blanket peat may well have been the result of the activities of neolithic man as he invaded these uplands, cutting and burning his way across the north of Britain. In Ireland, most blanket bogs date from early bronze-age times, as do many in central Wales, whereas on parts of Dartmoor and Exmoor in south-west Britain there are some of later origin. During the Iron Age, there was another deterioration of the climate to cooler and wetter weather, further encouraging the growth of peat bog at the expense of trees. Since then, the climate of the British Isles has not changed dramatically. There have been periodic fluctuations in average temperatures and rainfall, but conditions have been fairly stable for 2500 years. To maintain their soggy nature, blanket bogs must have a steady supply of rainfall. The poorly drained uplands of Britain and Ireland are not only lacking in nutrients but also blessed with that persistent damp atmosphere on which the bog vegetation thrives. It is not surprising that blanket bog is commoner and more extensive in these upland areas of the British Isles than anywhere else in Europe.

Where blanket bog has dried out with changes in climate or has been burnt or drained by man, it is transformed into upland heath which we recognise as moorland. In other parts of our hill and mountain country, similar heather-covered moorland has developed following the widespread destruction of the wildwood over the last three or four thousand years. This forest clearance, burning, grazing and gradual soil deterioration seems to have been started at different times in different regions of Britain. The North Yorkshire Moors and the moorland of central Wales date back nearly 3000 years to the late Bronze Age and on the moors of the south-west Lake District there are burial cairns and stone circles from the same period. Much of the rest of the Lake District was not deforested until 1500 years ago, when many hill farms sprang up there and also in the Galloway hills of southern Scotland. Other moorlands of even more recent origin include the southern Lake District, where Viking and Norse colonisation led to extensive development of the valleys for grazing. All these places are still dominated by heather. As well as the ubiquitous ling, there is usually bell heather and its close relatives bilberry, cowberry and bearberry. Where the moorland is intensively grazed and regularly burnt, a variety of grasses and upland herbs appear, including such common plants as tormentil and heath bedstraw, both of which are widespread on lowland heaths of southern England. As on these warmer heaths, the main wild consumers of the moorland

Red deer, formerly creatures of the forest, have been forced to adapt to a way of life on the bleak northern moorlands where the bellowing of the stags heralds their autumn rut. In winter they seek shelter in the valleys where they often damage young crops and forestry plantations.

vegetation are the insects – thrips, bugs and leafhoppers – which feed on the plant sap. Red deer and mountain hares may often be seen among the heather but it is the more nutritious grass and herbs that they seek, and not the hardy heathers.

The one creature that feeds almost exclusively on young heather is the red grouse – the bird that has pride of place over much of the moorland of Britain and Ireland. These handsome birds, so favoured by sportsmen with shotguns, are perfectly adapted to moorland conditions. The adults feed on the shoots, flowers and fruit of heather but the chicks feed mainly on insects, which provide them with protein for their rapidly growing bodies. By wintertime, the young grouse have graduated to the heather itself. Even when the moorland is under a blizzard, they reach the young shoots by burrowing into the snow. The red grouse that is resident here in Britain is essentially the same species as is found in Scandinavia. There it is known as the 'willow grouse' because of its predilection for the young shoots and fruits of the willow, birch and bilberry, which grow on

In spring the moorlands echo to the crowing calls of the male grouse as they establish territories. Where the heather and its associated insect-life is rich, the territories need only be small; management by regular burning ensures a high density of these game-birds.

the open margins of the northern forests. Such landscapes there today are probably very similar to the early tundra of upland Britain just after the ice. The willow grouse would have been one of the first birds to seek its fortunes in these exposed northern regions of the British Isles. As the wildwood advanced from the south, such open vegetation became more scarce and the willow grouse would have been confined to patches of suitable habitat further north or nearer the tops of mountains. But as moorland expanded, the grouse was able to extend its range once again. In place of willow shoots, it took a liking for the heather that now coloured the uplands with its purple hue. In time, the grouse that came to the British Isles lost the white summer wing colour of its Scandinavian cousin and became the heather-eating 'red' race that is the symbol of moorland Britain and found nowhere else in the world. Its call is one of the most distinctive sounds of our uplands and its welfare attracts more money to the hills than any other bird. Today, a well-managed grouse moor can support as many as eighty pairs of red grouse on every square mile of heather. To keep the right balance of young shoots for food and mature bushes for shelter and nesting, the heather is systematically burned in rotation. At the end of the winter, as you trek across the moors of northern Britain, you may see the plumes of smoke rising from this upland wilderness. The fires kindled by our ancestors seem strangely close.

CHAPTER SEVEN
FRESH PASTURES

Wherever you go in the British Isles you will find grass. It is the hallmark of our countryside and for many people it is the most essential ingredient of our green and pleasant land. Grass is favoured by the temperate climate of these islands and by the high rainfall; in some western areas of Britain and Ireland, the grass grows for nine months of the year – a natural crop that has fashioned the face of our landscape and dictated the style of our farming.

There are more than 150 different species of grass growing wild in the British Isles – more than any other family of flowering plants. Along with many herbs and ferns, these grasses would have first graced the early forests – thriving wherever sunlight broke through the leafy canopy and struck the forest floor. Here, in natural glades, grazed by the wild creatures of the forest, grasses would rapidly multiply – their delicate wind-blown seeds borne on the air to colonise any open, sunlit corner of a landscape that was still primarily the preserve of towering trees. Only on a few coastal areas, mountain-tops and inland gorges where trees were sparse or absent was there any terrain that we would recognise as grassland. It was from such outposts that many of the typical grassland species of plants would have spread to establish themselves wherever the forest would let them in. Ever since the ice retreated, there has been a continual battle for space and light between grass and trees and so often the sun-loving plants on the ground had been the losers. Their new lease of life – their awakening – came with the arrival of the first farmers. With their axes and their fire, these agricultural pioneers laboriously felled the forest to let in the light. From the clearings they created or enlarged sprang the essence of the fresh pastures which provided grazing for the domestic stock of cattle and sheep they had brought from mainland Europe. The natural history of grasslands in Britain and Ireland is the story of a very close partnership between man and nature.

Natural grassland, unaffected by the influence of man or his grazing animals, is hard to find anywhere in our islands. On the steep sides of the Avon Gorge and Cheddar Gorge there are small pockets of grass and herbs growing in places which, because of their inaccessibility to sheep and cattle, have probably never been grazed by domestic stock. The thinness of the limestone soils and the exposed outlook have prevented the growth of trees. There are similar sites around the coast – notably on the west of Pembrokeshire where there has probably been grass ever since the climate was warm enough for it to flourish. But such examples are rare. The most likely beginnings of the grassland of these islands were probably natural glades in the wildwood. You can come across such places deep in the New Forest which, although created in the last 1000 years, has a feeling of antiquity. In spring and summer these glades have quite a different character from the surrounding woodland. The floor is carpeted with delicate and colourful herbs and the normally scant grasses form a dense green sward. Butterflies, bees and hoverflies forage between the flower heads and from the grass is heard the song of grasshoppers. Even the woodland birds seem less subdued as they emerge from the forest and explore the vibrant atmosphere of this warm and airy clearing. If you wait silently downwind, out of sight on the edge of a New Forest glade, the larger creatures of the wood may emerge to graze on the lush grass. As well as the ponies, you may see fallow deer or, if you are lucky, red or roe deer – all cautiously venturing out into the open to feast on the fresh natural pasture of this 'oasis' in the forest. Such glades in the ancient wildwood of Britain would have been a Mecca for the wild herbivores of the forest – not, of course, today's ponies and fallow deer, but the red deer which were abundant, roe deer, wild horse, perhaps bison but certainly the aurochs. These wild cattle were extremely common throughout much of Britain at the time when neolithic man first crossed from Europe. The aurochs had large

Bird's-foot-trefoil is now one of the most widespread grassland plants of the British Isles. Seven thousand years ago, when the wildwood covered most of the land, this and other plants of open ground would have been restricted to exposed cliffs and tops of mountains.

horns with a span of nearly four feet and must have been awe-inspiring creatures. They were never domesticated in Britain but remained forest game until they became extinct. The last European aurochs perished in Poland in 1627 but here in Britain they had probably disappeared by the Iron Age more than 2000 years before. In their place, as the forests were cleared and the grassland spread, the domesticated breeds of cattle and sheep which were brought across from Europe became the main beneficiaries of the newly created grazing. It was these tame herds and flocks and the domesticated pigs rooting in the soil that helped keep the forest at bay. In any one area their numbers were far greater than the wild herbivores of the forest and through their intensive grazing and foraging the new pastures of the forest soon increased in size. We know that they were fed with the foliage of elms and other trees – which would have been pollarded by those early farmers to provide a constant supply of young leaves and twigs. Wherever neolithic people settled with their domestic stock, the woodland dwindled and much of it was converted to land for growing grass or planting cereals and other crops brought from the mainland. Britain was becoming a pastoral land.

Today's farmers maintain the grasslands of the British Isles by grazing their stock and by making hay and silage. From the buttercup-meadows to upland sheepwalks, we have a great range of grassland habitats which reflects the long history of man's influence on the landscape.

For naturalists and for the wildlife they observe, the attraction of grassland is not simply the grass; it is the vast array of other plants which make up the sward giving it variety and colour. Unlike the familiar grass of our lawns and playing fields, which form a functional green cloak for the soil, the grasslands of the countryside are rich, living communities, often spangled with an intricate diversity of flowers and insects. Most of the familiar examples of grasslands rich in plant species are to be found on such open country as the chalk of the Sussex Downs and the limestone of the Yorkshire Dales but the most spectacular of all is the famous 'machair' of the Outer Hebrides. This is a grassland without parallel elsewhere in the British Isles and is a habitat to experience rather than describe. It has an ancient, natural feel about it. The archipelago of the Outer Hebrides comprises well over a hundred islands, including Lewis, Harris, North and South Uist, Benbecula and Barra. The east coasts of these islands, facing the mainland of Scotland, have much in common with the moorland of the Highlands but the western seaboards are, by contrast, vibrantly fertile. The Atlantic rollers break endlessly on long, white beaches of shells and sand, which form the basis of the machair. This Gaelic name describes the entire coastal strip, in places stretching a mile or two inland. It is the chalky content of the sand derived from wave-pounded shells that gives the soil fertility and lightness. In some places the calcium carbonate content of the sand is over eighty per cent and the plants that grow there are lime-loving species familiar to anyone who walks over chalk and limestone hills. The machair is vital to the crofting economy of the islands. It is grazed in spring and summer by sheep and cattle and some parts are cultivated in strips on a rotational system, the main crops being cereals and potatoes. Traditionally, these cultivated strips were fertilised with seaweeds cast up by winter gales but in recent years chemical fertilisers have become more widespread. What makes the machair unique is its traditional form of management whereby strips are cultivated for a year or two and then left fallow. This mosaic of cereal crops and fallow pasture creates a very varied habitat which has encouraged the grassland flora and fauna to flourish much as it has done ever since man first came to these remote islands.

Spring comes late to the Outer Hebrides. The winters are wet and windy and there is very little plant growth before May. Then, very suddenly, the machair comes to life. By mid-June it is ablaze with plants of almost every hue and the overall impression is one of a land of flowers rather than grass. For those of us more accustomed to the uniformity of modern farmland, the variety and abundance of the plant life is breathtaking. On the tiny Monach Isles, just to the west of North Uist, as many as 220 different species have been recorded – a living tapestry that celebrates the richness of the machair. But this is not the work of nature on her own; it is the result of man's management to promote summer grazing for his livestock and a crop of hay to see them through the winter. The composition of this fodder must rank as the most exotic of vegetarian diets! In addition to grasses such as red fescue, sweet vernal, cock's-foot, false oat and Yorkshire-fog, there are many leguminous plants including bird's-foot-trefoil, kidney vetch and white and red clovers. It is one of the most fascinating

When they landed on the Western Isles of Scotland, the first farmers created a coastal strip of grassland on which to feed their livestock. Over the millennia the Machair has been extended by grazing and cultivation to provide the basis of today's crofting economy.

attractions of this grassland that its overall hue changes as the season advances. There is silverweed and hawkbit, the blues of harebell and germander speedwell, the purple of selfheal, the pink of stork's-bill and the deep pink of thyme. In areas that are more damp and sheltered, orchids grow in profusion. Here in summer, against a dazzling backdrop of blue sea and white sand, is a galaxy of wild flowers that looks almost too good to be true.

The natural history wealth of the machair is not confined to its flora. Its birdlife is just as remarkable. From the beginning of March, the west coasts of the Outer Hebrides become alive with the sounds of waders returning to breed on the coastal grasslands. Six species are particularly numerous – the oyster-catcher, the lapwing, the ringed plover, the redshank, the dunlin and the snipe. Dotted between the nests and scrapes of these waders are the nests of other grassland birds including meadow pipits, wheatears and the emblem of open country – the skylark. So close is the proximity of the nests of the usually retiring skylark to those of dunlin, that you can sometimes hear the skylarks adopting the reeling call of the dunlin in their own melodious song. The main reason that all these birds thrive so well on the machair is the perpetuation of traditional crofting methods of agriculture and, in particular, the late cutting of the hay. It is usually well into July before the strips of grassland, with their profusion of plants, are ripe enough for harvesting; by then the waders have raised their broods and can seek refuge in the cereal crops and marshy vegetation that fringe the machair itself. It is this taller cover of sedges and iris that is the favoured haunt of the Hebrides' most celebrated grassland bird – the corncrake.

Little is known about the habits of the corncrake. More often heard than seen, this secretive bird – also called the landrail – is favoured by traditional farming still practised on the Hebrides and in parts of Ireland.

152

Only two or three decades ago this species was widespread on the mainland of Scotland and was considered common in some parts of pastoral England. Now the only places in Britain where you can be assured of hearing its characteristic rasping call are the Orkneys and Hebrides. Corncrakes spend winter in Africa and when they arrive back on the machair in early spring the best cover available to these shy birds is that offered by the beds of iris. From here they move into the lush vegetation of the meadows to raise their young when the grass has grown. If the iris beds were to be drained or the machair grass cropped early as silage, then this last stronghold of the corncrake would instantly lose its attraction. Such is the delicate balance between the activities of man and wildlife on the grasslands of the British Isles.

By the beginning of the Bronze Age, large tracts of southern England had been cleared of trees. So had the coastal plain of north-west England, and in Scotland bronze-age people had cleared areas such as Strath Tay and as far north as the Outer Hebrides and the Orkneys. In Ireland much of the east had been converted to grassland, and even Co. Mayo on the Atlantic coast had been transformed to open country. But there was still a marked regional contrast between north and south. Then from Europe came the technology of iron. Not only were iron axes more effective in felling trees but the process of smelting demanded an increasing quantity of wood for charcoal. Throughout the Weald of Sussex the charcoal burners' fires would fill the ancient wildwood with a haze of drifting blue wood-smoke and to the south the Downs were conspicuous for their nakedness. It was here, on the higher ground safe from attack, that earlier the neolithic farmers had settled; now with the iron plough and multiple teams of oxen, their successors continued to transform the gently undulating chalkland into a mosaic of grass and crops. A spectacular legacy of the Iron Age is the series of fortified hilltop camps which stretched across the Downs from Caburn, east of Lewes, to Wiltshire and Dorset and the ancient fortress of Maiden Castle. From these vantage points the Celtic people of the south looked out over a new landscape of fields and grassland, interspersed with remnants of the wildwood. By now, sheep had become the most numerous domestic animal. Cattle were mainly used as draught animals but the sheep provided plentiful meat and wool, and dung for fertilising arable plots. Across the chalklands of southern England, vast flocks nibbled the rich vegetation, turning it into the characteristic springy turf over which we can walk today.

The slopes of the Downs are at their most colourful in early summer. If you look in detail at the close-cropped sward, you may be able to distinguish as many as thirty different species of plant in any square yard of turf. Such variety is typical of chalk and limestone soils, which are usually rather shallow but rich in humus. Paradoxically, such soils are often very infertile, lacking in nutrients such as phosphorus, nitrogen, potassium and iron but having ample calcium. Such conditions do not encourage rapid plant growth but favour the small, relatively slow-growing species. It is the sheep which suppress the growth of the more vigorous plants by grazing the sward to a uniform height. Unlike other flowering plants, the leaves of grasses have growing points at the base of the plant and are therefore not killed by nibbling. Grazing by animals not only favours the growth of grasses and sedges but also small perennial herbs such as salad burnet, rough hawkbit, mouse-ear hawkweed, plantains and the stemless thistle, which grow close to the ground. Annuals are uncommon in chalk grassland – the soil is just not rich enough to nourish them to maturity in one season. The diminutive chalk eyebright is an exception – as is the yellow rattle. Both plants seem to be partially parasitic on the roots of other herbs and grasses which accounts for their survival. Familiar-sounding herbs such as wild basil, thyme and marjoram add to the aroma of the turf, bringing an extra sweetness to the summer air. As the season advances, the delicate harebells make their appearance, waving in the soft August breezes on their slender stems that hold the deep blue heads proud above the turf. It is perhaps though for orchids that chalk grassland is best known. In June, some slopes are covered by carpets of fragrant and common spotted-orchids and later in the summer the pyramidal orchids can be extremely common. One of the most admired is the bee orchid, with its rose-pink sepals and lower lip decorated in uncanny resemblance to the bumble-bee. For botanists, it is not just the beauty of orchids which makes them so fascinating, it is their extraordinary way of life. They all produce minute seeds which contain very little in the way of food reserve. The growth of the seedling is slow and the first flowers may not appear for several years. The bee orchid, for example, takes six to eight years to bloom. During this time it is dependent on food substances absorbed from a fungus which grows in association with its roots and which in delicate partnership with the orchid also benefits from the strange liaison. In time, the orchid stores enough food in its underground tubers to become independent of the fungus. Many grassland orchids such as the spotted-orchid then produce flower spikes for several years in succession, while others, such as the bee orchid, have stored only enough food to produce one magnificent floral head which, having shed a multitude of minute seeds, usually dies along with the whole body of the plant.

One of the most prominent features of downland turf is created by one of its smallest inhabitants. Those grassy hillocks which you can find scattered like cushions across the sward are the citadels of the yellow field ant. Each dome conceals a honeycomb of passages and chambers which is home to perhaps 25,000 ants. The mounds are the breeding centre for a colony and link with other passages that spread into the soil and turf beyond. A sweep of downland may take in hundreds of anthills, the size and number of which can be a good indicator of the antiquity of the grassland. In several places on the downs of Wiltshire, it is thought that the individual mounds are 150 years old and would have been well-established centres of downland life when Hardy's Gabriel Oak tended his flocks across these fabled sheepwalks of Wessex.

It is entirely due to the countless generations of shepherds who have grazed their sheep across southern England since the Bronze and Iron Ages that downland has become such a feature of our natural and social history. It is difficult to think of the gentle chalk hills of the south without that close-cropped turf.

Here is the long-established home for many of our most treasured insects — especially the butterflies, which reflect the rich diversity of the chalkland flora. Commonest is the meadow brown butterfly, which appears in June and July, often in huge numbers and whose caterpillars feed on a variety of grasses. The adults of the small heath appear earlier as do the equally abundant common blue, which can be found throughout the summer and whose caterpillars feed mainly on the leaves of bird's-foot-trefoil.

Many orchids have flowers which so resemble insects that they attract males in search of a mate. Inadvertently, the insect picks up sticky parcels of pollen which it delivers to the next floral hoax. Despite its convincing mimicry, the bee orchid seems to have abandoned this insect-pollination in favour of a more assured self-pollination.

155

Two other members of the blue family of butterflies, the chalkhill blue and the adonis blue, have an extraordinary liaison with ants. Chalkhill blues spend the winter as eggs, which the females have laid on the grass and other plant stems late in the summer. Within each egg is a fully developed larva which hibernates until the warmth of the spring. The eggs of the less common adonis blue, laid in late summer, hatch out after a week or so and then over-winter as microscopic caterpillars, attached by a silken pad to the underside of the vetch leaves. By April, the caterpillars of both species have emerged to feed on these leaves. Those of the chalkhill blue tend to feed after dusk, whereas those of the adonis, which will often occupy the same patch of turf, feed during the day. It is during the early morning that if you look carefully with the help of a hand lens you might witness one of the most fascinating of relationships in the insect world. When the caterpillars of the adonis butterfly are no more than a quarter of an inch long, their bodies become coated with honeydew. This sweet, sugary liquid, rich in amino acids, is secreted by microscopic glands all over the caterpillar and particularly by a gland on its tail. Here, quite large droplets form and next to the gland is a pair of slits from which two minute structures periodically protrude – rather like a sweep's brush emerging from the top of a chimney. All this unlikely behaviour has a dramatic effect on the ants of the immediate neighbourhood. The sweet honeydew is evidently highly attractive to the ants, which swarm over the caterpillars to drink their fill of the secretions. In the early morning you might see up to thirty worker ants feeding from one caterpillar after it has emerged to feed itself on the vetch plants. The adonis caterpillar is frequently attended by tiny red ants of *Myrmica* species and they

will defend their charges against other species which are likewise attracted by the addictive sweet offerings of the infant butterfly. But what does the caterpillar gain from this strange relationship? It seems that the answer is simply care and protection. The ants are constantly attentive to the young insect that they collectively adopt. Once discovered in the grass, they never leave its side even at night. When the sun goes down, the caterpillar descends the stem of the vetch to the safety of the soil, where the ants often bury it in a specially formed cell in the earth. Here it is attended by ten or twelve ants which continue the 'milking' through the night. In the morning the caterpillar emerges to continue feeding, oblivious of the increasing number of excited ants that shadow its every move. The most vulnerable time for any caterpillar is when it sheds its skin to moult into a larger stage; it is during the three or four days of each moult that the caterpillar gains greatest benefit from the protection afforded by its attentive custodians. Eventually, the caterpillar seeks out a crevice in the soil to pupate. It forms into a chrysalis and undergoes the tissue reorganisation from which it will emerge as the adult butterfly. Even during this dormant stage of its life, the creature continues to secrete honeydew and the ants continue to look after it, often incorporating the cell of the chrysalis into the underground passages of the ant colony. Then the chrysalis opens and the adult form emerges. Reaching the surface of the soil, it expands its shimmering blue wings and soaks up the warmth of the downland air. Around it swarm the tiny red ants that have nursed it to adulthood. Until the moment it flies, the ants guard their benefactor, scurrying around until it finally dries the tips of its wings. Then, suddenly, the perfectly formed adonis lifts off into the summer breeze.

Left The aptly-named chalkhill blue butterfly is abundant on the chalk and limestone grasslands of the southern half of England throughout late summer. Its caterpillars usually feed on the horseshoe vetch which thrives on grazed downland. In Lincolnshire it became extinct soon after myxomatosis reduced the rabbit population.

Above The pupa of the Adonis blue secretes honeydew, ensuring the continued protection of ants during this vulnerable stage of its life cycle.

Compared with earlier times, the animal now conspicuously absent from the downs is the sheep. In Thomas Hardy's time, a century ago, countless flocks roamed the green hills from Kent across to deepest Wessex, keeping the turf in constant trim in the tradition first started by bronze-age people. Now arable farming has replaced much of that ancient grassland and what sheep remain are concentrated on modern fields of rye-grass. The camps and burial mounds of the downland tribes have been deserted by domestic animals. Had it not been for the rabbit, probably introduced to these islands in Norman times, the close-cropped carpet of the downs would have long since reverted to a tangle of hawthorn scrub and eventually woodland. During the early part of this century when sheep flocks were dwindling, their role as grazers of the downland sward was adopted by the increasingly large populations of feral rabbits, which had escaped from fenced-off warrens. Although unpopular with the arable farmers, the rabbit helped maintain the nature of the turf by cropping it short and nibbling away the seedlings of invading shrubs. With the introduction of the myxomatosis virus in 1953, the rabbit population was reduced in just two years to less than one per cent of its former level. Although they have made a come-back, the once familiar rabbits of chalk downland are no longer holding the woodland at bay. Over great tracts of the downs of southern England the scrub has already returned and with it the immigrants from the forest edge. On a morning in early summer you can hear the difference. In place of grasshoppers and skylarks, there is now the song of willow warblers and whitethroats heralding the return of woodland. Here the landscape, left to itself, is turning full circle back to the tangled forest that our ancestors so painstakingly cleared.

Rabbits were an important part of the economy of Norman Britain. Managed in huge warrens, the adults – originally called coneys – were valued for their meat and fur. Over the centuries they escaped to become the most familiar wild mammal of the countryside; their proverbial breeding habits led to their persecution as pests and to the eventual unofficial introduction of the myxomatosis virus which drastically reduced their numbers.

There has been a monument at this site for nearly fifty centuries. The present Stonehenge is the third stone circle to have been built in this now remote part of the Salisbury plain and dates from 3500 years ago. Whatever its original purpose, it stands as a symbol of man's increasing domination of the landscape. Throughout the British Isles as far west as the Atlantic coast of Ireland and north as the Isle of Lewis, our ancestors erected impressive megaliths – landmarks which celebrated a change from their former nomadic way of life to a more settled agriculture.

The hay meadows of the Dales have a very different character from the grass-lands of the south. Bounded by stone walls, each has its own mix of grasses and herbs which bloom in turn until the time for making hay.

The wildwood of northern England survived much longer than the forests of the south. It was not really until the Iron Age, 2500 years ago, that the axe took its toll in the wooded uplands of Yorkshire and Derbyshire at the foot of the Pennines. Here on the varied soils of the Dales, the first extensive grasslands did not appear until nearly 2000 years after neolithic man created the grass-scapes of the south country. The grazing created by the northern pioneer farmers took on a very different character. The mountainous landscape and the cold, wet climate fashioned pastureland with a nature of its own. Many of the grasses and herbs that became established after the trees were felled came from the tops of the Pennines where, as we have seen, there would have been a natural grassland flora surviving as a relic from the end of the Ice Age. Upper Teesdale is renowned for its rare but rich limestone flora but the pastures of many of the northern Dales have a mix of more common plant species which would have been very familiar to those first northern farmers. Today, each pasture in the Dales has its own particular character – the tapestry of streams on the surface and the variety of bedrock beneath ensure that no two parts of a field contain the same mix of plant species. This mosaic of pastureland, with its ever-changing floral patterns, gives the Dales their special attraction.

In spring, there is an influx of wading birds which come to breed. Many of them are the same species that are found at this time of year further north on the Hebridean machair. They come from the estuaries on the coast to rear their young among the grass stalks of these man-made pastures. The snipe, redshanks, golden plovers and lapwings must all rear their offspring as quickly and safely as possible before the brief summer ends. As the days shorten, there is an innate urgency to complete the reproductive cycle and see the new generation fend for itself. By August, these upland pastures are quiet again. Most of the birds have flown to the milder climate of the estuaries; soon it will be too cold up here even for the grass to grow. The livestock – by whose grazing these pastures were created – would quickly starve if there were no alternative supply of food. As long ago as the Iron Age, our ancestors devised another, more assured source of winter fodder – the hay-meadow.

The working hay-meadows that survive in the Dales of northern England are among the most beautiful of all our grasslands. Traditional stone walls criss-cross the verdant slopes, excluding the cattle and allowing the herbs and grasses to flourish unimpeded by rasping tongues and trampling hooves. The science of haymaking is very sophisticated and has endured for centuries. The grass is allowed to grow, without grazing, until the flowering heads appear, by which time the herbage has reached its maximum yield without becoming tough and fibrous – the timing is critical. The traditional country names for the plants of the meadow reflect the character of each species: the globeflower recalls its shape; the yellow rattle, the sound of its ripe seed-heads waving in the summer breeze; and the pignut, the attraction of its nutty-flavoured tubers. Each species flowers in turn; if all goes according to the natural cycle, most plants will have shed their seeds before the arrival of the farmer with his mower.

161

THE MOWER MUST WAIT

Beneath the shade of old ash trees the mower stands idle until the grass is ready to cut and the plants and animals have completed their annual cycle in the meadow.

Among the colourful meadow flowers the hayrattle will signal the time for mowing. The dry seed-cases have a characteristic rattle when the crop is ready. A week or two before mowing many of the plants are still in flower including yarrow, frog orchid, meadow buttercup, red clover, salad burnet and lady's bedstraw, but their colours will be fading by the time haymaking starts on these northern fields.

The meadow is enclosed by stone walls and will not be grazed until after the hay crop is taken. Elsewhere in the Pennine Dales sheep roam freely over short-turfed grassland flecked with the dainty flowers of tormentil and eyebright.

The meadow grasses of the dry limestone soils are dominated by sheep's fescue, cock's-foot, common quaking-grass, false brome and meadow foxtail. The scented vernal grass will produce the familiar sweet smell of new-mown hay.

The abundant, closely-packed foliage of so many plants provides the ideal habitat for leaf-eating mammals and insects. In the tangled vegetation mice, voles, beetles, bugs and insect larvae of all sorts munch through the greenery before it is felled and dried. Immature frog-hoppers screen themselves from the summer sun with a sticky fluid which they blow into frothy cuckoo-spit.

The ruined monastery of Clonmacnoise stands in the 'Meadows of the Sons of Noise' in the heart of the Irish midlands and looks out over a sweeping curve of the River Shannon. When you stand among its Celtic crosses and beneath its round tower, looking out over the generous floodplain of Ireland's longest river, it is easy to understand why it has remained such a powerful symbol of early Christianity since it was founded in the sixth century. When Pope John Paul II preached there on his Irish pilgrimage in 1979, he spoke of the enduring character of the view from that fortified hill. Below the monastery are ancient meadows which for almost half the year lie under the floodwaters of the Shannon. It is not until well into spring that the local farmers can venture out on to their traditional strips of meadow. There is time for only one cut of hay but, because of the rich alluvial deposits left behind by the winter waters, the crop is lush. The pioneering monks who brought the new Christian gospel came with progressive ideas about agriculture. To them, these herb-rich callows must have been one of the attractions of this remote corner of Ireland.

The combination of winter flooding and the consequent late haycropping has resulted in a particularly rich association of plants – giving these Irish flood-meadows a distinctive character of their own. Alongside many of the familiar plants of hay-meadows you will find meadowsweet, sneezewort, marsh cinquefoil and the rare marsh pea – all indicators of prolonged damp conditions. To walk from the banks of the Shannon up towards the ruins of Clonmacnoise, knee-deep in flowers and grasses of delicate shapes and vivid hues, is an unforgettable experience. It transports you back in time to an era when much of the grassland of the British Isles must have been as diverse and colourful as this. If you visit in early summer you may hear the rasping call of the corncrake – for here in deep-est Ireland, land of grass, this shy bird still finds a refuge. As with the grasslands of the Hebridean machair, its presence here by the Shannon is a sure sign that farming ways have changed very little since the monastery and callows were founded nearly 1500 years ago. The Emerald Isle still has fresh pastures, the wild beauty of which would surely delight the Sons of Noise.

In southern England there are still a few flood-meadows which, because of their traditional cropping, are particularly spectacular and rich in plant life. They are used to grow grass for hay and are then grazed for the rest of the season after the hay has been cut. The timing of the haymaking is critical for it dictates which species of flower grow there. Many of these hay-meadow species were welcomed by the farmers because they added sweetness and nourishment to their hay. Such old-style meadows owe their continued existence to com-plexities of ownership which have prevented their conversion to intensively managed hayfields. The fritillary meadows of the Upper Thames Valley and the rich meadows of Yarnton and Pixie Meads near Oxford are classic examples of how an outmoded form of farming has protected rare botanical beauty. Many have remained unchanged for centuries and their antiquity is indicated by the presence of species such as cowslip, meadowsweet and yellow rattle along with commoner meadow plants such as meadow buttercup, dandelion, oxeye daisy, knapweed, creeping thistle, ribwort plantain and common sorrel.

The snake's-head fritillary was once the familiar flower of flood-meadows in the south and east of England. Drainage and changes in grassland management have made it a rarity. It is now mainly confined to a handful of meadows along the Thames; over 80 per cent of the national population is found in this one field at Cricklade in Wiltshire.

Most of these relic hay-meadows have been accorded the status of nature reserves but their botanical value would disappear if the style of haymaking changed. The ancient partnership between man and nature has created a natural work of art.

For centuries man has lived with the natural rhythm of flood-meadows – grazing his sheep and cattle in the spring and autumn and making hay from the rich flush of summer grass. In the winter he left the wet meadows to the fishermen and the wildfowlers and to the birds. To improve on this natural system, he has built drains and ditches to change the water-tables and canalised rivers to control their flooding. There are now very few natural floodlands left in the country, and the modern draining of Britain and Ireland has highlighted the importance of the idiosyncratic man-made flood-meadows called the Ouse Washes. In the middle of the seventeenth century a Dutchman, Cornelius Vermuyden, drew up an ambitious scheme to drain the Fens of East Anglia. Two straight, parallel rivers were cut at different times from Earith to Denver, just inland from King's Lynn, to bypass the Ely branch of the Great Ouse. These two great drains – the Old and New Bedford Rivers, as they became known – run for about twenty miles, never more than 1000 yards or so apart. They enclose a strip of land which in winter acts as a 'safety valve' for Vermuyden's scheme and takes the surplus floodwater. It is this area which forms the Ouse Washes, so famous for its wildlife. In summer, the rich pasture is grazed by cattle but in winter the flooded fields are the exclusive domain of water-birds. From September,

Left Goat's-beard – a larger relative of the familiar dandelion – is found on a wide variety of grassland; its fist-sized seedhead is also a feature of roadside verges.
Above The pace of agricultural 'improvement' has been slower in Ireland, where you can still find many wet-meadows with their lush communities of plants such as marsh ragwort.

the wildfowl begin to arrive from the summer breeding grounds. In November, the first Bewick's swans fly in from Siberia to feed on the wet or submerged grass. By Christmas, these wild swans number nearly 1500 forming the largest flock in Britain. Thousands of wigeon and pintail abound here, together with other dabbling ducks such as mallard, teal and shoveler, many of which stay to breed on these meadows after the floodwaters have subsided.

It is in the spring when the true character of a traditional wet grassland like this is most striking. Beyond the boundary river the arable land of the Fens is a monotonous silent prairie of young wheat stems. In contrast, the vivid green washlands are vibrant with the calls of grassland birds. High in the air the pure song of the skylark is constantly interspersed with the bleating of the snipe as it drums its way through its aerial territory. On the gateposts that only weeks before were lapped by water, the redshank calls to his mate while from the long grassy tussocks wafts the distinctive nuptial call of the black-tailed godwits as they stake this year's claim on their only regular breeding ground in Britain. Perhaps most specific to this disappearing grassland paradise is the spring ritual of the ruffs. Throughout most of the year these birds are a dull brown colour but in May the males are transformed by the growth of their ornamental ruff of feathers around their heads. Out on the grass sward of the Ouse Washes the males then congregate on their display grounds, the leks. Here they compete for the attentions of the admiring females, the reeves, with frenzied displays of their

The natural home of the ruffs is wet grassland: they breed now only in East Anglia.
The conspicuous 'ruff' of the male grows in spring in preparation for the ritualised combat of the lek.

plumage and ritualised combat with each other. With apparent disregard for all this male exhibitionism, the reeves wander casually across the lek. Delicately touching her selected mate on his ruff with her bill, a reeve will signify her approval to mating. Those males nearest the centre of the lek attract the most attention and secure the greatest number of mates. It is an ancient ritual that celebrates the arrival of spring.

Elsewhere on the grass-scapes of the British Isles the farmers are cutting their first silage. Highly productive, temporary leys are now the most common type of grassland in all but a few parts of the lowlands. Only a handful of grass species are sown, often a monotonous monoculture of rye-grass or Timothy grass – neither of which is particularly attractive to insects. Wild flowers are excluded by the use of herbicides, and artificial fertilisers help to promote the growth of the hybrid grass which outstrips the less tenacious species of yesterday's meadow. The early and frequent cutting of the grass precludes most creatures from becoming established in this alien world. Even the domestic stock is fenced off from this green revolution. At the end of the season after it has finished producing its successive crops of grass, the ground is turned over by the plough and prepared for another year. In place of grass the field may next produce a yield of peas or sugar-beet, kale or oilseed rape. Or perhaps it will become a sea of waving corn. In today's farming economy, grass is just another crop – part of the relentless cycle of the plough.

CHAPTER EIGHT
UNDER THE PLOUGH

Autumn can be a very sad time. The vitality of spring and summer pales all too soon. There is a reluctance in the air. Out in the farmland, next year's crop is thrusting through the soil of the wheatfield, almost before the trees and hedgerows have brought this year's growing season to its natural end. In another field the rye-grass has surrendered its final crop of silage; exhausted, it waits for the plough. Where the two fields meet there is a straggling hedge of hawthorn, and by the headland where this meets the road a few ash and elm trees form a modest copse. Here in the early spring a colony of rooks had raised their young. Through the dampness that hangs heavy in the air, their early morning cawing is the only sound to be heard in the otherwise still and silent landscape.

In time, the farmer comes to turn the soil. His 250-horsepower tractor wields a reversible plough that simultaneously cuts seven furrows, creating a swathe of dark-brown earth almost ten feet wide. For him, this field of grass will barely be a day's work – by evening there will hardly be a trace of green. As the steel ploughshares course almost effortlessly through the ground, they bring to the surface the hidden creatures of the soil. For a few minutes after the plough has passed, a host of earthworms, leatherjackets, grubs and beetles, eelworms, mites and millipedes writhe on the cut surface of the field. From their vantage point in the copse, the rooks swoop down to feast on these hordes of invertebrates before they can burrow back into the rich dark world of the soil. Before the ploughman has reached the headland to turn his massive machine, the rooks have been joined by flocks of other opportunist birds – black-headed gulls, lapwings and jackdaws – all greedily tumbling and leap-frogging in the wake of the plough.

By clearing the vegetation and then exposing the flora and fauna of the soil, farmers with their ploughs introduce more opportunities for nature. Yet, at the same time, the normal processes of natural succession by which open ground eventually reverts to woodland are constantly interrupted by cultivation. By ploughing his field every year, the farmer holds back succession at a very early stage, so giving the species that he chooses to plant a much greater advantage. This annual ploughing of the soil also favours certain species of *wild* plants and animals. Wherever the plough cuts through the soil for the first time, opportunities are created which had barely existed since the ground was first turned over by the retreating glaciers. Many plants, such as the dock and ribwort plantain, first flourished in the glacial tills left at the end of the Ice Age. In time, these pioneers were overtaken by a succession of more permanent vegetation which had, in a way, been waiting in the wings. When man again broke the surface of the ground, these opportunists made a comeback that was so successful they became the weeds and pests of arable farming. In contrast, other wildlife species – particularly those adapted to deep woodland – have had almost insuperable problems of survival; for them the impact of the plough has been disastrous. These revolutionary changes to the landscape and its wildlife were started over 5000 years ago when the new colonisers of Britain first scratched the surface of the soil to plant the seeds of their chosen crops. The farmer and his plough have radically changed the course of natural history.

The story of our arable land is one that runs parallel with that of our grasslands. We cannot be sure where our first farmers settled to establish true farmland around their dwellings but they were already versed in the technology when they arrived from Europe. With them they brought the seeds for their crops and their own breeds of domestic sheep and cattle – so dispensing with the constant need to follow wild herds or to search for the natural harvest of the forest. These farming tribes of the New Stone Age scratched the cleared surface of the soil with branches and antlers in order to sow their seeds but repetitive cropping of the same small plot exhausted the land and forced the groups to move on. By 4000 years ago, the climate of southern Britain was becoming warmer and drier. The Beaker people of the Bronze Age brought new strains of wheat and barley from the Mediterranean region, which did well here in the climate of that time. But with the seeds of the corn came the seeds of other immigrant species – the poppy, for example – many of which were invasive

Of the plants that have taken to arable land, the poppy is the most opportunist and persistent. As soon as the farmer relaxes control over his crops, the dormant seeds of the poppy spring up between the young shoots of the cereals – a scarlet reminder of nature's tenacity.

colonising annuals. These earliest of arable plots must have contained a remark-ably colourful collection of plants – a mixture of the crops wanted by the farmer and also the weeds he had inadvertently encouraged. With less competition from the shrubs and other perennials of the woods and grasslands, species such as corn marigold, corncockle and cornflower, together with the poppies, added a blaze of yellow, red and blue to the ripening corn.

Today, you can see the same proliferation of colour wherever the fields of modern cereals have escaped the farmer's herbicides. The most conspicuous weed is still the seemingly indestructible poppy. This plant owes its tenacity to the way its life cycle is pre-adapted to the annual cycle of arable farming. Each poppy plant produces as many as 20,000 seeds which, when shed on the ground and buried by the plough, can remain dormant for many years. Their germination is induced by light and they start to grow rapidly as soon as they are turned up to the surface of the soil. Poppies and most other arable weeds do so well in the newly turned soil that, unless sprayed or weeded out, their growth often outstrips the cultivated crops. Although there are not many of these opportunist species, they have flourished under the plough. In contrast, for numerous other species of plants and animals, our arable farmland has never been an adequate substitute for their original woodland habitats. Their varying fortunes closely follow our own social history and the changing fashions of our farming.

The hillsides of western Britain must have enjoyed many more long hot summers than they do today. In the far south-west, notably on Dartmoor and Bodmin Moor, tribes of the late Bronze Age set up villages and established permanent fields. The populations of these uplands were probably far greater than they are now and it was these industrious people who left on the landscape many of the ceremonial circles and avenues of standing stones that you come across today. As they cleared the ground they used the smaller granite boulders to make walls – so creating distinct fields. They lived in stone huts with separate rooms and around their settlements the fields extended for many acres. Near St Ives in Cornwall, close to sites of bronze-age finds, are the remains of an un-usual ancient field-system which, remarkably, is still in use. As in many other parts of this enduring county, we can see the intimate scale of the first patches of ploughland. The 'infield' around the homestead was permanently farmed and you can still see the irregular pattern of small square-shaped fields. The 'outfield' had larger enclosures and was cultivated in rotation, returning the exhausted land to fallow until it had recovered its fertility. Just as it is today, the conspicuous denizen of these fields would have been the rook. This noisy, gregari-ous woodland bird needed the trees of the forest. Nesting high in the elms of the wildwood, the rooks would have witnessed the creation of open land and very soon the whole colony would have established a pattern of flights from the swaying platforms of twigs to the cultivated fields. Here, these omnivorous opportunists would forage for any kind of available food – from spilled grain to leatherjackets – and return to the rookery to feed their young. Today, as then, their incessant cawing starts an hour before dawn, followed by an outward

Of all the birds that have adapted their
woodland way of life to the regime of
the plough, the rook is the most conspicuous. Gregarious and opportunist,
it feeds both on the animal life turned
over in the soil and on the grain left
after the harvest.

drift of the first few birds commuting to their favoured arable land. Then the main exodus from the woodland follows a predetermined flight path from the trees, as if the flock had received an early morning briefing about the best fields to raid for their daily rations.

The closeness of the woodland and its wildlife must have dominated those early settlements. Deer would have trampled and eaten the crops, wolves and foxes preyed on the livestock, and great flocks of finches and other seed-eating birds, such as pigeons, consumed much of the annual yield of cereal. Britain was still a wooded country and the constant presence of these woodland creatures was an everyday part of farming life. It was not until the middle of the Iron Age that woodland clearance became so extensive that farmland became more remote from the surviving tracts of wildwood. The process was accelerated by the assertive settlement of Celtic tribes from Belgium who brought with them the skills of iron-working. With this new technology, the people of Britain could now fashion ploughshares that could turn the heavy soils. The plough was the most powerful invention of agriculture – a wedge to divide the soil, and a lever to lift and turn it. The coming of iron to these islands forged a tool with which those Celtic farmers could at last tackle the rich soils of the remaining unexploited lowland valleys. Iron does not need casting; unlike bronze, it can be reheated after smelting and, while red-hot, hammered on the anvil into almost any shape. Just as the iron sword of the Celtic culture dominated life in southern Britain, so their iron ploughs imposed the new arable regime on much of the countryside. What had been woodland or grassland was now new fields of waving corn.

The attractive seed-heads of teasel decorate the margins of arable fields. In autumn, flocks of goldfinches invade the farmland to reap this natural harvest.

175

By the end of the stormy centuries of the Iron Age, England had become an exporter of grain and other food to the mainland of Europe, and the extensive arable fields in the south were attracting the attentions of the Romans. After several tentative sorties, they eventually came to stay in AD 43 and over the next 350 years helped transform southern Britain into a granary for their Empire. Below the Sussex Downs at Bignor, there are impressive remains of a Roman villa built in the fourth century. The spectacular mosaics are reminders of the wealth and importance of the site. It was the headquarters of a huge farming and horticultural estate and had vineyards of red grapes which grew well in the warmth of those days. Bignor now stands in a landscape of rolling arable land, much as it did in Roman times, but the only vines cultivated near by are white-graped because of our cooler climate. None the less, some of the wildlife of Caesar's time has survived. As well as the large edible Roman snail that the invaders introduced to England, you might still come across another of their favourite delicacies – the quail. This secretive, dumpy little bird was sought after by the Romans for its subtly flavoured meat and eggs, and the three distinctive notes of the male's call would have been familiar in the wheatfields around Bignor.

Less than 100 years after Bignor was built, the Roman garrison was withdrawn from British shores and the villas of the south lost much of their export market. Many were abandoned in the wake of the victorious Anglo-Saxon coalition; others survived to be integrated into the Saxon agricultural system. A landscape of cereal crops interspersed with scrub was ideal country for the corn bunting. It is only during the spring that you notice this small, inconspicuously-marked bird; it attracts attention through its jingling, territorial song proclaimed by the male from prominent perches above the growing corn. Bushes, trees and, in recent times, telegraph poles and overhead wires are vital landmarks for the corn bunting in featureless arable terrain.

By the middle of the eighth century, the landscape of more than half of lowland Britain was dominated by large, open farmland. It was worked communally under the Saxon system and each manorial estate had two, three or sometimes more fields on which barley and wheat were grown in rotation with one field resting fallow. Many of these expanses of arable land extended over hundreds of acres without much relief from trees and hedges. They were attractive to only a very limited number of animal species. Beneath the rising larks, hares raced across the strips of crops, unimpeded by hedges. The local people working on these fields would have known the traditional March trysting place of the hares and, as the farming year progressed, they would also have noticed the seasonal movements of the harvest mice. Secure in the shelter of the distant hedgerows and grassland at the woodland edge, these mice – our smallest and most attractive rodents – would then move out into the ripening corn until harvest time. Here, they would ingeniously build their domed nests, skilfully suspended

Right The harvest mouse was formerly able to rear its young in the crops before they were reaped; now with earlier harvesting, these diminutive rodents are increasingly confined to the field margin.

in the growing crop. Now with changes in the pattern and timing of cereal crops, these graceful acrobats of the corn stalks are rarely found on arable farmland.

In a rural part of central Nottinghamshire on the heavy clay soils so typical of the English Midlands, there is a last remnant of that open-field system. The village of Laxton continues to be farmed in the Saxon way. Its three great fields are ploughed in strips now almost a thousand years old and still have the common grasslands called 'sykes', colourfully rich in meadow flowers. If, in spring, you stand at the top of the enormous Mill Field and cast your eyes over the hedgeless, treeless expanse of growing corn, you might well conclude that nature had been permanently banished to the edge of cultivation, and that only the woods on the horizon and the boundary hedges and lanes offered any real retreat.

Nature has never been completely subdued by agriculture. Its potential to recolonise arable fields rapidly was dramatically demonstrated to the farmers of medieval Britain. In the summer of 1348, the first victims of the Great Plague had died and this remarkably virulent disease was spreading unchecked through the villages of England. Within a generation it had killed a third of the population, devastating the workforce on the land. Village after village was abandoned as the survivors regrouped in an effort to continue their traditional farming life. Thousands of acres of arable land were left unploughed and immediately the plants of heath and woodland began to return. The silence of the deserted villages was soon broken by an explosion of birdsong, as the thrushes, warblers, tits and finches celebrated the reprieve for their depleted woodland homes. Today, archaeologists are unearthing villages and farms which have lain under grass and heath ever since that great exodus from the land; there must be many more waiting to be discovered.

Wherever arable land has been abandoned, the shrubs of the woodland edge, notably the hawthorn, are the first to recolonise. Densely branched and armed with spiky thorns, hawthorn withstands the browsing of wild and domestic animals and can be used to establish a hedge so quickly that countrymen call it the 'quickthorn'. In many parts of lowland Britain, it is the planted hedges which give relief and diversity to an otherwise open landscape. For centuries they have been used to separate crops and impound domestic stock; they are the living boundaries of farmland. Many of the earliest hedges were simply linear tracts of the wildwood, coppiced and then left to form a natural stockade around the cleared ground. Some of these ancient hedgerows survive today and have histories that may well go back to the late Iron Age. Many of the hedges on the clay soils of the English Midlands have their origins in Saxon times – but these were probably specially planted. To the quick-growing hawthorn, the farmers would have added other spiky shrubs such as blackthorn and holly, both good deterrents to livestock and people. In time, the young hedge would be enriched by the arrival of seeds of rose and ash, which soon become established in the shelter of the hedgerow. Elm has always been an important hedgerow tree because of its use as fodder for cattle, and it was often planted by the farmer – if only as a boundary marker. Hazel and field maple are both slow to seed themselves, even if there are mature trees near by. Their presence in hedgerows is a good indication of antiquity – as are species of woodland herbs such as dog's mercury, wood anemone, bluebell and primrose. Many of the glorious hedges on the embankments along the lanes of Devon are rich in such plants. Although clearly the shrubs and trees would have originally been planted, they have, over the centuries, acquired the floral diversity of the oldest hedges. More than 500 species of plants have been recorded in the hedgerows of the British Isles and many of these have their associated insect species which in turn attract small mammals and birds. Hedges are important reservoirs of wildlife – especially on arable land, where there is precious little other cover for food and nest sites. They link many isolated copses and field corners, so providing a living network of corridors along which wildlife can spread across the farming countryside. In spite of the ravages of the last few decades, the hedgerows of the British Isles still total more than half a million miles.

The spring splendour of bluebells and red campion in the ancient hedgerows of Devon reflects the wildwood origins of these field boundaries.

HEDGEROW HIGHWAYS

Linking the woods and copses over the north Midlands
farmland, hedges are vital as nature's highways, providing
the routes by which woodland plants and animals spread
into the open countryside.

In the changing history of agricultural landscapes the planting of hedges has played an important part in providing
substitute habitats for woodland which has been felled over
the centuries, and for creating the attractive, intimate
landscapes with which we are familiar. Hedgerow trees
such as the ash, crack willow and oak are as important for
their wildlife as for their amenity.

The typical tangle of hawthorn, blackthorn, elder, bramble, ash and maple is a concentration of the native shrubs normally found on the woodland edge. Climbers such as the honeysuckle, traveller's joy and black bryony help to form a dense cover for nesting birds. Yellowhammers, whitethroats, blackbirds and chaffinches sing from the hedge tops; wrens and dunnocks (the hedge sparrow) sing from the lower layers where they nest.

Though rarely seen or heard, the mammals of the hedgerow are often numerous and include mice, voles, shrews, stoats and weasels and of course the aptly-named hedgehog. Extensive tunnel systems of the burrowing animals weave between the hedge roots.

Safe from the annual cultivation of the plough, the roadside verges and strips along the hedge sides are permanent extensions to the hedgerow habitats. Typical midsummer plants by the hedge include ragwort, meadowsweet, herb-Robert, fat-hen and cornflower.

From April to October you can find many butterfly species enjoying the sunshine and shelter of the hedge. Each has a special plant association for feeding or breeding and as the year passes brimstones are seen on buckthorn, orange-tips on Jack-by-the-hedge, peacock and small tortoiseshell visit the nettles and thistles, and gatekeepers feed on the bramble blossom.

In flight the cuckoo can easily be mistaken for a bird of prey. Hedgerow birds appear to make the same mistake – rising into the air to mob a passing cuckoo. Perhaps the female cuckoo takes advantage of unguarded nests of birds such as the hedge-sparrow to lay her eggs. The resemblance of the parasitic cuckoo to predatory hawks may be no coincidence.

Ours is not the first century to have witnessed the rapid wholesale destruction of many wildlife habitats in the interests of agricultural gain. The losses during the seventeenth and eighteenth centuries were unprecedented. As the demand for food increased with the growing population, so it became viable to farm heath, moor and fen – the 'wastes' as these wilder parts of the countryside were called. The miles of new hedgerows created by the awards of the Enclosure Acts clearly made the large fields they divided more hospitable to the local woodland wildlife but their contribution was almost irrelevant to the overall balance. The general trend has continued until the present day. More and more land has been pressed into intensive agriculture which is now characterised by increasing specialisation and mechanisation. No longer are crops grown where they are needed but where they can most economically be cultivated. This leads to the monoculture type of landscapes typical of East Anglia and its prairies of grain, or south-west England and its vast acres of grass. Gone is the diversity of habitats which for 3000 years or more had been the hallmark of farmland. The effects on wildlife – particularly the species of the woodland edge – has been to make much of our farmland into a ghetto. The plants and animals that have survived – even flourished – are those which can adjust their life-styles to the unrelenting annual cycle of modern farming. Some species have become so successful that they are victimised by the farmer. Wild oats and docks have been under attack for centuries but we have failed to eliminate them. Woodland émigrés such as rooks, carrion crows and wood-pigeons have fared so well that they have become followers of the plough and its dominating regime. These opportunist 'pests' of farmland may be very numerous but there are only a few such species that have taken advantage of this man-made habitat. Most of our native plants and animals cannot survive in habitats which are so different from their ancestral woodland home. The Old English for 'field' is 'feld' – literally a felled area,

Over much of the British Isles the green mantle of the wildwood has been replaced by vast golden prairies of barley and wheat. The large fields offer little to the native woodland wildlife of our islands. In place of the ancient diversity, we have a modern monoculture.

Farming fashions are now more dictated by international political economics than by local domestic demand. The intensive yellow of oil-seed rape fields is a conspicuous reminder of this latest episode in the arable story.

stripped of its trees. For many of our native woodland species, the saving grace of today's farming countryside is the network of hedges and copses that punctuate the land.

As you walk along the edge of an arable field in autumn, flocks of brightly coloured birds bounce ahead of you, keeping in touch with each other by their twittering flight calls. These finches – greenfinch, chaffinch, goldfinch and linnet – are all essentially birds of wood and heathland. At this time of year they collectively raid the spilt grain of the fields, the seeds and fruits of the autumn hedgerow and the thistles on the headland beyond the line of the stubble. Their numbers are swelled by parties of yellowhammers, twites and even reed buntings which, together with house sparrows and tree sparrows, cash in on this brief seasonal harvest. The appearance of these noisy flocks of birds over the open fields attracts the attention of the predatory sparrowhawk. Drawn away from the seclusion of its distant wood, this skilful flyer has perfected the art of surprise. Low over the hedgerows, it dashes towards the flocks and, undistracted by their scattering, makes a swift, decisive kill. As the finches regroup and continue their gleaning of the empty fields, a fox patrols the hedgerow. In the evening light, the richness of his fur echoes the golds and browns of the autumn woodland from which he came. In the field on the other side of the straggling hedge, the ploughing is complete. Finding little of interest in the thin line of hawthorn, the fox paws at the fresh soil, devouring the last of the worms and beetles before they disappear below the bare but fertile furrow.

CHAPTER NINE

SHELTERING WITH MAN

Seeing a fox at night arouses in us mixed feelings of suspicion and admiration. Part of us is wary of the creature's intent, of its predatory nature and of its reputation for slyness and cunning; another part of us is thrilled by the unexpected encounter with this, the most elegant and largest native carnivore of the British Isles. For the majority of us who live an urban way of life with no poultry or livestock at risk, the fox is no longer seen as a competitor. It can come and go as it pleases; we almost feel privileged by its presence. Anxious not to disturb it, eager to see more of this very private creature, we stand motionless in our tracks. Its sleek, athletic body and cat-like gait give it an aura of grace and agility; its long, pointed muzzle, erect ears and glinting eyes impart it with an air of astuteness and purpose. As we watch it going about its nocturnal business, we have an instinctive respect for this ancient survivor of the wildwood.

Ever since man first returned to these islands, his dwellings, his places of work, his clothes and the surface of his body have harboured organisms. Many came with him, others followed in his wake to stake a claim in the new world he was creating. From the wilderness of the land he had invaded emerged all manner of plants and animals to explore the new habitats that were developing around him and his novel way of life. The animals that were already long-established natives were mostly woodland species. In the wildwood, birds such as the robin picked insects from the forest floor and snatched grubs and worms unearthed by wild pigs rooting in the soil. For the robin, today's suburban gardener with his spade is equally effective in turning up another meal. Here, in the British Isles, we have developed a relationship with the robin which is unique; elsewhere in Europe the same species is still exclusively a bird of woodland. In the caves where our ancestors sheltered from the vagaries of the climate and seasons, there were roosting bats and birds and insects who continued their way of life side by side with these new neighbours, much as they still do today in the roofs and attics of our contemporary houses. Ever since we first set up home here, we have unwittingly offered food and shelter to many of the other residents of these islands.

Around the camp fires of these neolithic people prowled their hunting dogs. The earliest evidence of domestic dogs in Britain comes from Star Carr, a site in Yorkshire that dates back 7500 years. Here, on the slopes of a low hillock of glacial gravel, early hunter-gatherers set up camp by the edge of a lake. A brushwood platform of axe-felled birch trees and branches bridged the gap between the open settlement in the forest and the water of the lake, which was bordered by dense reed-swamp. From the relative security of this camp, they would have ventured into the wildwood in search of the natural harvest of plants and their fruits and in pursuit of wild game. With them went their dogs to join in the hunt and share in the kill. Complete skeletons of dogs have been found on other later sites, from which it is assumed that these early domesticated dogs were about the size of a terrier but resembled the dingo. Like all modern breeds of dog, they were descended from the wolf of the forest, a process of domestication and selective breeding that probably started in southern Europe and Asia 12,000 years ago.

The remarkable kinship that exists between man and dog today has developed as a reflection of the common hunting ancestry of ourselves and the wolf. The social structures and patterns of behaviour of humans and wolves are very similar and have evolved to meet the demands of working as part of an efficient team of hunters. At the end of the Ice Age in Europe, wolf and man were competing for the same food and shelter and it is not difficult to imagine how a workable alliance formed to mutual benefit. Like us, prehistoric tribes would have adopted pets, particularly young animals – maybe the orphans of the mammals they hunted. But of all the species taken into the camp, it was the young wolves which had instinctive social patterns most naturally compatible with human society. Here is the basis of the empathy between man and dog – one that distinguishes this relationship from the many other alliances formed over the years between wildlife and ourselves.

As they moved through the country, clearing the trees and tilling the soil, the farmers of the New Stone Age unwittingly became the prime distributors of animal and plant species. The house sparrow thrived on the shelter and nourishment that could be gleaned from the human way of life. Compared to the tree sparrow, its forest cousin, the house sparrow had long since adapted to life in the shadow of man. So, too, had the house mouse, an uninvited companion on the great trek north into Britain. This opportunist creature probably reached our shores 5000 years ago, hidden in the grain and cargoes brought across the Channel on board those skin-covered boats. Wherever early man built a shelter for himself, the house mouse set up home. Its success is now inextricably linked to a life with man – as was shown on St Kilda. When, earlier this century, the last people left that remote Scottish island, the house mouse became extinct there; only the less domestic wood mouse was able to survive without man.

As with traditional farms and smallholdings today, a concentration of buildings and livestock in neolithic times would have encouraged a profusion of insects, particularly in summer. As he tended his cattle, the neolithic farmer would have heard the scream of swifts above him as they sieved the air, collecting food for their nestlings. When people began to build more permanent homes of timber and stone, the swifts took to building their nests near to their source of food and found man's buildings an admirable substitute for caves and other traditional sites. So, too, did the house martin, which was originally a

Left The working dog was one of man's first companions. Using the natural hunting instincts and sociable nature of the wolf, our ancestors forged a partnership which has remained unparalleled in our relationship with wildlife.
Above The house sparrow has a world-wide distribution; it followed wherever man set up home. Often unwelcome pests, these birds are supreme opportunists.

cliff-nester but which has, in comparatively recent times, adopted a preference for the eaves and overhangs of houses. But where did the swallows nest before man provided them with convenient sites? Occasionally today they will set up home in the roofs of caves and very rarely on the branches of trees or, perilously, on the underside of the larger nests of birds of prey. But both swifts and swallows are birds of open country preferring to live near water, and their numbers must have been very small before people began to create suitable habitats. Bronze-age man with his clearings and settlements of thatched huts must have given them a new lease of life in the warm, dry summers of that time.

The Romans, coming as they did from a well-established urban civilisation, brought new standards of town life to Britain. The towns they expanded were not simply to house their garrisons but were designed to convert the indigenous population to Roman ways. The urban way of life had come to stay and around it wildlife adjusted to the new regime. Some plants and animals kept to their rural roots and shunned the bustle of the town; others found its hospitality irresistible. Already addicted to the urban scene was the black rat. Once thought to have invaded Britain in medieval times, this unwelcome cohabitant of towns is now known to have come across from Europe with the Romans. Bones of *Rattus rattus* – sometimes called the 'ship rat' because of its successful spread by sea – have been unearthed in Roman archaeological sites in the City of London and are quite distinct from those of the brown rat, which did not arrive in Britain until the late seventeenth century. There are many records from Roman and Anglo-Saxon times of unidentified 'pestilences' which correspond to the rat-borne plagues that swept through Europe at that time. It is certain that Britain suffered outbreaks of these diseases long before the infamous Black Death of the fourteenth century. Wherever there were concentrations of people with stores of food and simple systems of sanitation, rats and other pests moved in. Cockroaches and larder beetles pillaged the Roman kitchen; bedbugs, fleas and mites pestered the Roman soldier in his bed. As our towns grew into cities, the uninvited house guests gave cause for the human population to think of wildlife as alien and evil.

Among the vagrants and immigrants of the animal world came jackdaws and rooks from the countryside, to take their pickings from the town. At first they would have made the daily trek to and from their roosting and nesting grounds. In time, they often became permanent residents like the rooks that persist in nesting noisily in the trees along Cheltenham's smart Promenade. Surprisingly, the starling's predilection for towns is a very recent phenomenon; it has only become common away from the countryside in the last 200 years. Now every city has its great starling roosts, particularly in winter when the warmth of buildings such as Temple Meads station in the heart of Bristol attracts countless thousands to the girders and parapets above the lines. Even the wary magpie finds comfort in city life; the trees of parks and gardens resound to its

Left In its many guises, the house mouse shares our homes – either as an unwelcome guest or as an amusing pet. Such is the ambiguity of our attitudes to wildlife.

Dublin is famous for its winter roost of pied wagtails which flock in at night to the trees of O'Connell Street; here the chattering throng congregates in the warmth of the city centre.

raucous call. At night in Dublin's O'Connell Street, about 1000 pied wagtails come to roost in the plane trees. Perhaps most unexpected of all is the way that the otherwise rare black redstart has taken to nesting in our inner cities. They first nested regularly in the coastal towns of Sussex in the 1920s but it was the Second World War that boosted their population in London. The gutted buildings were adopted as secluded nest sites and the ants and flies in the rubble were a plentiful source of food. These unlikely converts to the urban way of life show just how attractive our man-made jungle can be to other species.

The symbol of the city street is now the feral pigeon. Because its more recent forebears were domesticated dovecote birds, it is easy to forget that it is descended from the rock-dove whose ancestral habitat was coastal cliffs – almost identical in structure to the ledges and sills of the cityscape. There is always a niche for a vegetarian scavenger in a modern city and the feral pigeon has occupied it more effectively and more numerously than any other bird. It is a real opportunist, foraging in gutters and wastelands, around dockland and lorry-parks, stealing from roadside stalls and restaurants and appealing to the sentiments of nature-lovers in parks and squares. The modern pigeon seems to have exploited the city and its human inhabitants to the full. In London they are said to commute on the tube trains, alighting at one station and leaving at the next, in search of new pickings. Unlike farmers and others who still make their living from the land, we often regard the impertinent pigeon with tolerant affection. That it will eat right out of our hand helps us overlook its scavenging ways.

Five hundred years ago, the avian scavengers of London included large numbers of ravens and, notably, kites. There were thousands of these handsome red raptors in the capital during the Middle Ages and they were so fearless that they would feed on scraps offered in the hand. The streets of London were littered with rotting vegetation and offal and would have been intolerable were it not for the cleansing effect of the bold ravens and kites. An Act of Parliament made it a capital offence to kill them – a status which they retained until the eighteenth century. Their scavenging role has now been taken by the gulls which rummage over the city refuse dumps. Black-headed, herring, and lesser black-backed all regularly congregate at these tips in search of scraps. Flocks several hundred strong wait for the refuse vehicles to disgorge their bounty and then greedily surge over the mountain of handouts. In the evening they leave the feeding ground to roost on the water in gravel pits and reservoirs on the fringes of our cities. Their modern way of life on our doorstep seems a far cry from the sea. But for us, winter in the city has taken on a new, less bleak look as these large white birds tramp back across the evening skyline.

The success of many species in adapting to town life has gone hand in hand with our changing attitude to them. Cities such as Bristol now harbour denser populations of foxes than the animals' original rural homes – a reflection of the human residents' tolerance and affection for their wild companions. In the country, the fox is hunted for sport and shot as vermin; there it is still thought of as a competitor – much as the wolf was once regarded throughout the land. With the wolf exterminated and the wilderness tamed, our Tudor ancestors had time

Above Our throwaway lifestyle attracts the natural scavengers; gulls are just as much at home following in the wake of the rubbish cart as they are behind the trawler at sea.

Right Whatever our attitude to adult foxes, the unexpected appearance of their cubs in our gardens is a delightful encounter. During their infancy they will even play in broad daylight, giving us a glimpse of the very private lives of these ancient inhabitants of our islands.

to reflect on the appeal of the more natural world and the way they had distanced themselves from it. From the beginning of the sixteenth century, stable government had eliminated the need to fortify country houses, and their owners turned back towards the landscape around them. They created fashionable mansions in beautiful gardens and enclosed great tracts of countryside as parkland. Here, with resourcefulness, they could select the trees and large animals, such as deer, that they preferred to see. This was the beginning of the English landscape movement which, by the end of the eighteenth century, had turned the art of landscape gardening into the creation of extensive informal and romantic landscapes. For much of the native wildlife surviving precariously in the remnants of ancient woodlands and the marshes of lowland England, these estates with their trees and open grassland, their lakes and ponds, acted as unofficial nature reserves. Though it was not the intention of their patrons, these idealised tracts

of new countryside offered refuge to a wide variety of birds, insects and small mammals that were less conspicuous than the fallow deer grazing peacefully beneath the stands of imported sycamores and chestnuts. Then the fortunes of such creatures turned yet again as these 'naturalised' scenes of English landscape gave way to Victorian formality. Wild plants had little chance of escaping the gardener's trowel and the strict regimentation of parks and gardens banished all but the most tenacious birds and mammals. In 1876 the grey squirrel was introduced from North America to beautify these Victorian parks and gardens. Following repeated importations over the next fifty years, it rapidly colonised much of the British Isles. The once fashionable immigrant was declared a national pest, and there was a bounty on its tail.

For the most part, our city parks still reflect the formality of the Victorian attitude to nature more than the liberal outlook of Capability Brown and that earlier generation of landscapers. Most are manicured so clinically by pruning knives and mowing machines, and by the use of weed-killers and pesticides,

Above The Capability Brown landscapes of parkland, such as Petworth Park, were created to give an illusion of countryside; their informal but organised design is not only pleasing to our eyes but is also attractive to woodland wildlife.
Right The grey squirrel is now a feature of our city parkland, where it subsists on handouts from its human neighbours.

that there is no illusion of wilderness. But not all municipal parks are like this. Regent's Park in the heart of London is large enough to retain a variety of habitats which satisfy the day to day needs of the human and wildlife populations that use it. Apart from the open areas enjoyed by Londoners, there are numerous wild corners in this park where plants and animals flourish unharassed. Tawny owls nest in the old hardwood trees and there are ample fruiting shrubs to provide more than twenty species of song-bird with food and nest sites. On the pond is found the wildest corner – a wooded island which is inaccessible to most. Here, in this secret oasis, the naturalised giant hogweed with its huge cartwheel heads on ten-foot stalks grows as a tangled jungle on the edge of the water and, in the privacy of the island's copse, a few herons have taken to nesting – inner London's first modern heronry. In winter, the handful of resident birds are joined by other herons which lope in from the countryside outside London to share in the spoils of the well-stocked lake, which like most urban ponds seldom freezes over. To see these great grey birds flapping their way in to the heart of the capital is one of London's most reassuring natural scenes.

This century has also witnessed a great migration outwards from the city centre – of people setting a new life-style in sprawling suburbia. Culminating in the boom of the 1930s, town and country have met in the half-way houses that are now the dormitories of every major city. On a spring day when you walk along the tree-lined pavements of any residential street of any suburb in the British Isles you will hear, above the rumble of the traffic, the song of woodland birds. Chaffinches and blackbirds, great tits and robins, warblers and thrushes proclaim their approval of these 'garden cities'. Behind the house with its neatly hedged front garden lies a private nature reserve of trees and shrubs, a patch of grassland and perhaps even a miniature plot of arable land that together mimic the main ingredients of a woodland-edge. Like the real thing, many gardens can be hostile places for wildlife; like farmers, gardeners often regard wild flowers as unwelcome weeds, and wild animals as pests. Where only a few chosen cultivated plants are allowed to flourish, and insects and other invertebrate animals are deliberately banished with chemicals, the monotonous regime of modern arable land prevails. As with grass leys, a neat close-cropped lawn, free of weeds and brilliant green with fertilisers, is a barren wasteland to most wildlife. But for every desert patch there is a nearby wilderness where disorder reigns supreme! Fortunately for our suburban wildlife, the differing attitudes of householders to their gardens leads to biological diversity and where one species fails to find what it needs in one garden, it will seek out a more attractive habitat near by. It is not just town gardens which can be valuable wildlife habitats; villages are often marooned by arable farmland and their gardens and churchyards offer sanctuary to many woodland species. This mosaic of private landscapes occupies a very significant proportion of the British Isles. There are fourteen million assorted patches of vegetation which together account for nearly a million acres – substantially more than the size of most counties and three times greater than the sum of all the officially recognised nature reserves of Britain.

URBAN OASIS

For many of us, gardens are the most familiar wildlife habitats, providing a substitute home for an amazing variety of plants and animals. Plants such as buddleia and *Sedum spectabile* attract butterflies, while bees are drawn to lavender and foxglove. Shrubberies and hedges provide nesting sites and winter berries for garden birds. By the late autumn the rubbish heap holds a multitude of insects and perhaps a hibernating hedgehog. Even the shed itself is occupied by the robin family, spiders, beetles, ladybirds and perhaps a mouse or two.

199

Wildlife conservationists used to undervalue gardens on the assumption that introduced species of plants are seldom attractive to our native insects and other animals. But, as most gardeners will confirm, there are many ornamental bushes which are favoured by butterflies. Buddleia, which was introduced from China at the end of the last century, has become a conspicuous weed of building sites and wasteland in cities. Whether cultivated in gardens or growing wild, it always attracts nectar-seeking insects in a way unrivalled by any native plant. During the summer it will be constantly visited by hoverflies and bumble-bees as well as a great variety of butterflies, which have given this shrub the common name of 'the butterfly bush'. In July and August, when the flowers are at their best, buddleia bushes swarm with almost every species of butterfly to be found in towns – large and small white, peacocks and red admirals, small tortoiseshells and even, in some summers, painted ladies. In all, more than twenty species might visit the same bush in a well-established English suburban garden –

Left For woodland birds the mature shrubs of the suburban or country garden are as attractive as the woodland edge. Resident with us throughout the year, the robin has a special place in our affections.
Above An individual toad can take up permanent residence in a suitable corner of the garden. An ally of the gardener, this amphibian hunts for slugs and insects as well as earthworms.
Overleaf The hedgehog, known in the country as the urchin, has taken to life in the towns – finding shelter and food in the diverse habitats of our suburbia.

201

which is a third of the total species from the whole of the British Isles. Other plants attract other insects which, in turn, provide a source of food for insectivorous birds. On warm nights, herbaceous borders are visited by hundreds of moths of dozens of species, most after nectar but others to lay eggs. The caterpillars that eventually hatch add to the army of aphids and bugs, spiders and flies that form the staple diet of many garden birds including blue tits, goldcrests, blackcaps and the spotted flycatcher that sallies from its garden perch to catch insects in mid-air above the borders.

Other plants and shrubs attract seed- or fruit-eating birds – often to the gardener's displeasure. In spring, pairs of bullfinches strip the young buds off fruit trees and later in the year the seeds of weeds are raided by goldfinches and greenfinches. In the middle of winter it is the bird-tables and bird-feeders that help support this large suburban population of woodland birds. Of the larger garden birds, it is the collared dove which has become especially conspicuous in the last few years. They were unknown in Britain until 1952 when they came across from Eastern Europe. The first pair known to nest here did so in Norfolk in 1955, since when the species has spread throughout the whole of Britain and most of Ireland. Its incessant *coo coo-o cuk* call threatens to become one of the more annoying permanent features of suburbia!

Maybe the boom in garden birds will be checked by natural predators. Until recently, the only carnivore to have any significant effect on birds in the safety of the suburbs has been the domestic cat. Unlike the dog, our feline pets are an integral part of the urban ecology and whether we condone their behaviour or not they, too, are merely responding to the call of the wild. But now we have kestrels, and the sight of their flickering wings and fanned tails hovering over the urban skyline is a reminder of their success in adjusting to our urban environment. Their food is mainly small mammals such as voles and mice, but they have even been known to take kitchen scraps from the back doorstep – a behaviour pattern reminiscent of the red kites of medieval London. Sometimes almost out of nowhere swoops a sparrowhawk – an unexpected bandit from the forest edge. In pursuit of its traditional prey – finches, tits and sparrows – this short-winged, long-tailed bird of prey has also discovered the rich hunting grounds of suburbia. Darting low over the garden fence, it will snatch sparrows from lawns and blue tits from bird-tables. But in the main, gardens provide relatively safe refuges for wildlife. Hedgehogs seem to fare just as well snuffling around compost heaps as they do in the leaf litter of country woodland. Another animal that now depends largely on the private garden for its survival in many parts of Britain is the common frog. In many rural areas this amphibian has become such a rarity that the description 'common' is a misnomer. Drainage, pollution and the use of insecticides in the countryside has forced the species to rely on the sanctuary offered by garden ponds. Originally designed to stock ornamental goldfish, these miniature wetlands have taken on a national responsibility; their role in the wider ecology of twentieth-century Britain is poignantly symbolised by the surprise sighting of a heron standing sentinel by the garden pond.

In the last fifty years, our attitude to wildlife has changed more fundamentally than at any previous time in our social history. As our countryside has been increasingly dominated by the business of providing us with food, our villages, towns and cities have taken over the role of satisfying our aspirations for contact with nature. We plant shrubs for butterflies and we feed the birds – our hospitality is extended to hedgehogs and badgers and even to our traditional enemy, the fox. As suburbia spreads further away from the centres of our cities, an inner sanctum has been created where many species of wildlife have established themselves as permanent city dwellers. The feral pigeons and the sparrows that earn a living by day in the inner city are joined in the evening by great flocks of starlings returning to roost in the shelter and warmth of office rooftops and the parapets of churches and other city landmarks. Since dawn, the starlings have been probing the lawns of suburbia and noisily raiding the bird-tables and doorsteps for scraps. As the city worker commutes home on a winter's evening, these modern opportunists flock back in the opposite direction, to spend the night in the heart of the city. As they settle down in the trees of a London square or under the bridges of the Thames, their chatter drowns the roar of the traffic.

It is at this time that the fox emerges to patrol his urban beat. For him the city also offers warmth and shelter, food and security. He has overcome his instinctive mistrust of man to exploit a man-made world that in essence is not too far removed from his traditional rural home. Out in the farmland beyond the city limits, his country cousin is on the run. Much of the countryside we have refashioned in the last fifty years has no place for the fox or many of the other native woodland creatures of the British Isles. Like the fox, they have discovered that our villages and towns, and even our cities can be a welcome substitute for their own depleted homes.

CHAPTER TEN
NEW LANDSCAPES

High on the north-facing slope of the mountain range of the Carneddau, the last glacier in Wales is thought to have finally ground to a halt. In its wake it left the massive debris of its progress – countless granite boulders strewn over the steep slopes that fall towards the Llanberis Pass. Further down this glacial valley are the scarred rock faces left by generations of Welsh quarry-men as they tore slate from their mountainside. The combined effect of man and nature has created one primeval-looking scene.

At 1000 feet above Llyn Peris is a corrie-like depression in the mountain-side – no larger than a football pitch – so recent in origin that it does not appear on many maps. It is the quarry hewn in the 1970s to provide the material for a dam that now holds back the head reservoir of the Dinorwig pumped storage scheme. This giant 500-million-pound electricity generating station was, for aesthetic reasons, sunk out of sight in the largest man-made cavern in the world. In off-peak periods, surplus electricity from the national grid is used to pump water from Llyn Peris up to the head reservoir. At times of peak demand, the water is released and surges down through the mountain to drive the hidden turbines. The only tell-tale signs on the landscape are the approach road and the small quarry that provided hardcore for the dam. Here, the jagged rock face with its green-grey slate cut by the force of explosives and giant machines still looks bare and raw. But only a few seasons after it was blasted from the side of the mountain, this quarry had been invaded by nature. On a ledge half-way up the man-made cliff, a pair of ravens set up home. It seemed that the aftermath of the blasting still echoed round Snowdonia and the dust had hardly settled. Yet the ravens had returned, built a nest and raised another generation. In time, other colonisers – the pioneering plants that first gained a hold in the scant soil after the ice – would invade the cracks and crevices of the quarry to begin the familiar process of succession. Here, in this small man-made scar on the land, our natural history is being repeated.

Wildlife is extraordinarily tenacious and often far more adaptable than we would credit. Throughout their history, animal and plant species have adjusted to the new conditions imposed on them by changes in the climate, the soil and the vegetation of the landscapes in which they have lived. For some species which followed in the wake of the ice, our climate and terrain is now too temperate and they have moved northwards to the lands of the arctic; others which came when these islands were warmer and drier than now, have retreated south. Such species have been lost from the British Isles. But the great majority of the plant and animal species that established themselves here after the Ice Age have remained permanent residents. In the face of continual changes in the physical nature of the landscape of the British Isles, they have managed to adjust and survive – and in certain cases to flourish more widely in greater numbers year by year, century by century. For the last 2000 years or so our climate has fluctuated relatively little; the most dramatic changes inflicted on our flora and fauna have been those of our making. The wholesale restructuring of the landscape during this twentieth century looks like being the most testing for the tenacity of our wildlife.

Yet, up and down the country, naturalists are constantly amazed by the discovery of some rare plant or endangered insect found thriving in the most unexpected places – many of them the seemingly inhospitable new landscapes of our industrial complexes. Rare and beautiful orchids, including spotted- and marsh-orchids and autumn lady's-tresses, bloom in the lime tips of Billingham's

Above Oxford ragwort was introduced to Britain at the end of the eighteenth century. It escaped from the Oxford Botanic Gardens and quickly spread along the newly created railway system to colonise most of the country. Now it is a common sight on waste ground – such as the cooled slag of this blast furnace on Teesside.
Right Wildlife capitalises on every new opportunity. For this pied wagtail the incongruous industrial backdrop to its adopted home is of no consequence.

chemical works; carpets of sea thrift colour the heavy metal shingles of Tyneside. Even the glaring white china clay spoil around St Austell is being gradually clothed in green. On the colliery wastes of mines near Derby you can find nests of the little ringed plover and on industrial buildings, including the famed Baltic flour mill at Newcastle, colonies of kittiwakes have discovered a secluded substitute for sea cliffs. Nearby at Wallsend, kestrels regularly nest in the crane gantries high above the clatter of the docks, and in Northampton a brewery yard is host to hundreds of pied wagtails that roost nightly among the jungle of metal beer barrels. Travellers taking off at Dublin Airport are delighted by the sight of Irish hares nibbling at the perimeter turf, apparently oblivious of the monster overhead, and as the jet banks towards London it passes over the golf course on Bull Island, which in winter has more brent geese than golfers.

For most wildlife it is the detail of their habitat that counts, not the general appearance. What is wasteland, even poison, to us may be very tolerable to lime-loving orchids or shingle-loving thrift. For the natterjack toads that breed in the pools created during the construction of Windscale, the nuclear establishment that looms above them is of no consequence. More important is the secure perimeter fence that keeps us out and gives them privacy. Each no-man's-land of modern industry has attracted and protected a specialist flora and fauna of its own – an act of benefaction more by accident than design.

Perhaps the most familiar but unexplored no-man's-land of modern Britain is the motorway – or at least the grassy verges and embankments that separate the tarmac from the landscape beyond. Each mile of motorway absorbs twenty acres of countryside, of which nearly half are reseeded with a mixture of cultivated grasses and clover. There are now many thousands of acres of verges which, year by year, are developing into grassland habitats. These verges, banks and cuttings are rarely disturbed and only infrequently cut. Not surprisingly, many older motorway grasslands on sandy soils have been colonised by such wild species as heath bedstraw, tormentil and even harebell, while on the edge of motorways such as the M4 that cut through chalk downland, there are invasions of vetches and bird's-foot-trefoil. Where salt has accumulated from winter gritting, plants more familiar on coastal salt-marsh spring up miles from the sea. Like the railways of Victorian times, today's motorways are the linear highways along which many species have extended their range across the country. The conservation value of these continuous areas of grass is principally their potential as sanctuaries for wild plants and small animals which are elsewhere losing their traditional habitats. Beyond the fence of the motorway, the countryside is almost invariably cultivated land with little respite from the intensive farming cycle, but here in this new grassland is a once-familiar community of plants and insects. On a summer's day, against the constant rumble of the traffic, bush-crickets and grasshoppers sing for mates. On the grasses and the vetches, butterflies lay their eggs and ants search for caterpillars anointed in honeydew. Poisonous burnet moths flash their brilliant spotted wings to warn off the insect-eating birds that have also discovered this narrow grassland paradise. On the edge of the tarmac, rooks and crows deftly dodge the traffic in search of the bees and beetles that, together with the night-time carnage of moths, litter the kerb. Nothing goes to waste; even the unfortunate hedgehog or barn owl, struck down by the relentless passage of cars and lorries, is consumed by carrion-eating birds. The left-overs are carried back to the verge by hordes of ants and beetles that emerge from the jungle of the roadside grass. There in the lush world of leaves and stalks, the field vole is surrounded by its favourite vegetarian diet. Above it hovers the watchful kestrel – often the only sign we notice of the natural wealth of this man-made reservation.

Left For some species, the new landscapes that we are now creating offer new opportunities. These ornamental plum trees, planted to relieve the monotony of an urban roadside, have been ravaged by a plague of caterpillars of the browntail moth – normally an insect of coastal scrub.

NEW RESERVATIONS

As you speed across the new agricultural landscapes of open arable land you can see how the motorways have provided strange new reserves for wildlife. These noisy strips of grassland are rarely disturbed by man and there are high populations of voles, mice and shrews to attract the familiar silhouette of the hovering kestrel.

Even newly-planted hedges and new scrub areas soon attract birds such as yellowhammers, dunnocks, thrushes and linnets. These places may form the site of new rabbit burrows or hedgehog territories. Members of the pigeon and crow families collect grit from the edge of the tarmac to aid their digestion.

The body of an animal killed by the traffic is often picked by the scavengers – magpies, crows, gulls and rooks. So intent on their meals, they are sometimes knocked over themselves, to become their companions' next meal.

The banks and slopes of the motorway can be a blaze of colour as wild flowers gradually move into the new grassland. The mixture of native species can be encouraged by sowing special seed mixtures. Many of the plants have particular associations with certain insects: cinnabar moths on ragwort, honey-bees on clover, soldier beetles on hogweed. Even the grasses themselves provide food and shelter for leaf bugs, grasshoppers, burnet moths, meadow brown butterflies, skippers, spiders and many others.

The broadlands of Norfolk, with their 120 miles of rivers and fifty shallow lakes, have so much the look of a natural wild stretch of countryside that their beauty and quietness attract a million holidaymakers every year. But, like so much of the British Isles, this patchwork of broads, carr-woodlands and marshes is essentially the work of man over more than 1000 years. This gently undulating landscape left by the retreating glaciers was originally a vast reed-swamp. Its natural succession to woodland was interrupted by periods when the rising sea flooded inland, but by the time man arrived there would have been a very varied mixture of swamp, fen, marsh and dry land – rich in wildlife. For people, it must have been very inhospitable but early tribes might have grazed livestock on the drier areas and managed the swamps and marshes for reeds and hay. The sparse wildwood of the higher land between the river valleys soon disappeared under the axe. The great depth of peat was then the most sought-after natural resource of the region, and by medieval times it was being extensively worked. With his deep 'open-cast' workings, man was adding the final ingredient of the broadland landscape – the broads themselves. These shallow lakes were created as the peat workings flooded with water – particularly during the fourteenth century, when a rise in sea-level increased the inundations. In all, it has been estimated, 900 million cubic feet of peat were removed in medieval times. By his hand alone, man rapidly transforms the face of the landscape!

Today, the broads have changed again. They retain much of their attractive wildness but have lost most of their characteristic wildlife. During the summer

When they were first created as peat diggings, the Broads were undoubtedly an inhospitable scar on the East Anglian landscape. Centuries later, they had become one of the strongholds of freshwater life – including the elusive otter.

months there are more than 2000 hired motor boats and another 3000 private craft surging through the placid waters of the rivers and broads. This ceaseless traffic erodes the fragile banks and stirs up sediment around the flowering plants in the shallow water. The constant disturbance has harassed the shy otters and kingfishers, to such a degree that a sighting has become an enthusiastic talking-point on the cruisers. What was very recently a paradise for fishermen and birdwatchers has been depleted of its wildlife attractions. Into the broads pours sewage from the treatment works and artificial fertilisers that have leached out from the farmland of the river catchments. As a result, many of the water-ways have become clouded with millions of minute algae, blocking out the sunlight and so preventing the growth of larger plants. Only where there has been ecological management, such as that at Hickling and Cocksfoot Broads, has this unique man-made waterscape regained its rich and varied flora. Here in the reed-beds, which are cut in rotation for their commercial crop for thatch-ing, the bearded tit and the reed bunting make their nests; in the drier beds of sedge there are large numbers of brightly coloured dragonflies, damselflies and beautiful moths and butterflies. Many of the plants are equally vivid – except perhaps the rare milk-parsley, which is the food-plant for caterpillars of the swallowtail butterfly. From late May until mid-July, visitors to Hickling Broad may catch a fleeting glimpse of these loveliest of fenland insects which are the largest butterfly resident in the British Isles and which symbolise the importance of this fragile, ancient man-made habitat. It is now their only home.

The one-time 'new landscape' we now know as the Broads has become one of the last refuges of the swallowtail butterfly in the British Isles. Perhaps we should not dismiss the potential of today's new landscapes.

This gravel pit was last worked thirty years ago; since then it has matured into a rich fresh-water community which provides a replacement home for animal and plant species threatened by our extensive agricultural land-drainage schemes.

The broads are really 'industrial wastelands' that have come down to us from medieval times and, in a way, their modern equivalents are the pits and quarries excavated for sand and gravel. Demand for these raw materials to build roads and motorways, houses and factories, increased rapidly in the 1950s and 1960s, reaching a peak of 110 million tons in 1972, at the height of the motorway boom. Most of the sand and gravel has been taken from the deposits in the Thames and Trent valleys and from the floodplains of the Ouse and its tributaries. Much of this natural geological legacy dates from the last Ice Age. Because the depth of these pits reaches well below the water-table, it has been difficult and expensive to restore them to agricultural or other uses, and they have been allowed to flood naturally with water – so creating the man-made lakes which have become such a familiar part of our contemporary landscape. To our eyes, they relieve the uniformity of arable farmland, or punctuate the sprawl of the urban fringe. For many people, they offer an accessible area for watersports and leisure. For wildlife – particularly waterfowl – these new man-made wetlands have become almost indispensable. In Britain, the total number of wildfowl on flooded gravel pits doubled during the 1970s and now accounts for more than ten per cent of the population of such species as gadwall, tufted duck, pochard and Canada geese. One of the most spectacular sights on the gravel pits that fringe the M4 near Reading is the spring courtship of the great crested grebes as they perform their ritual dance against a backdrop of excavating grabs and conveyor belts. Their extravagant sequence of postures and head-shaking establishes recognition and is often accompanied by offerings of weed. Engrossed in their courtship, the pair are totally oblivious of the incongruous setting for their passion!

Throughout the British Isles, the reservoirs created during the last 100 years to provide for our apparently insatiable demand for water have added to the range of wetland habitats. The high altitude, dammed-up reservoirs of Wales and Scotland and northern England are on poor soils and have little associated wildlife; but those in the lowlands are often rich in vegetation around their long perimeters and attract large numbers of resident and migratory water-birds. Most reservoirs were created in the second half of the nineteenth century and the first three decades of this one; but the most ecologically valuable are those fashioned from the landscape during the last thirty years. Rutland Water was flooded between 1975 and 1979 and is particularly impressive for its population of wildfowl. It was constructed in an area of arable land and part of it was designated as a nature reserve even before there was any water. Existing habitats around its edge were retained and new shallow lagoons were created especially for waterfowl. Of the older reservoirs, Chew Valley Lake in Avon is notable for its mature appearance and diverse wildlife to delight birdwatchers and anglers, and in winter the sight of thousands of wigeon, pochard and tufted duck concentrated on the patches of open water in the ice is proof of the year-long value of reservoirs to waterfowl. The new waterscapes we have created to supply our own domestic and industrial needs not only provide important refuges for wetland birds but also welcome retreats for ourselves.

The reason that the most recently constructed reservoirs have proved more ecologically successful than their forerunners earlier this century is essentially one of changing attitudes – both public and official. Management for conservation of habitats is a new philosophy, and the professional ecologist is quite a new breed of naturalist. If current attitudes and skills had been prevalent at the time when the Forestry Commission was set up in 1919, there is no doubt that their first plantations would look very different today. Since the First World War, hundreds of thousands of acres of Britain – and there have been similar schemes in Ireland – have been planted in huge stands of softwood tree species, many of them in upland areas of marginal farmland and moorland. Gradually, the forest cover in Britain has been increased until it now occupies about 10 per cent of our land – higher than at any time in the last 1000 years. But most of the plantations are of conifer species that are alien to the landscapes of the British Isles and to the wildlife that lives here. Usually in blocks of single species, such as spruce and lodgepole pine, these forests are uniform in character – dense, dark and quiet. The ground beneath is cold and acidic and supports little in the way of shrubs and ground flora. The debris left from the 'brashing' of the lower branches, when trees are fifteen or so years old, reduces the diversity of the habitat still further. But whatever we think of these unnatural forests, they have added a measure of variety to our landscape and to our wildlife. In their infant stages, the plantations play host to a surprising variety of species including many heathland insects and even nightingales and nightjars. Then, as they grow, the sunlight is shut out and with it disappears the richness of more traditional woodland and heathland habitats. But, like all woodland, these new plantations have a relative permanence and stability that is absent from the

rapid turnover of contemporary arable farmland. Like the water authorities, the Forestry Commission, creator and custodian of so much of our woodland, is now responding to the contemporary attitudes to landscape and wildlife. Perhaps the 'new forests' it is planting now will be the new landscapes we celebrate in the twenty-first century.

But such tree-scapes will never be able to re-create the diverse structure and wildlife of the old woodlands of these islands. It is their very antiquity and historical continuity that have made them what they are. We may be able to plant the same species of trees but it is the detail of the woodland that gives it ecological diversity and richness. In many parts of the British Isles, the flowers that we particularly associate with woodland – the anemones, the bluebells, wood-sorrel and yellow archangel, dog-violet and herb-Paris grow only in places which have been wooded for centuries. Such places often have a continuous woodland history that can be traced back to the wildwood that first developed after the Ice Age. Ecologists refer to these patches as 'primary' woodland. The tree cover on such places may have been cut down several times in their long history but the soil in which they have grown has never been ploughed; no matter how intensive has been the human management over the centuries, these primary woodlands have retained the basic floral ingredients of ancient forest. The main reason why such species are restricted to primary woods seems to be their poor ability to colonise new woodland growing on land that has been ploughed. Even if they reach the newer 'secondary' woodland, which may have the same trees, these often delicate species almost invariably cannot compete with the more vigorous plants such as nettle, bramble and ground-ivy. Sadly, we cannot easily re-create a bluebell wood.

Left The regimented ranks of conifer that now march across the moorland created by our ancestors are no real substitute for the wildwood that they felled.
Above The young plantations are invaded by a few pinewood specialists – such as coal-tits which probe for insects among the larch needles. Even they will shun the forest's gloomy interior.

As we have seen, nearly all the habitats in the British Isles today are of man's making or management – with the exception of the very tops of mountains, our seas and coasts, some lakes and rivers and, of course, that ancient woodland. By far the greatest part of our landscape is made up of the heaths and moors, the meadows and pastures, the fields and hedges, and the towns and villages that we and our predecessors deliberately moulded from the land and its vegetation. Even our richest wetlands, such as the Ouse Washes, are of our collective making. All these habitats were 'new' at some time, and during their history they have continued to change in response to the vicissitudes of climate and man's activities, or simply to the passage of time. Throughout its natural history, wildlife has adjusted with remarkable tolerance to these changes. It is only when the speed and scale of the transformation is uncompromisingly great that wildlife is unable to adjust and species continue to survive only in the remnants of the habitats to which they are naturally adapted. It is the sanctuary offered to these threatened species of plants and animals that is the scientific, aesthetic and moral basis for wildlife conservation – the most novel of all the stages in man's long relationship with the plants and animals of these islands.

The story of Wicken Fen – one of the few surviving remnants of the East Anglian Fens – is a graphic example of the changing attitudes to nature conservation during the last 100 years. As we have seen, the fenlands had been originally created by a complex sequence of geological and climatic changes but these wild, marshy expanses have, for centuries, been the handiwork of ambitious 'venturers' and industrious East Anglian farmers. Towards the end of the nineteenth century it was noticed that, almost by chance, Wicken Fen had escaped the most recent impact of this agricultural 'improvement' because it was still being used by villagers for harvesting sedge. Amateur insect collectors swarmed in from all parts of the country in pursuit of the swallowtails and other fine fenland species; so, too, did the plant hunters who heard of its rich flora. Today, there is a great vogue for bird life – and Wicken is a paradise for ornithologists on the track of fenland birds – but at the beginning of this century, bugs and beetles, moths and butterflies and delicate plants were pinned and pressed into the collections of people with time to find them. In the interests of preserving this national treasure, the National Trust acquired Wicken Fen in the sincere belief that ownership would ensure its survival intact with its valued flora and fauna. It was one of the first nature sanctuaries in the country and was left to itself without the threat of drainage and other modern agricultural practices. Almost before the eyes of the naturalists, the swallowtail declined and finally disappeared and the fen violet was lost from the checklist of rare Wicken plants – and in neither case were collectors to blame. What the well-intentioned conservationists had failed to recognise – or at least to put into practice – was that Wicken would have to be managed in the same traditional way if it were not to change its nature. The inconspicuous milk-parsley, vital for the swallowtail caterpillars, flourished where there was regular management and harvesting of the fen sedge, which for generations had been used by local people as material for finishing off thatch, bedding for cattle and faggots for

To maintain landscapes as they were in the past, we must continue the traditional practices that created them. Regular sedge cutting on Wicken Fen not only provides material for thatching but also is essential for the conservation of the fen habitat.

winter fuel. It was not just the presence of milk-parsley that was vital – it was the way the habitat was managed around it. In short, the swallowtail butterfly had declined soon after these rural practices came to an end. By the early 1950s it was extinct at Wicken Fen. Since then, informed ecologists and skilled fenmen have worked together in an attempt to turn back the clock. The water-table is being raised back to its former level and the woodland that grew up in place of the fen-carr is being gradually cleared to make way for fields of common-reed and purple moor-grass, which are managed and harvested in the traditional way. In 1982, large numbers of the fen violet were found growing on disturbed peat where bushes had been recently cleared. If you look among the vegetation that is again being encouraged to grow in the sedge fields, you will discover the feathery leaves of milk-parsley. There will be a well-earned celebration at Wicken if at last the swallowtail butterfly returns. In the meantime, this oasis of fenland, distinctly different and physically separated from the vast desert of drained agricultural land that surrounds it, has, at every season of the year, an atmosphere of its own. It transports you back to a time when much of East Anglia had the same rich variety of fenland plants and animals in the same distinctive mix of habitats. Wicken Fen is like a 'time-capsule' preserved from the past – witness to a bygone era of our country's natural history. It is a remnant of a once more widespread landscape and has a rarity value to be treasured.

The vast swampland of East Anglia has been drained over the centuries by the cutting of lodes and by ambitious pumping schemes. Wicken Fen was created as a working landscape to provide local people with sedges, reeds and food for their livestock.

222

Like so many of our native reserves, Wicken Fen is open to the public; we are welcome there to explore for ourselves its natural wealth and beauty. Such treasured places are so often the product of man and nature working in partnership, and the scene created is a natural work of art. As we visit and experience these reserves, each of us looks on the detail with a different eye. For some, these are places for scientific research; for others, they are a naturalist's paradise in which to observe and record the richness of wildlife. For everyone, they are places of simple beauty and refreshment – part of the living heritage of the British Isles to which we, as new inhabitants and custodians, now belong.

There are, though, some plants and animals whose way of life is so specific that they cannot survive in the absence of their ancient habitats. Such species came to these islands in that 'wilderness period' between the end of the Ice Age and the transformation of the landscape by man. These wilderness corners of the British Isles have dwindled with time and have been eroded by our increasing monopoly of the land. They are true sanctuaries where long-established species can continue a way of life that is not pressured by our own. Their sanctity is clearly not negotiable.

Raised bogs – those curious, fragile communities of heathers, bog-mosses and sundews that, over thousands of years, have grown in the rain-lashed western parts of the British Isles – are particularly vulnerable. Once destroyed, they can never be re-created. Ireland once had so many that their value was counted only as turves to be cut from the peat; today there are very few intact. The most pristine raised bog in Wales is the one near Borth on the Dyfi estuary. For many years the Nature Conservancy Council has monitored and protected this extraordinary domed tract of bogland as part of a National Nature Reserve that embraces the lower reaches of the estuary and the Ynyslas sand dunes. This area has great fascination for the naturalist and was once the hinterland of that sunken Celtic land reaching out into Cardigan Bay. At low tide you can walk along the sand and discover the petrified stumps of trees which date back 6000 years to the time when dense forest covered the land. Holidaymakers spending a summer week or two at the small resort of Borth can explore the special plant life of Ynyslas by way of board-walks that the NCC wardens have laid across the shifting dunes. Each year thousands of people visit this small and fragile dune system and the information centre set up to explain its history and plans for its conservation. But the ancient raised bog, Cors Fochno, with a history almost as old as the sunken forest, is out of bounds. Nevertheless, it is reassuring to know that such rare and fragile areas of our ancient wilderness continue to exist.

To succeed, nature conservation must involve us all – both nationally and locally. As well as the Nature Conservancy Council, the government body which promotes nature conservation in Great Britain, we have forty-six Nature Conservation Trusts working in different parts of the country under the umbrella of the Royal Society for Nature Conservation. These, together with several national voluntary and charitable organisations, such as the Royal Society for the Protection of Birds, identify and, where possible, purchase or manage areas in need of special attention. In Eire, the government Forestry and Wildlife Service and organisations such as the Irish Wildlife Federation work in a similar way. Through them, anyone can take part in cherishing and conserving the typical or special habitats and wildlife of their own part of the British Isles. It is no coincidence that the first nature reserves and conservation trusts were formed earlier this century in Norfolk and Lincolnshire and other nearby counties, where the impact of intensive cultivation was becoming more apparent. During the last two decades, the issues of nature conservation have largely polarised around the problems of farming and wildlife, but realism and compromise are beginning to replace over-reaction and conflict. Increasingly it seems that substantial areas of land will have to be specially set aside for the welfare of wildlife and that our national and local priorities for its conservation will be embraced in the overall economic equation of our lives. Fortunately, because our farmers are so efficient, more and more marginal land is no longer required for production and is becoming available for purchase or management as nature reserves. But behind this concept of setting aside exclusive areas for wildlife – no matter how accessible they may be to people – is the danger that the rest of the country will lose the diversity and richness of its wild plants and animals, by default. It is in the familiar, contemporary, functional parts of our land that we most need and appreciate contact with nature. All the reserves together add up to only a small fraction of the land we have, and to omit from our conservation policy the ordinary, undesignated working landscapes of these islands would be to break faith with history.

In their long natural history, our animals and plants have survived great changes in their habitats – many of them more disastrous than those of today. The localised impact of bronze-age man, 3000 years ago, was far more devastating on the wildwood and its wildlife than the new 'improvements' of our twentieth-century farmers on contemporary landscapes; the revolutionary regime of the plough was imposed by the discovery of iron, not by the development of the modern tractor. What was different in the past was that our wildlife had more opportunity to shift and adjust to the changes in the landscape and its habitats. We have to see today's scene in the right perspective – in the longer-term context of six millennia of intervention by man. We have continuously been changing the course of natural history and will go on doing so for many more millennia. The difference now is that we have a knowledge of the past which alters our view of the present. The future chapters in the natural history of these islands will not only tell the continuing story of our shaping of the landscape and its wildlife, but will also be written with increasing hindsight. We are at the crossroads of conservation. We have to decide whether conservation intervention is always justified. We may have to be prepared to lose some habitats for good, just as our predecessors did. Many of the habitats that they created as part of their way of life have become outmoded and are artificially preserved by us as curios of the past. When they were first fashioned as part of the working landscape, such places as hay-meadows and hedgerows, pastures and ponds were never designed by their creators to become permanent treasures for the nation. We have to decide which and how many of these we should try to safeguard as part of our natural heritage. Although we may deplete or destroy some outdated habitats, we are, after all, continually creating new ones where, as we have seen, many threatened species can regroup and adjust and perhaps, with help from us, even flourish.

We are continually adding to the montage of habitats that has been compiled over the millennia. Each has a continuity with the past. Each different landscape with its unique community of plants and animals gives us direct contact with history. To explore the varied mosaic of the living landscapes of these islands, to sense their atmospheres, appreciate their textures and their colours, to observe them through their different seasons, and to understand the way they have been shaped by time and by the lives of people, is to set out on a journey through their natural history. It is a travelogue through time – each part of the pattern is a landmark in the story of the making of the British Isles as we know them today. It has been a dramatic tale of never-ending change – one that continues and one which will have many more equally eventful chapters.

When, 10,000 years ago, the ice finally retreated, it left here a barren landscape – a blank page on which we and the other wildlife invaders from the south have made our mark, transforming this land into 'The Living Isles'. That epic story – a natural history – is recorded all around us.

There are many nature reserves throughout the British Isles. The Farne Islands have changed little since they were created by the rising seas after the Ice Age; they are a 'time capsule' from that wilderness period before man came on the scene. Today they and their wildlife are preserved for us to visit and enjoy – we are transported back to one of the earlier chapters in our natural history.

A·GUIDE·TO·THE NATURAL·HISTORY OF·BRITAIN AND·IRELAND

The landscapes of the British Isles are among the most varied in the world. It is this diversity which gives them their special appeal. The natural history of Britain and Ireland is unique. Exploring it provides the opportunity for everyone to follow their particular interests – whether they be geology and the history of landscape, archaeology and our own social history, botany, ornithology or the wealth of other wildlife studies.

There are several thousand nature reserves and other sites which have been designated for their national importance or local interest – or simply for their natural beauty.

This gazetteer lists nearly 450 of these – all of which are open to the public. They are grouped in regions and have been selected not only for the way they reflect the character of each area but also for the way they illustrate the story of our landscapes and wildlife since the end of the last Ice Age.

With this gazetteer as a guide and companion, you can, region by region, explore the past and present natural history of 'The Living Isles'.

HOW TO USE THE GAZETTEER

The 20 regions derive from the natural boundaries and character of the land. Each has its own distinctive land-scapes and natural history: the grass downlands of Wessex, the dramatic mountains and coastline of the High-lands and Islands, the steep valley woodlands of South Wales, the glacial eskers and lush pastures of the central plain of Ireland. The map of the British Isles shows these twenty natural regions – each of which may be either your own part of the country or an area you are planning to visit. From the description of the region and the series of twenty to thirty sites selected within it, you can pin-point where to discover and enjoy its natural history.

CHOOSING WHICH SITES TO VISIT

depends on your particular interest in the natural history of the region. The series of sites has been arranged to follow the sequence of the ten chapters in this book – each of which is a stage in the natural history of these islands and is characterised by one type of habitat.

For example, Chapter I describes the British Isles just after the ice-sheets melted; all of the twenty regions in the gazetteer have sites of ice-age relics and these are denoted by the symbol **1**.

In the same way, if you wish to explore the woodlands of the region, look for the symbol **3**: several of these sites were mentioned in Chapter 3, 'Beneath the Greenwood'.

Not every region has examples of every main habitat but all the regions reveal how the landscape has unfolded.

Some sites contain more than one habitat and are therefore illustrative of two or more chapters. Where this is the case, you will see more than one symbol against the site entry. The symbol that appears first represents the most characteristic habitat of the reserve.

The ten habitats corresponding to the ten chapters of the book are:

1 *Glacial features of the landscape*: corries and cwms, eskers and drumlins, arctic and alpine relic flora and fauna – impressions of the British Isles 'After the Ice'.

2 *Streams, rivers, lakes, marsh and fenland:* the succession of freshwater habitats and wildlife communities that developed when the melting ice became the 'Streams of Life'.

3 *Forests, woods and copses:* the woodlands that tell the story of our trees and the wildlife to be found 'Beneath the Greenwood'.

4 *The marine world that encircles the British Isles:* its colonies of seals and sea-birds, underwater nature reserves and offshore islands – the sea-life of our 'Island Waters'.

5 *Towering cliffs, estuaries and salt-marshes, sand dunes, shingle spits and rocky bays:* the ever-changing coast-line and its diverse wildlife – all at the mercy of 'Time and Tide'.

6 *Heath and moorland, blanket and valley bogs:* wild, open tracts of country with rare and dramatic communities of plants and animals – landscapes fashioned by our ancestors 'Out of the Flames'.

7 *The grasslands of chalk downland and limestone hills, hay-meadows and flood-meadows:* each with its rich plant and insect life, birds and mammals that inhabit these 'Fresh Pastures'.

8 *Agricultural landscapes:* arable land and orchards, ancient field systems and farm museums – the intimate world of the hedgerow and the wildlife of open country that has come 'Under the Plough'.

9 *The habitats of towns and villages:* churchyards and public parks, the grounds of stately homes and the tree-lined streets and squares of our cities – all have wildlife 'Sheltering with Man'.

10 *Twentieth-century landscapes:* reservoirs and flooded gravel pits, water parks, forestry plantations and the terrain of modern industry – the wildlife that flourishes in these 'New Landscapes'.

HOW TO FIND THEM Each regional section of the gazetteer has a map which shows the general location of each site. You can then pin-point its exact position from the description of the nearest main roads and towns, and, in England, Scotland, Wales and Northern Ireland, from the Ordnance Survey National Grid Reference Number that accompanies the site entry. All OS maps explain how to use the system. The sites in Eire are accompanied by the relevant Irish grid reference.

IF YOU WANT TO KNOW MORE about the site and its wildlife or wish to check details of access, you should refer to the organisation that manages it. Each entry includes the abbreviation for the organisation that is primarily respon-sible for looking after the reserve; this is not necessarily the owner of the site. There may be seasonal or other restrictions to access which are not detailed in the gazetteer.

The organisations are:

Abbreviations used in the Gazetteer Regions
AT   An Taisce (National Trust Eire)
AWA   Anglian Water Authority
BNS   Bristol Naturalists Society
BPT   Bradgate Park Trust
BWC   Bristol Waterworks Company
C   Commonage (Ireland)
CC   The appropriate County Council
C Com   Countryside Commission
CEC   Crown Estate Commissioners
CEGB   Central Electricity Generating Board
CT   The appropriate County Trust for nature conservation
DC   The appropriate Local District Council
DOC   Duchy of Cornwall
DOE   Department of Environment
DOM   Duke of Marlborough
DTP   Department of Transport
EHCP   Elsham Hall Country Park
F   Foreshore (Ireland)
FC   Forestry Commission
FS   Forestry Service (Northern Ireland)
FSC   Field Studies Council
FWS   Forestry and Wildlife Service (Eire)
IWC   Irish Wildbird Conservancy
KAMT   Kenneth Allsop Memorial Trust
LT   Landmark Trust
LVA   Lee Valley Regional Park Authority
LWT   London Wildlife Trust
MOD   Ministry of Defence
NCC   Nature Conservancy Council
NPA   The appropriate National Park authority
NT   National Trust (including Northern Ireland)

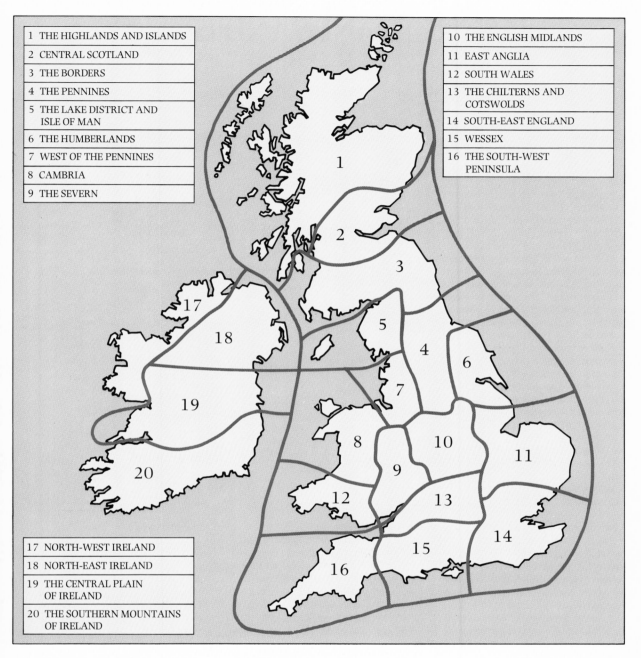

1 THE HIGHLANDS AND ISLANDS	10 THE ENGLISH MIDLANDS
2 CENTRAL SCOTLAND	11 EAST ANGLIA
3 THE BORDERS	12 SOUTH WALES
4 THE PENNINES	13 THE CHILTERNS AND COTSWOLDS
5 THE LAKE DISTRICT AND ISLE OF MAN	14 SOUTH-EAST ENGLAND
6 THE HUMBERLANDS	15 WESSEX
7 WEST OF THE PENNINES	16 THE SOUTH-WEST PENINSULA
8 CAMBRIA	
9 THE SEVERN	

17 NORTH-WEST IRELAND
18 NORTH-EAST IRELAND
19 THE CENTRAL PLAIN OF IRELAND
20 THE SOUTHERN MOUNTAINS OF IRELAND

NTS National Trust for Scotland
NWNT North Wales Naturalists Trust
OPW Office of Public Works (Eire)
P Private land in Ireland, open to public or viewed from roads and paths
PDC Peterlee Development Corporation
PbDC Peterborough Development Corporation
RC The appropriate Regional Council (Scotland)

RSPB Royal Society for the Protection of Birds
S State (Ireland)
SE Sandringham Estate Limited
SgE Strangways Estate
SWT Scottish Wildlife Trust
WdT Woodland Trust
WMCAAG Wembury Marine Conservation Area Advisory Group
WT Wildfowl Trust

1 THE HIGHLANDS AND ISLANDS

One of the last great wildernesses of Europe, the Scottish Highlands have the most dramatic and distinctive combinations of scenery and wildlife of any region in the British Isles. It is the region most sparsely populated, least affected by man and with the landscapes of the grandest scale and beauty. The Highlands can be intimate and sheltered or wild and exposed. They are far larger, more remote and inaccessible than we imagine. They support many habitats which are unique to the region or are the best examples of their kind. Mountain summits, vast desolate moorlands, extensive bogs, beautiful upland lochs and rivers, and fiord-like sea lochs all provide homes for a range of species distinctly associated with Scotland.

The Islands are an integral part of the Highlands and we cannot fail to be impressed by their remarkable cliffs of sea-birds and a wealth of other natural habitats which include the incomparable Hebridean machair.

On the subarctic summit of Cairngorm or at the top of St Kilda's sea cliffs you are looking at some of the best natural history stories in the world.

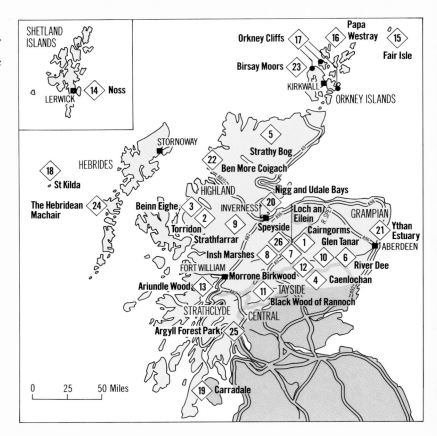

1 Cairngorms Highland NCC

We start, quite naturally, on our largest nature reserve. Stand on the Cairngorm summit and the breathtaking view below covers a hundred square miles of high mountains. This forms the most extensive area of land over 3000 feet high in the British Isles. With an arctic chill even in July, only the toughest plants and animals can survive the exposure. This is the land of red deer, wild cat and golden eagles. There are no trees or shrubs. The flowering plants are small, tough, arctic species with ferns, mosses and lichens covered in snow for most of the year. Roseroot, mountain sorrel and other flora shelter in the corries ● NJ010040 take Ski Road via Glen More from Aviemore, Speyside. ▪

2 Torridon Highland NTS

Between Lochs Torridon and Maree on Wester Ross is an area of over 150 square miles which is typical of the best of the Highland wilderness, shaped by the power of ice. First appreciating its scale and beauty from a distance, we venture to penetrate this land of rocky coasts, mountains, moorlands, freshwater hill lochs and coastal sea lochs to appreciate the individuality of the Highland wildlife. It seems as though the divers and eagles of Torridon are locked in a time-capsule with the pinewoods and arctic flowers which were obliterated from the warmer south thousands of years ago. An exciting collection of true Highland habitats not to be missed ● Via A896 and A832 north-west of Achnasheen. ▪

3 Beinn Eighe Highland NCC

The summit of Torridon's wild landscape is an awe-inspiring mountain of considerable biological importance set in superb Highland scenery. There is a valuable remnant of Caledonian pine forest on the north-eastern slopes, together with fine moorland and bog communities. The higher levels of the mountain have arctic alpines and other unusual species including dwarf cornel and moonwort. Birds and animals are hard to see but ptarmigan, red deer, mountain hare, golden eagle and merlin are present ● NG952610 immediately west of Kinlochewe. ▪

4 Caenlochan Tayside NCC
Mountain animals are somewhat less difficult to find here. Red deer, fox and blue hare are on the high mountains with ptarmigan. Dunlin and golden plover breed on the high moorland. Eagles soar over the glens. The cliff ledges on the corries display a special flora of arctic alpines including alpine bistort and northern bedstraw with montane willows. Lichens, sedges and mosses are abundant on the summits ● NO200750 above the Devil's Elbow on A93, 10 miles south of Braemar. From June to October access is restricted. **1**

5 Strathy Bog Highland NCC
To see one of the best remaining blanket bogs in Britain involves a long walk in spring over some of the most remote land in Scotland to a site now surrounded by commercial afforestation. The trek is rewarded by a great variety of bog species, dwarf birch, sundews and bearberry ● NC790550, 8 miles west of B871 on the upper reaches of the River Strathy. **2 6**

6 River Dee Grampian
The epitome of Scottish rivers, the Dee is clear, fresh and free of hydroelectric interruptions. Famous for its salmon it also has trout, eels, mink and otter. The middle section of Deeside is clothed with superb woodlands which are the haunt of pine marten, crossbills, buzzard and deer ● From Braemar downstream to Banchory. **2**

7 Loch an Eilein Highland NCC
Set in the Cairngorms amidst native pinewoods, this beautiful loch has all the Highland characteristics from white water-lilies to a ruined castle island. Birds feed on the shallow bays and water meadows; brown trout, pike, eels and otters are held in the deeper waters; insects are abundant in the brief summer warmth ● NH898085 off B970 at Polchar about 2 miles southeast of Craigellachie. **2**

8 Insh Marshes Highland RSPB
As you stand on the perimeter road looking down on the most important tract of flood plain mire in northern Britain you will see extensive habitats of lowland fen and marsh with willow carr, small pools and old drainage ditches which fortunately failed to work. Whooper swan and northern sedge are two of the exciting range of northern species. The story of Loch Insh and its marshes is told in Ch. 2 ● NN775998 off B970 near Feshiebridge. **2**

9 Strathfarrar Highland NCC
If you want to see one of the most memorable wildwoods of Britain there can be few more compelling scenes than the native pine forest of Strathfarrar. It clings to the deep gorges and spreads around the alder marshes which persuaded successive generations of fellers to leave it untouched. Fine, mature pines are mixed with birch and open areas of heather and bilberry in a colourful mosaic. The plants and animals of the once extensive Caledonian Forest described in Ch. 3 are present, including crested tit, roe deer and pine marten ● NH270375 vehicular access is controlled at Leishmore, access via Glen Strathfarrar off A831, 6 miles north of Cannich. **3**

10 Glen Tanar Grampian NCC
The native Scots pine are naturally regenerating in this eastern section of the Caledonian Forest, even spreading on to adjacent moorland. Juniper, rowan, aspen and birch are scattered throughout, representing the range of post-glacial colonising trees. Typical pinewood plants include chickweed wintergreen, and creeping lady's-tresses. Crossbill, siskin and capercaillie breed, red squirrel, otter, fox and wild cat are present ● NO480910 at Braeloine, south of B976 about 6 miles east of Ballater. **3**

11 Black Wood of Rannoch
Tayside FC
Despite its gloomy name the Black Wood is one of the finest remnants of Caledonian pine and birch forest with an exciting range of plants and animals of the wildwood. Capercaillie, black grouse, siskin, Scottish crossbill, redstart, spotted flycatcher and tree pipit are all breeding here. The forest and the Camghouran birch woods to the east are of international importance for their species of rare moths and other insects ● NN570550, south of Loch Rannoch off B846, 28 miles west of Pitlochry. **3**

12 Morrone Birkwood Grampian NCC
A rare woodland type in Britain today, this is our best sub-alpine birch–juniper woodland with a surprisingly rich ground flora. There are 280 species of flowering plants and ferns, most notable being those otherwise restricted to open mountains: alpine cinquefoil, Scottish asphodel, alpine rush and hair sedge. Mosses and lichens are numerous in this woodland of Nordic character ● NO143911 off A93 west of Braemar, paths from car park at this point. **3**

Loch Maree, from Beinn Eighe National Nature Reserve

13 Ariundle Wood Highland NCC/FC
A distinctly different wood in the wildness of Sunart's sea loch scenery shows how the natural woodlands of the highlands are more than just pine and birch. In Strontian Glen oak was once coppiced and grows with birch, hazel and rowan. The high humidity and heavy rainfall result in luxuriant growth of mosses, liverworts and lichens ● NM835645 near Strontian on A861 12 miles west of the Corran ferry. **3**

14 Noss Shetland NCC
The view down the sheer 600-foot cliffs, covered in sea-birds, is stunning. One of the most spectacular sea-bird colonies in Europe (described in Chapter 4), there are 10,000 gannets, 20,000 kittiwakes, 63,000 guillemots with fulmars, black guillemots and great and arctic skuas ● HU550400 by boat from Lerwick via Bressay in summer. **4**

15 Fair Isle Shetland NTS
The natural aggression of great and arctic skuas can be turned on to visitors who walk over their rough hill ground territories on this magnificent bird island. From Siberia and North America windblown rarities find themselves on Fair Isle and the species list is fascinating. The bird ringing station has handled 150,000 birds of 250 species, some of which have reappeared in Greece, Siberia and even Brazil. But the real treasure of the island is its breeding sea-bird colonies which include 30,000 puffins, 50,000 fulmar, 40,000 guillemots and as many as 100 pairs of the storm petrel which comes ashore only at night ● HZ210720 between north Ronaldsay, Orkneys, and Sumburgh Head, Shetlands. **4**

16 Papa Westray Orkneys RSPB
The rather mundane heathland of North Hill is brought to life each spring by the return of over 10,000 arctic terns in one unusually large and impressive colony. Harassed by the skuas, the terns disgorge their food which is eagerly eaten by their pursuers. Gulls, ringed plover, eiders and dunlin also breed here. The best maritime sedge heath in northern Scotland draws botanists as well as birdwatchers ● HY500550 north part of Westray Island, contact RSPB warden at Gowrie before entering reserve area. **4**

17 Orkney Cliffs Orkney RSPB
Copinsay, Marwick Head and Noup Cliffs together form one of the most spectacular collections of cliffs with breeding sea-bird colonies. As a group they hold internationally significant numbers of many species; individually they are a most enthralling experience to reward the Orkney visitor. The birds make use of the rich feeding grounds of the Atlantic, with seemingly endless supplies of sand eels for the auks, and are protected by the inaccessible security of high cliff ledges ● Marwick is on western mainland Orkney, Noup Head is on Westray and Copinsay is southeast of the mainland, offshore. **4**

18 St Kilda Outer Hebrides NCC/NTS
St Kilda is a world of its own. It is the epitome of an oceanic island: isolated, beautiful, rugged, dramatic and totally dominated by the sea. It is now inhabited and accessible again, following its abandonment between 1930 and 1957. In 1840 it may have been the last refuge of the great auk before extinction. Today it has its own subspecies of wren and long-tailed fieldmouse, feral herds of Soay and blackfaced sheep, and the

St Kilda, with gannets

breeding sites of the rare Leach's and storm petrels and of Manx shearwaters. And the cliffs? It is hard to imagine sheer drops of over 1300 feet, clothed in roseroot, primrose, honeysuckle, moss campion and purple saxifrage, and all around the noise and smell of the largest gannetry in the world, the largest colony of fulmar in Britain and thousands of sea-birds of a dozen other species ● 41 miles west of North Uist. Unless you have your own yacht, access is only available through membership of the annual NTS work parties which are organised to conserve and restore the buildings of the old village community. **4**

19 Carradale Strathclyde SWT
From the low cliffs of this grassy peninsula, porpoise, white-beaked dolphins, bottle-nosed dolphins and killer whales can be seen in the Kilbrannan Sound while otters are often seen on shore. Grazing is undertaken by a curious herd of white feral goats ● NR815375 off B842/B879 on east side of Kintyre. **4**

20 Nigg and Udale Bays
Highland part NCC
On opposite banks of the Cromarty Firth these bays are part of north-east Scotland's major wintering and migration sites for wildfowl and waders. The estuary flats are extensive and hold good numbers of goldeneye, pintail, scaup, wigeon, whooper and mute swans in winter. Autumn brings roosts of greylag geese from the fertile arable land around ● NH750720/NH710675, view from roads near Barbaraville, Nigg and Balblair, south and east of Invergordon. **5**

21 Ythan Estuary Grampian NCC
The dunes and moorland close to the habitats of the estuary are the perfect combination for the eider ducks to breed in their largest numbers. Shelduck make use of the old rabbit burrows; sandwich, little, arctic and common terns nest on the Sands of Forvie. A marvellous example of a large dune system undisturbed by man ● NK025275 on A975 about 12 miles north of Aberdeen. **5**

22 Ben More Coigach Highland SWT
If you want to see the range of moorland and heathland habitats from the edge of cultivation to the mountain tops, this site is ideal. The rolling western moorland is covered in deergrass and cottongrass blanket bog with sundews; the higher slopes are of heather. The sandstone slopes of Beinn an Eoin rise steeply from the heather-grass moorland typical of the Highlands and dramatic in scale. The cultivation of the crofts has ceased and they have reverted to grazing land for stock, and visiting barnacle geese ● NC085040 on Coigach west of the A835, 6 miles north of Ullapool, via Achiltibuie. **6 8**

23 Birsay Moors Orkney RSPB
Both the hen harrier and short-eared owl need extensive areas of moorland heath for hunting, a habitat declining in Orkney as the heather and deergrass are replaced by cultivated grasses and clovers. But here on this moorland nature reserve they are secure with skylark, snipe, redshank and wheatear among other breeding species. The area has lochans, peat banks and shallow valleys to add interest ● HY370194 from lower Cottasgarth. **6**

24 The Hebridean Machair Hebrides
You can read the fascinating story of this beautiful, semi-natural grassland in Ch. 7. Lime-rich shell sand has been blown inland on to low-lying marshes transforming the land into a magic carpet of botanical interest. The vivid colour patterns of the summer machair vary with the type and intensity of farming. It is difficult to imagine how

nature could use the colours to greater effect, varying the shades of hybrid orchids from cream to deep red. Yellow seaside pansies and pink stork's-bill stand out on the sandy patches. The hay meadows and barley fields contain corn marigold, poppies, small bugloss and important populations of corn-crake, twite, corn bunting and breeding waders ● NF707707 Balranald RSPB reserve is excellent, west of A865 south of Tigharry, North Uist. **7**

25 Argyll Forest Park Strathclyde FC
Established in 1935, Argyll was the first forest park in Great Britain and demonstrates exceptionally well how commercial forestry can be combined with recreational and tourist uses and nature conservation interests. In fact, only half the park is afforested, the remainder being left as valuable moorland, wetlands and montane habitats ● NN272034 at Ardgartan and elsewhere north and west of Loch Long. **9 10**

26 Speyside Highlands
Superimposed on a once remote and still delicate habitat of montane species is a new and potentially destructive land use. The introduction of intensive recreational and sporting use of the Cairngorms is based on the centre at Aviemore and the increased facilities of Speyside. Roads, buildings, pylons and the paraphernalia of the ski slopes and thousands of trampling feet on the mountain tops have already begun to erode the environment the visitors travel to see ● NH980060 follow road to Cairngorms from Speyside up to Glen More and beyond. **10**

If we had to tell the natural history of our islands from one region only it would have been Central Scotland. For here is the drama of mountain scenery with arctic relics, the power of roaring river torrents and the richness of lowland lochs. Remnants of a varied wildwood contrast with the wave-battered oceanic isles. All the shoreline habitats are represented on the east or west coasts. Heather moorlands and upland grasses are grazed by sheep on the rugged hills. Here, the twentieth-century landscapes of coniferous forests are not as new as we may think. There is the essential link between the rich arable land of the lowlands and the wild geese which winter here. Other wildlife species have adjusted to living with man in the great Scottish cities and with our help in new nature reserves.

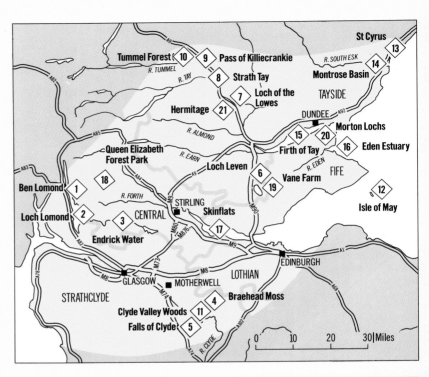

1 Ben Lomond Central

With all the splendour of the Highland peaks to the north, Ben Lomond towers over its loch to mark the end of the Lowland hills of Central Scotland. The flora of this mountain is remarkable in its richness. High on the crags and corries are the arctic alpines: fairy flax, alpine meadow-rue, sibbaldia and cyphel. The colourful campions, saxifrage and mountain pansy embellish the highest crags but the wealth of mosses, ferns and grasses are less striking. The most arctic of our birds, the ptarmigan, is found on the summits with raven and ring ousel below. Red deer, mountain hare and merlin are present in this splendid introduction to the montane habitats, readily accessible from the Glasgow area ● NM370025, a five-hour return trek will take you to the summit, access from Loch Lomond (*see* 2 below) or Queen Elizabeth forest park (*see* 18 below). **1**

2 Loch Lomond Central/Strathclyde

NCC *et al.*

In the largest freshwater lake in Britain it is not surprising to find a unique aquatic life typified by an unusual fish. The powan, or freshwater herring, is quite rare in Britain and swims with salmon, brown and sea trout in the loch. Roach are confined to the richer waters of the southern end, where the wintering wildfowl also tend to concentrate. Around the edges are fine spreads of reed swamp, lagoons, fen, willow carr and other wetlands. The islands provide ideal sanctuaries for wildlife and the largest, Inchcailloch, has a nature trail with fine sessile oak woodland with alder and birch. During low water levels the exposed shoreline mud attracts a variety of waders ● NS420910, the south-east section and islands are the most interesting and include a nature reserve, B837 off A811 at Drymen. Only 22 miles from the centre of Glasgow. **1 2**

Loch Lomond, with Ben Lomond behind

3 Endrick Water Central
In its short dash across Central Scotland from the Carleatheran Bog to Loch Lomond, the River Endrick portrays each stage of a river's story through time and space. High in the grouse moors the rills and burns gather speed to erode ravines. The hill streams support brown trout, dipper and grey wagtail. The high waterfall at the Loup of Fintry obstructs the migration of salmon and sea trout further upstream. The lower reaches are subject to sudden spates, from which the river takes its name. There are ox-bow lakes where it slows down. It never reaches the sea but spills out into the freshwater richness of Loch Lomond where otters and herons fish the mouth of the river ● NS650865 on B818 to NS473875 on A811 south of Drymen. **2**

4 Braehead Moss Strathclyde NCC
The best local example of both raised and blanket bogs is now a nature reserve having been undisturbed by burning, forestry or farming. Rarer species of bog mosses are found among the typical bog plants. The area is open to public access on foot but can be extremely wet. A rare opportunity to appreciate the bog habitats ● NS955510 on B7016 adjacent Braehead village, 6 miles north-east of Lanark. **2** **6**

5 Falls of Clyde Strathclyde SWT
The power of the Clyde in spate is dramatic indeed, as it roars over a series of falls. It carved the valley and gorge where mink, otter, grey wagtail and dippers now feed. It drove the New Lanark watermills with the crystal-clear waters, still stocked with minnow, trout, grayling, pike and lamprey. The spray-drenched cliffs have developed mosses and ferns and their ledges grow butterwort and purple saxifrage. There are two delightful nature reserves, one on each bank, with excellent flora in woods rich in birds, fungi and insects ● NS880415 on minor roads south of Lanark. **2**

6 Loch Leven Tayside NCC
The importance of this region's coastal sites for wintering birds is admirably complemented by the national significance of the breeding duck of Loch Leven. Perhaps 1000 pairs of duck (about half of them tufted) nest on the shores and islands of this enormous freshwater loch. Waders, especially lapwing, oystercatcher, curlew, snipe and redshank, use the surrounding wetlands for breeding. These species are joined by large numbers of other waders in winter and the main wildfowl interest is the herds of pink-footed and greylag geese. But the breeding successes are tempered by the significant changes in the loch's water over the last few years. Algal blooms have indicated the increased richness of the water caused by run-off from the agricultural land drained by the Leven's feeder streams. Reed-beds and pondweeds are seriously depleted; stonewort has virtually disappeared along with dragonflies and mayflies. Although the duck's diet of pondweed has declined, the larvae of the chironomid midges is still an abundant food source ● NO150010 between A911 and M90, access at Kirkgate Park, Findatie, Burleigh Sands and Leven Castle, together with Vane Farm (*see* 19 below). **2**

7 Loch of the Lowes Tayside SWT
This very attractive loch's wildlife is special because it combines, as nowhere else, the species of the Central Lowlands with some from the Highlands. The breeding osprey, red-breasted mergansers, great crested and little grebes are some of Scotland's treasured birds. The shallow waters, woodlands and marsh habitats have a wealth of plant species from the quillwort, shoreweed and bogbean of highland nutrient-poor lochs to the yellow water-lily and amphibious bistort typical of the nutrient-rich waters of the lowlands. Reed-beds hide the secretive water-rail and roe deer. Fringing woodland has the same species composition as the native wildwood with oak, ash, hazel, holly, alder, willow and cherry ● NO050440 south of A923 a mile east of Dunkeld. **2**

8 Strath Tay Tayside
The rolling landscapes of Central Scotland break at Dunkeld, on the line of the Highland Fault, with a range of low but rugged hills. Three rivers form the complex valley system of Strath Tay, U-shaped in profile with steep sides to a heathery plateau between Dunkeld and Pitlochry. Beyond are the foothills of the Highlands and a narrow gorge through the Pass of Killiecrankie (*see* 9 below). This area is of outstanding interest for wildlife for it contains many Highland species as well as Lowland plants and animals in extensive forests of exceptional beauty. There are oakwoods and mixed and coniferous plantations, forests planted by the Dukes of Atholl for amenity and timber as far

Loch of the Lowes

235

back as 1738. On the shingle islands of the valley floor Scots pine, willow and alder freely regenerate. Many of the steeper and higher sites have held the tree species of the wildwood: birch, juniper, oak and pine. The woodland birds are of particular interest ● A9 from Dunkeld to Blair Atholl, public access by many waymarked trails and paths. **3**

9 Pass of Killiecrankie Tayside NTS
This pass to the Highlands is a dramatic wooded gorge following the River Garry. Oak dominates an attractive forest with bird cherry and a fine ground flora including wood vetch, stone bramble, melancholy thistle, giant bellflower and orchids. Redstart, wood warbler and spotted flycatcher will be seen during the spring and summer when the visitor centre is open to explain the wildlife of the area. The centre also has information for the Linn of Tummel between the pass and Pitlochry with excellent wooded walks ● NN917627 on the A9 north of Pitlochry. **3**

10 Tummel Forest Tayside FC
Oak, ash, hazel, alder and birch are the principal species of this deciduous woodland, overlooking Loch Tummel. There are small lochs around the forest which add the interest of waterside plants to those of the forest. Redstart, spotted flycatcher and woodpeckers breed in the broadleaved woods, capercaillie, black grouse and goldcrest in the conifers with mallard, teal and wigeon on the lochs. There is a Forestry Commission information centre at Queens View ● NN865597 off B8019, 5 miles north-west of Pitlochry. **3**

11 Clyde Valley Woods
Strathclyde NCC
The upper Clyde Valley has a group of important broadleaved woodlands with a wide range of native tree species of oak, elm, ash and alder. Many uncommon plants occur in these lowland glens including rough horsetail, wood fescue, herb-Paris, and stone bramble ● NS895455 off minor roads north of Lanark. **3**

12 Isle of May Fife NCC
One of Scotland's premier birdwatching sites, this island in the North Sea, at the mouth of the Firth of Forth, has a growing colony of grey seals on its northern tip. Almost any migrant bird can drop exhausted on to the safety of the rock and the observatory has recorded an amazing species list since its establishment in 1934. The fascination of May, however, is in the dramatic changes in the composition of the seabird colonies. Forty years ago the island was covered in thrift and sea campion with ten times as many breeding terns as gulls. Thirty years later the vegetation was a tangle of chickweed, sorrel and scurvygrass with 40,000 gulls, and no terns. Management now attempts to balance the gull and tern populations but other changes have occurred. Puffin numbers have risen from 7 to about 8500 pairs in 30 years and shag increased from 6 to 1000 pairs in 50 years. The spectacle of this massive colony of oceanic birds is completed with razorbill and guillemot and several thousand pairs of kittiwakes and an expanding population of fulmar ● NT655995 by boat during the summertime from Crail, Anstruther or Pittenweem. **4**

13 St Cyrus Grampian NCC
This narrow strip of the east coast has a superb range of habitats associated with the shoreline. Of the 350 flowering plants and ferns several are on

their northern limit of distribution. The salt-marsh, dunes and cliffs carry typical species with rare examples of the Nottingham catchfly, annual soft clover and rough clover. The dune pastures are still rich in flowers despite the decline of the rabbit population. The tenuous nature of some of the coastal habitats is witnessed by the virtual destruction of the salt-marsh plants following a major sand blow in 1967. Eider ducks and little terns are two of the 47 breeding bird species. Insect populations are also important ● NO745645 at St Cyrus on A92, 5 miles north of Montrose. **5**

14 Montrose Basin Tayside SWT/DC
In this great circular basin of estuarine mud the annual cycle of bird migration provides interest for over seven months. Each of the main species reaches peak numbers at a different time, from the curlew in August to the dunlin in February. Oystercatcher, redshank and snipe stay on to breed. While the waders are attracted by the small animals of the mud, the ducks feed on eelgrass and glasswort. Mallard, teal, wigeon and pintail come in large numbers in the winter. Eider and shelduck breed. Some of the grey geese which winter in the Central Lowlands will fly into the winter dusk to roost in the basin. Salmon, sea trout, eels and mussels are traditionally harvested in the mouth of the South Esk ● NO694575 west of Montrose. **5**

15 Firth of Tay Fife
Whilst the Firth holds internationally significant numbers of wintering wild-fowl and waders, including 20 per cent of the British population of eider ducks, watching for them over this vast expanse of estuary can be a cold and frustrating pastime. The secret is to know when and where to be. Low tide is not a good time as the birds are too far away and too dispersed to identify. Try Kingoodie or Port Allen for autumn waders in Invergowrie Bay, and the minor road from Newburgh to Balmerino for flighting pink-footed and greylag geese, overhead, at dawn and dusk. Diving duck and mute swans collect round the sewage outfall at the Stannergate and near Monifieth. The eider, scoter and divers which normally winter off the Abertay Sands will come close to Tayport and Newport in severe weather ● From Perth to Monifieth (including Dundee, Newburgh, Newport and the Carse of Gowrie). **5**

16 Eden Estuary Fife DC
Common seal will haul out on to the sandbanks between Shelly Point and the mouth of the Eden and their amusing, if somewhat lethargic, antics will brighten any birdwatcher's visit to this estuary. Sheltered with a range of coastal habitats, the Eden attracts godwits, redshank, dunlin and knot in good numbers. Views of the eiders and scoters in St Andrews Bay or the estuary can often be enjoyed more easily than from the Firth of Tay (*see* 15 above). The black and white patterns of both shelduck and oystercatchers are always around ● NO455188 main access at Out Head 2 miles north of St Andrews, or from Coble Shore or Guardbridge, on A919, 4 miles north-west of St Andrews. **5**

17 Skinflats Lothian RSPB
The risk of losing these internationally important mudflats on the south bank of the Inner Forth Estuary is partly reduced by a 1000-acre nature reserve over some of the best wintering grounds. Knot, redshank, shelduck, dunlin and golden plover are all counted in thousands ● NS930835 east of A905 between Grangemouth and the Kincardine Bridge. **5**

18 Queen Elizabeth Forest Park
Central FC
A clear impression of the Highland moors to the north can be gained from the open land around Ben Venue. While the oak and conifer woods are the principal interest to the visitor, heather- and bracken-covered moorland rolls for miles around the rising land. Cross-leaved heath is common and the moors are spotted with struggling birch and straggles of bog myrtle. The subtle changes in vegetation over the wetter or rockier patches are reflected in the colour mosaic of the moors. All the birds of the moorland and upland scrub are present with good insect populations in the sheltered parts ● NN520015 David Marshall Lodge Centre above Aberfoyle. **6 3 10**

19 Vane Farm Tayside RSPB
The close relationship between the wintering herds of geese in the shelter of Central Scotland and the crops of the arable land is well known. For generations the grey geese have flown to these feeding fields beside Loch Leven at dawn, and returned to estuaries, lochs and other safe places at dusk. It is an exciting spectacle when two or three thousand honking geese fly over in wavering echelons in the twilight. They can, however, cause problems for farmers by feeding on growing crops.

Here at Vane Farm they are welcomed and the arable land which forms part of the reserve is managed to provide autumn gleanings from barley and potatoes for pink-footed and greylag geese ● NT145987 on B9097, 2 miles east of Junction 5 on M90. On the banks of Loch Leven (*see* 6 above). **8 2**

20 Morton Lochs Fife NCC
The wildlife richness of these man-made lochs was originally accidental but has now been recognised and enhanced. The management of the old fish-rearing lochs has left the south loch to show how the open water was abandoned and colonised with rushes, reeds, alder and willow. The other pools have been restored with new islands and promontories to increase the bank area, and this has already attracted many nesting birds. Migrants and wintering birds, including heron, use the lochs and surrounds ● NO465260 east of B945 about 1 mile south of Tayport. **10**

21 Hermitage Tayside NTS
Not all of our coniferous forests are recent and this site is a rare opportunity to illustrate the wildlife and indeed the amenity, of long-established plantations of Douglas and silver fir, Norway spruce and larch. Alder, birch, oak and wild cherry inevitably find a niche on the river-banks, providing food for a wide range of woodland birds. Dipper, grey wagtail and salmon may be seen in the gorge ● NO013423 access directly off A9 1 mile west of Dunkeld. **10**

Grey seal on the Isle of May

The line of the border between England and Scotland is entirely artificial and ignored by wildlife which spreads across the uplands of Northumberland and the Borders, Dumfries and Galloway. Here the boundaries of the natural habitats do not follow any of the lines we have drawn through history.

The Borders are exciting, their scenery is dramatic and remote, ancient or very recent indeed. The coastline is superb, with some of the finest offshore islands, cliffs and bays in Britain. From the montane flowers of the Cheviots to the submarine kelp forests off St Abb's there is a clear, clean beauty in the region's complex vegetation patterns. The gannets of Bass Rock are no more or less exhilarating than the geese of the Solway Firth. They are different and it is the fact that they both occur here that matters. It is a very special region to those who live here or stay long enough to discover its scenery and wildlife.

1 Goat Fell Strathclyde NTS
Rising to nearly 3000 feet, the scenic ridges and corries of Goat Fell crown the mountain habitats of Arran. On the island's granite summits are found arctic alpines: starry saxifrage or mountain sorrel and the alpine buckler-fern. Dwarf junipers survive the cold exposure at higher levels than the birch or oak of Merkland Wood. Raven, golden eagle and golden plover breed in these montane landscapes ● NR990415 on A841 north of Brodick. ▯

2 The Cheviots
Northumberland/Borders
Magnificent views stretch out across the Borders and the Northumberland countryside from the peaks of the County's National Park. Round the summit of the Cheviots grow plants with ingenious ways of surviving the cold, windy and snow-laden peaks. Most important is to stay close to the ground

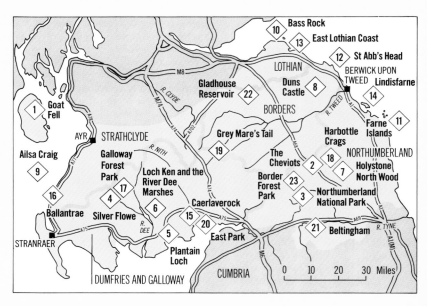

The Cheviots, from Alnwick Moor

like the parsley fern, dwarf male-fern, chives and maiden pink. Where there are lime-rich rocks on the Cheviots, globeflower, roseroot, alpine saw-wort and mossy saxifrage occur, with hairy stonecrop in wetter patches. All of them have been here for thousands of years, since the arctic tundra of post-glacial Britain ● NT910205 between Wooler on the A697 and Carter Bar on the A68. **1**

3 Northumberland National Park
Northumberland CC
Scattered throughout the National Park are small lakes, or loughs, formed by the glaciers over-deepening the depressions they made in the ground, then, as they thawed, filling the dip with ice-cold water. Some are still open water with sparse or rich vegetation depending on the local soil. Others have naturally infilled with vegetation to form willow-wooded mires. The upland streams may be fed by these loughs or simply charged by the rainwater from the hills. They flow over waterfalls and in powerful torrents where dipper and grey wagtail feed on a wealth of insects.

Everywhere the water spreads there are mosses and lichens, sedges and waterside herbs ● NY763796 the Blacka Burn Lough has acid swamp and feeds the Blacka Burn in the conifers of the southern park. **2**

4 Silver Flowe
Dumfries and Galloway NCC
On the least disturbed and most varied acidic peatland in southern Scotland an important system of blanket mire has developed. The surface of the bog is extremely sensitive to trampling and no access is provided. However, as you look down from the hillside the seven bog areas are clearly visible, each with its series of shining pools from which the reserve derives its name ● NX470820, fairly remote to the east of Glen Trool in fine walking country. **2** **6**

5 Plantain Loch
Dumfries and Galloway FC
The rich delight of this shallow upland loch is its wealth of dragonflies. When they are victims of the many oblong-leaved sundews they can be studied closely. The species include common

aeshna and four spotted libellula, with large red, common ischnura, green lestes and common blue damselflies. These colourful insects are out hunting July to September ● NX841602 near Dalbeattie. **2**

6 Loch Ken and the River Dee Marshes
Dumfries and Galloway RSPB
A narrow sinuous loch edged with forest and farmland is an important wintering refuge for wildfowl including the largest mainland flock of Greenland white-fronted geese. The marshes of the River Dee and their associated wet meadows have breeding snipe, curlew, redshank and lapwing with mallard, teal, shoveler, sedge warbler and reed buntings. Tufted duck, goosander and great crested grebe nest on the loch shore. There are many other birds to be found in the wide variety of other habitats along the river and loch ● NX638765 and NX695694 from A713 and A762 south of New Galloway. **2**

7 Holystone North Wood
Northumberland CT
Many of the oaks have a somewhat stunted appearance, others spring from contorted boles, thought to be the result of coppicing many years ago. They are part of an excellent upland sessile oak-wood in acid conditions with bracken, mosses, wood sorrel and the rare chick-weed wintergreen normally restricted to Scottish hill pinewoods. Wood warbler and redstart are typical summer visitors ● NT945028 turn off B6341 at Flotterton on to minor roads via Sharperton and Holystone village. **3**

8 Duns Castle Borders SWT
In the shelter of the Lammermuir Hills, the wooded surrounds of Duns Castle are picturesque and exceptionally rich in wildlife. Late spring displays carpets of ramsons, bluebells, red campion and purple wood crane's-bill. The show continues through the summer with meadowsweet, foxglove and water avens. Beech, oak and ash are the principal forest trees but poplars add to the amenity and insect habitats. Rarer plants can be found beneath the trees

Bristhie Bog, Silver Flowe

including toothwort, common winter-green and twayblade. Tits and pied fly-catchers readily occupy the nest boxes. The rides and glades are ideal for butter-flies and moths. An artificial loch adds to the richness and beauty of the site ● NT778550 at Duns, 12 miles south-west of Eyemouth. **3**

9 Ailsa Craig Strathclyde
As if adrift in an ocean, this rugged island with a 1000-foot-high dome of grassland lies remote and detached from the Clyde Islands and the mainland. Seventy thousand sea-birds return from their oceanic wanderings each year to breed on the cliffs. The gannetry has been here at least 400 years, for most of which it was a source of human food. Now 21,000 pairs of protected gannets incubate without the risk of egg gatherers ● NS020000, 10 miles west of Girvan. **4**

10 Bass Rock Lothian
Nine thousand pairs of *Sula bassana* (the gannet's scientific name is taken from this island) spread up the cliff ledges and on to the summit slopes of Bass Rock. There is still room for kitti-wakes, auks, shag and fulmar to breed here too, though they are hardly notice-able amidst the noise, smell and clamour of the gannetry. The top of the island is one of the best places to marvel at the gannet's aerobatic plunges for food be-neath the waves ● NT602873 daily summer sailings from North Berwick, subject to weather. **4**

11 Farne Islands Northumberland NT
During all but the highest tides 28 islands stand above the swell of the North Sea. Rocky outcrops of the Great Whin Sill all play a part in the success of the seal and sea-bird colonies referred to in Ch. 4. There are low, flat platforms for cormorant or shag to dry out and higher cliffs for the auks and gulls to nest on. The other stars of the Farnes are the grey seals. Their great mottled backs roll beneath the surface and their inquisitive, doleful expressions can be

clearly seen as they rise to inspect the passing boats. Noisy, awkward and aggressive on land, they are swift and graceful in the waves. The pups will clamber over the rocks as the cows doze from the security of their rocky shelves ● NU230370 spring and summer boat trips, some with landings on Inner Farne and Staple Island from Seahouses daily, subject to weather. **4**

12 St Abb's Head Borders NTS/SWT
A marvellous day's adventure discover-ing the wildlife of the sea could start with a visit to the unspoilt fishing village of St Abb's. For generations, fishermen, the last of the real hunters, have har-vested the rich marine life of the North Sea. Follow the coast northwards to see how strong tides sweep the shore to keep the submarine kelp forests and rich marine life including the arctic lumpfish free of pollution. Upon reach-ing St Abb's Head you will be struck by the exposures in the rocky cliffs. Not only do they make wonderful coastal scenery but the once horizontal lines of rock planes are now tipped and tilted like crumpled bedclothes to indicate the powerful forces of geological change. The grassland tumbling to the shore and clothing the cliff tops is of short turf on different soil types with correspondingly varied floras. Thyme, pink thrift, tormentil and wood sage, unlikely companions, all grow in close

proximity. To complete the experience of the sea over 15,000 sea-birds nest on the cliffs, mainly guillemots and kittiwakes ● NT914693 off A1107 at Coldingham, the Head is about 1½ miles north of the village. **4 5**

13 East Lothian Coast Lothian
From Edinburgh to Dunbar you can see how man has developed the coast-line and how wildlife has adjusted to the changes. Large numbers of waders roost on the ash lagoons of Cockenzie power station, grebes winter in Gosford Bay and the mudflats, saltings and dunes of Aberlady Bay host breeding shelduck and wintering geese. Gullane Bay doubles as a sea-duck refuge and popular seaside beach. Boats full of tourists go out to Bass Rock from North Berwick, but gannets can easily be seen from above the town's swimming pool and Tantallon Castle. Then follows a quiet stretch of shoreline largely access-ible only on foot as far as Dunbar where, to complete the links between land and sea, fulmars nest on the castle ruins and harbour buildings as if they were cliffs ● Edinburgh to Dunbar off A1 and A198. **5 10**

14 Lindisfarne Northumberland NCC
The inaccessibility of Holy Island at high tide makes us acutely aware of the importance of tidal movements to the coastal birds. The wildfowl and waders

Bird colonies on the Farne Islands

which frequent the fine dunes, salt-marshes and mudflats of Lindisfarne, especially in winter, make it a site of international importance. The largest wintering herd of whooper swans in England and good views of other uncommon wildfowl – eiders, mergansers, scaup and brent geese – make an exciting excursion across the causeway, with dunlin, knot and godwits on the shores ● NU095430 off A1 via minor road through Beal across island causeway. **5**

15 Caerlaverock
Dumfries and Galloway NCC
For six miles along the Scottish shore of the Solway Firth extends one of the largest unreclaimed salt-marshes in the British Isles. Grazed by cattle and geese the plants also have to withstand regular inundation by salt water. One of the finest sites for our wintering geese (including the entire Spitsbergen population of barnacle geese), the reserve is hunted by harriers and peregrines and used by thousands of migrating ducks and waders. The evening roost flight of geese from the fields to the foreshore is dramatic indeed, with skein after skein of calling geese flying at low level. A thriving population of natterjack toads is also present on the reserve. This site is immediately adjacent to site 20, East Park ● NY018653, 7 miles south of Dumfries. **5**

16 Ballantrae Strathclyde SWT
Terns, ringed plover and oystercatcher nest on the spit of flat grey shingles covered in sea campion, sea sandwort and oysterplant. Successive plant associations on the landward side include bird's-foot-trefoil and wild carrot ● NX085825 on A77 between Girvan and Stranraer. **5**

17 Galloway Forest Park
Dumfries and Galloway
Although about a third of the area of the Forest Park remains unplanted the establishment of the softwoods 20 to 30 years ago had a considerable impact on the landscapes and wildlife of the moorlands. Habitats of the curlew, golden plover, red grouse and skylark were rapidly depleted as the young plantations were established. But these species survive in reduced numbers and can be found with red deer and wild goats roaming acres of rolling heather-grass moorland and open bogs ● From Clatteringshaws Lock on A712 to Loch Doon on A713 and west to Glentrool forest. **6**

18 Harbottle Crags
Northumberland CT
If you stand on the crags themselves and look down the great sweeps of heather moorland and bogs of sphagnum moss you will see the result of a programme of regular burning. This apparently drastic action successfully maintains the typical heather cover of an upland grouse moor, long since cleared of its natural oak/birch woodlands. Red and black grouse, meadow pipit, wheatear, whinchat and short-eared owl are typical birds of these moors ● NT927048 turn off B6341 at Flotterton on to minor road via Sharperton and Harbottle. **6**

19 Grey Mare's Tail
Dumfries and Galloway NTS
A familiar site with an unusual flora gives us the opportunity to appreciate the grasslands of the uplands. Grazed by sheep its surrounding grass-heather moors change on the steep scree to a type of grass heath hard-grazed by multi-coloured feral goats of remarkable agility. But even the goats cannot reach the cliffs of the hanging valley. The sides of the Mare's Tail, a memorable waterfall nearly 200 feet high, have therefore developed a nearly natural flora including roseroot, harebell, wood-rush, scabious, goldenrod and wood sage ● NT182150 on A708, 9 miles north-east of Moffat. **7**

20 East Park Dumfries and Galloway
WT/NCC
Because of the vital link between the Solway's wintering geese and the arable land on which they feed, the farmland round East Park was purchased and included in the extensive coastal reserve. This ensures undisturbed daytime feeding as well as roosting on the merse. Excellent observation facilities are provided for the birdwatchers ● NY052656 off B725 at Bankend then minor roads via Blackshaw. Visits to the hides must be escorted. This site is immediately adjacent to site 15, Caerlaverock. **8**

21 Beltingham Northumberland CT
Silt charged with lead and zinc from the northern Pennines' mines has been deposited in the Rivers South Tyne and Allen on to beaches of shingle. The resulting 'heavy metal' vegetation includes mountain pansy, thrift, alpine penny-cress, spring sandwort and alpine scurvygrass. The sites are unique ● NY785641, 3 miles west of Haydon Bridge, turn off A69 and follow signs to Beltingham, then on to the flood plain. **10**

22 Gladhouse Reservoir Lothian RC
A man-made habitat, an escaped species introduced by man and migrant wildfowl and waders are the subjects of this drama about wildlife living with man. Thirteen thousand pink-footed geese enjoy the security of the reservoir, which no doubt substitutes for habitat they may have lost. But a decline in duck numbers was blamed on the appetite of the alien mink which is now controlled. Tufted duck, goldeneye and goosander are typical diving ducks ● NT300540 view from public roads off B6372, 9 miles south of Dalkeith. **10**

23 Border Forest Park
Northumberland/Borders FC
This great wilderness of the uplands has the drama and scale of natural landscapes, but is entirely man-made. Kielder reservoir is the largest area of water created by man in western Europe; the Kielder Forest of pine and oak woods, birch and rowan was cleared centuries ago to provide the vast heather moorlands for sheep and grouse. The modern forest park is a huge area of coniferous plantations now forming a structure of different aged blocks. The moors have grouse and merlin, the forest has badger, roe deer and red squirrel, siskin, crossbill and sparrowhawk. It is unlikely that the Kielder Water will take long to establish itself as a major wintering site for wildfowl. The Kielder Forest drive is a toll road for the adventurous motorist and runs through the heart of the forest ● NY633935 turn off B6320 at Bellingham to follow road to Kielder. **10**

For 150 miles the Pennines form a very distinctive region of uplands, identifiable at any point and yet composed of an extremely complex geology and scenery. The vast peat bogs of the northern uplands contrast with the rich limestone dales of the White Peak. The gritstone plateau of the Kinder is as different a scene from the leafy coastal denes of Durham as we could imagine. This fascinating diversity is an essential part of the Pennines' character and leads to a quite outstanding collection of habitats. Some are as fragile and rare as the arctic relics of Upper Teesdale. Others lie in endless sweeps over miles of moorland controlled for the grouse and the sheep.

The Pennines dominate the life and landscape of the north. The influence of man is everywhere. His farming and felling, drainage and industries have brought great changes to these impressive hills.

1 Upper Teesdale Durham NCC Chapter 1 describes how this National Nature Reserve is one of our most exciting 'time capsules', an arctic relic for us to enjoy in the twentieth century. This fragile community of flowering plants is unique in western Europe. If you walk from Cow Green Reservoir along the Birkdale Track nature trail to Caldron Snout you pass through an area where arctic plants have grown continuously for 10,000 years. Protected from grazing sheep, the limestone grasslands, flushes and meadows form a colossal carpet of colourful arctic alpine plants such as spring gentian, bird's-eye primrose, alpine bartsia, Scottish asphodel and saxifrages. These survivors are the last of species which were widespread when arctic conditions occurred in Britain at the retreat of the glaciers ● NY815310 off B6277, 16 miles north-west of Barnard Castle. Bowlees visitor centre NY907283. (*See* 5 below.) ∎

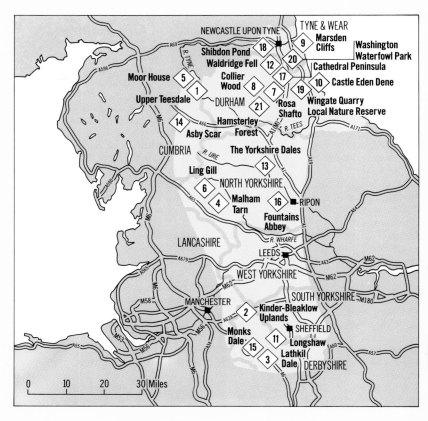

2 Kinder-Bleaklow Uplands Derby. The mighty processes of geological change are usually so slow as to be imperceptible. But on the high moors of the Dark Peak we can witness such changes and see for ourselves how geology, the weather, the influence of man and the high exposure of this area are dramatically changing the habitats. The meaning of the Dark Peak is obvious: a black, desolate, exposed, high plateau often with panoramic views, but an upland where few plants and creatures can survive. On the top of this hard block of millstone grit is a wide spread of blanket mire, an enormous peat bog – dying. The plants which built the bog were killed by industrial pollution a long time ago. Remnants of sphagnum moss can be found, there are small patches of bilberry,

cowberry and cottongrass here and there, but on the whole the peatlands are doomed. With no plants to hold them, the exceptional rainfall of the Kinder washes away the peat, dissecting the mire with ever wider gullies, cutting six feet down. The natural process of depositing peat has stopped. There is still sufficient cover to shelter the dunlin, merlin, ring ousel, golden plover and red grouse. The cloudberry normally favours mountain habitats and it does well here at the limit of its southern range ● SK090929 from the A57 east of Glossop. ∎

3 Lathkil Dale Derby. NCC
The Pennine landscapes are remarkably varied, reflecting the different rock formations which have left this spine of uplands down the centre of northern England. At the southern end the millstone grit of the High Peak changes to a soft white landscape of carboniferous limestone. But this is no less dramatic, for the glacial melt-waters cut deep valleys through the rock with steep slopes, cliffs and crags now overlooking very much smaller rivers. Broad-leaved woodland soon established in the shelter of the valleys but has been depleted by felling. Lathkil Dale with its rich mixture of grassland and woodland cover is typical of the White Peak. The river flows fast in the winter and spring. It is the only river in the White Peak which originates on limestone; the others flow down from the millstone grit. Purple loosestrife, sedges and marsh-marigold grow on the margins. Grey wagtails feed on the rich insect life of the clear waters ● SK205665 from the village of Over Haddon, 2 miles south-west of Bakewell via B5055. ▮ ▮

4 Malham Tarn Yorks. FSC/NT
High above the Dales of Yorkshire you will find a most important tarn which has been the subject of intensive field studies by generations of naturalists. The study centre and nature trail will introduce you to the various habitats associated with this lime-rich lake, including both bog and fen. The tarn represents a most interesting mixture of lowland and upland species associated with their northern and southern distributions in Britain ● SD890672 minor roads north of A682 via Airton and Malham. ▮

5 Moor House Cumbria NCC
Immediately north-west of the Upper Teesdale Reserve (see 1 above) is the largest nature reserve in England, over 10,000 acres of blanket bog representative of vast upland areas of the northern Pennines. From 10,000 to 7500 years ago birch and pine spread over these hills. The wetter climate of the next 2000 years meant that bogs overwhelmed the birch, and plant material only partly decomposed forming a layer of peat. The peat accumulated to a depth of 12 feet in places, formed by vegetation similar to that growing on the bog today: heather, cottongrass and sphagnum moss. The peat hags of these uplands are caused by the erosion of the peat by drainage, burning and grazing over the last 2500 years. The typical upland birds are present. Small trout and bullheads are in most of the streams. The reserve is rich in mosses, liverworts and lichens with fungi and algae too ● NY730325 off B6277, 8 miles south-east of Alston. ▮ ▮

6 Ling Gill Yorks. NCC
You will have to walk a short section of the Pennine Way to reach Ling Gill but a beautiful area of semi-natural woodland rewards the trek. You are free to wander over the boulder-strewn watercourse or the very steep valley sides to gain a marvellous impression of the native ash and elm wood of the limestone gorges of the Dales. Relatively inaccessible, it is virtually unmodified by man or grazing animals. The wood is renowned for its rich ground flora and mosses ● SD803778, 4½ miles from Horton-in-Ribblesdale along Pennine Way towards Hawes in Wensleydale. ▮

7 Rosa Shafto Durham CT
On the mid-Durham coalfields and within sight of the Pennines is a marvellous opportunity to compare the plant associations of different types of woodland. The Rosa Shafto reserve has a remarkable length of woodland edge around its H-shaped pattern and a wide diversity of species from beech high forest, and conifers to grassland and scrub. You will see how the plants change from drier to wetter areas, and from steeper to flatter areas with many of the familiar but now less common woodland species being present. Such a diversity attracts an excellent range of woodland birds, including the locally uncommon great spotted woodpecker ● NZ245350 on minor roads, 1 mile north of Spennymoor. ▮

8 Collier Wood Durham CT/CC
Seasonal changes in woodland character are important to our understanding of how the woodland ecology works. The nature trail at Collier Wood has a series of seasonal leaflets to illustrate the life of this mixed woodland throughout the year ● NZ129364 on the A68, ½ mile north of Harperley roundabout junction with A689. ▮

9 Marsden Cliffs Tyne and Wear DC
South of the River Tyne, the limestone rocks of the Pennines outcrop at the coast with a splendid cliff covered in cowslips, rock-rose and thrift. Despite the proximity of the urban conurbation inland, the site forms a most important colony of breeding sea-birds. The delightful kittiwakes sit for hours on their nests, providing one of the few oppor-

Alpine Lady's-mantle, Upper Teesdale

tunities to see these oceanic birds at close range. Fulmars too break their relentless flight to incubate their eggs here. The noisy herring gulls will leave you in no doubt that you are watching sea creatures uneasily holding temporary space on land ● NZ397650 South Shields. **4**

10 Castle Eden Dene Durham PDC
The Denes are coastal valley woods cut into the limestone plateau offering security and shelter for wildlife in quiet and beautiful valleys. A torrent of glacial melt-water from the uplands must have cut its way to the sea through these ravines, now narrowly edged with steep cliffs. Today, the waters rush down to meet the shingle banks thrown up by the North Sea tides. Castle Eden Dene is the finest of these valleys. Clothed with a superb mix of woodland it holds a most outstanding population of birds, insects and mammals. It is the home of the Castle Eden argus butterfly, one of four Lepidoptera species first captured at the Dene ● NZ410387, 3-mile-long valley to North Sea coast immediately south of Peterlee. **5 3**

11 Longshaw Derby. NT
Without suffering the exposure of the High Peak we can enjoy the typical acid moorland and heath of the mill-stone grits at Longshaw. Although it is 1000 feet above sea level this compact series of woods, meadows, pools and open moorland is sheltered by the high moors around and is easily accessible from car parks in the country park ● SK267800 on B6054/6055, 3 miles east of Hathersage. **6**

12 Waldridge Fell Durham CC
All the typical plants of the Pennine heaths provide a particularly rich insect population. Here a flora of heather, bell heather, crowberry and bilberry is enriched by bog plants such as bog-bean, water horsetail, cottongrass and sedges in the wetter areas. The country park also supports areas of semi-natural oak woodland and is a rich site for insects ● NZ254494 minor roads, $1\frac{1}{2}$ miles west of Chester-le-Street. **6**

13 The Yorkshire Dales Yorks.
The heart of the Pennines is formed from a series of limestone and gritstone layers. They are exposed by the wind and rain to form beautiful sweeping uplands with high and dramatic peaks; they are dissected by some of the most picturesque valleys in the British Isles, cut by clear rivers of great character and force. Every dale is different and each has its own special character, forming a unique blend of farmland, moorland, woodland and river. While many areas are dominated by the rugged beauty of gritstone landscapes, the Dales are also one of our richest compositions of limestone scenery. The remnants of natural woodland and of native plants on the scars and pavements are unequalled. But to most of the Dales' admirers it is the grasslands which make this part of the Pennines distinctive. Each Dale has the combination of open, grazed grassland together with valley bottom meadows enclosed by stone walls. Those meadows which have not been agriculturally improved are managed for hay and support a rich variety of flowering plants, forming some of the most colourful meadows in the country. On the many areas of limestone pavement is semi-natural grassland, untouched by grazing animals, with bloody crane's-bill, zig-zag clover and rock-rose on the clints, and wall lettuce, herb-Robert, dog's mercury and ferns in the shady and humid fissures ● North-west Yorkshire from Skipton to Richmond crossed by B6160, B6265, A684 and B6270. **6 7**

14 Asby Scar Cumbria NCC
The Vale of Eden is lined by a rim of limestone variously covered by the plant associations of the limestone pavement or by upland grasslands which are grazed by sheep. You can see how the protection of the pavement structure produces a richer flora than the grazed areas of Asby Scar and, indeed, how the exposed grey limestone rocks can be quite bare of any vegetation. A complex mosaic of habitats ● NY648103 on minor roads off B6260, 6 miles south of Appleby Westmorland. **7**

15 Monks Dale Derby. NCC
Since the first clearances of woodland from the Derbyshire Dales rich grasslands have developed on the thin limestone soils. They are full of characteristic species: wild thyme, common rock-rose, marjoram and bird's-foot-trefoil. Where the slopes have a southern aspect there can be over 50 species of plants in a square yard, a profusion of spring and summer colour which adds immensely

Swaledale, Yorkshire

hunt for the prolific insect life at night;
yellow wagtails and warblers do so in
the day. Waterfowl are abundant and
the secretive water-rail is often heard
in the reeds ● NZ195628 between
Blaydon and Swalwell via A69. 🔟 🔢

19 Wingate Quarry Local Nature Reserve Durham CC

The mounds, steep slopes and rocky
crags of Wingate were formed by limestone quarrying but support the flora
of the magnesian limestone unique to
this area. In spring and summer the
quarry resembles a wild rock garden
with cowslips, bird's-foot-trefoil, knapweed and orchids in flower. Newts,
frogs, damselflies and dragonflies are
at home in the ponds to be found in the
reserve ● NZ373376 south of A181
west of Wingate village. 🔟

20 Washington Waterfowl Park Tyne and Wear WT

An exciting demonstration of how
successful nature reserves can be linked
to other uses. In the built-up part of
the region the waterfowl collection combines the opportunities for visitors to
see the tame wildfowl at close quarters
and for declining species to be protected.
Wild areas with scrapes, ponds, river,
reed-beds and woodlands hold important numbers of wildfowl, waders and
land-birds, many of which use the areas
as a stopover while on migration ●
NZ330565 south of A1231 at Wash-
ington in the Wear valley. 🔟

21 Hamsterley Forest Durham FC

This is an interesting example of modern
coniferous plantations where the sheer
size of the area has meant the retention
of important animal species. Roe deer,
red squirrel, badger and fox are all
breeding. So too are the conifer specialists – crossbill, goldcrest and siskin.
Many areas of semi-natural broad-
leaved woodland were left to grow and
Pennington Beechwood is one of the
highest beechwoods in the country ●
NZ093312 minor roads north of B6282
at Woodland, about 8 miles north of
Barnard Castle. 🔟

to our enjoyment of these dales. Towards the top of the slopes the number
of species declines with increased acidity
and exposure, a subtle transition until
dominated by wavy hair-grass, sheep's-
fescue and the bilberry and heather of
the moors ● SK141735 north of
B6049 walking north from Miller's Dale
at this point. 🔢

16 Fountains Abbey Yorks. NT

Close to the hills of the Yorkshire Dales
stands the largest monastic ruin in
Britain – a Cistercian monastery founded
in 1132. In medieval times the Abbey
wielded great power over the management of its vast estates and contributed
to the deforestation of the region and
to the spread of sheep grazing in the
hills. The grounds of the Abbey were
landscaped between 1720 and 1740
with a lake and formal water gardens,
though the estate woods were restocked
by informal planting of broadleaved
woodland. The deer park remains and

the entire area is excellent for woodland
and farmland birds ● SE271683,
2 miles west of Ripon off B6265. 🔢

17 Cathedral Peninsula Durham CT/CC

Around the peninsula of Durham
Cathedral and following the banks of
the River Wear is an urban nature
trail showing some of the city's wildlife
close at hand ● NZ272422 Durham
City Centre. 🔢

18 Shibdon Pond Tyne and Wear CT/DC

The subsidence of land has created a
rich source of food and shelter for the
common and the less familiar of our
urban wildlife species. With a carefully
managed mix of habitat types ranging
from open water to marsh and acid
heath to scrub, the reserve attracts an
equally varied animal population. The
wetlands and water contain eel, coarse
fish, frogs, toads, newts and voles. Bats

Lakeland is more than a National Park, more than a landscape, however dramatic and splendid it may be. It is a way of life, a complete story of man and nature sharing the rigours of a hard existence. The story is set in a theatre of majestic beauty and scale. It is a region of moods, created by the scenery and exaggerated by the weather: in the spring sunshine it can be peacefully still, but at other times it can be as wild and inhospitable as anywhere in England. The offshore extension of the Caledonians makes the Isle of Man as rugged and beautiful as the Southern Uplands or mainland Cumbria.

As the Lakes mirror the mountain's images, so the wildlife reflects the moods and character of the region. The plaintive moorland piping of the golden plover enhances our solitude; the richness of the sheltered lakeside woods rings to the chorus of songbirds. For centuries the Lakes have drawn artists, poets, musicians and naturalists. If you walk from the lake edge to high fell you will know why they came.

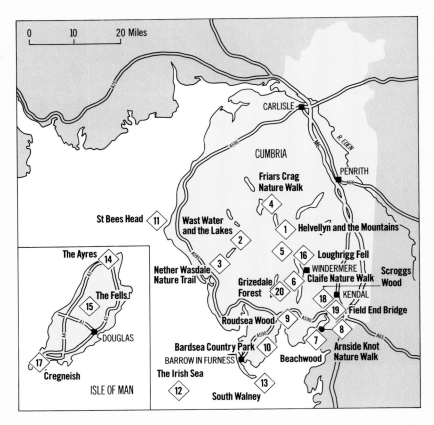

1 Helvellyn and the Mountains
Cumbria NPA/NT

From their Icelandic breeding grounds the wild whooper swans fly high over the Lakeland winter scene. It is covered by the first snows and these graceful arctic migrants will choose to settle on one of the great lakes radiating below them. If we had their vantage point we would understand how this complex region has been created. Millions of years ago, water flowed in all directions from the central heights of a great dome of ancient rocks. These streams were already shed when successive glaciations occurred, completely remodelling the surface of the dome. Stand on Helvellyn's Striding Edge and see to the west how the ice bulldozed the line of the tiny Wyth Burn into a deep valley, scooped a great hole in the valley bottom and, on thawing, dumped the

damming moraine and back-filled the depression of Thirlmere with ice-cold water. To the east lies a different view. Here the glaciers ripped two valleys from the side of Helvellyn so close together they left a blade of land with precipitous drops on both sides to form Striding Edge, one of the most dramatic paths in England. Red Tarn remains in the shadow of the mountain as a superb example of a glacial corrie.

By the time the glaciers had retreated the Lake District we know had been formed. At first only creatures and plants which could withstand the arctic cold of the tundra survived. Then the climate progressively warmed and more dominant plants of the temperate zones spread widely. But winters on the mountains here, where snow can lie for eight months of the year, have an arctic

bitterness which enables relics of the post-glacial years to survive. Wherever the sheep cannot graze, on ledges and screes, in cracks and crevices, alpine saw-wort, mossy and starry saxifrage, roseroot and alpine lady's-mantle represent some of the arctic flora. A special subspecies of juniper grows on the mountains, severely dwarfed by the exposure. Unbelievably, dwarf willows can mature at only one inch in height.

These mountains are the home of golden eagle and peregrine falcon, red grouse, wheatear and ring ousel. Red deer roam the hillsides, as do pine marten, though they are much harder to find.

On a sunny June day you may find a Lakeland treasure. On exposed damp mountainsides over 1 500 feet high, the small mountain ringlet butterfly searches the mat-grass for flowering plants. With a larval hibernation of ten months it concentrates the rest of its life into a few warm weeks in late spring, a real mountain survivor ● NY343153, A591, 5 miles north of Grasmere. **1**

2 Wast Water and the Lakes
Cumbria NT/CT
The deepest of the lakes is surrounded by steep fells, rising almost 3000 feet to the highest point in England, only two miles away. Although its surface is above the 200-foot contour the bed of Wast Water was scoured so deeply by the glaciers it now lies over 50 feet below sea-level. As described in Ch. 2, charr and whitefish are two of the glacial creatures which have survived being trapped in the Lakeland waters. At night another relic of glacial lakes, a tiny freshwater shrimp, rises from the depths of Ennerdale Water to feed on the surface. Each lake is different: Windermere has woods down to the shoreline; the wilder Haweswater has fells tumbling to the water's edge. Some of the shores are fringed with yellow loosestrife and common reed; others have water-lily and quillwort or shore-weed spreading in the shallows. Mallard, teal and tufted ducks, red-breasted mergansers, common sandpipers and grey wagtails breed at Wast Water, a typical range of Lakeland birds ● NY145045 Wast Water, minor roads from the south via Nether Wasdale. **1 2**

3 Nether Wasdale Nature Trail
Cumbria CT
Embracing all the characteristic scenery and many important Lakeland habitats, this delightful trail includes Wast Water lake, marsh, bog and woodland ● NY147048 from Nether Wasdale at the southern end of Wast Water. **2**

4 Friars Crag Nature Walk
Cumbria NT
An important part of the lakeland character is the combination of woodland and water habitats. Derwent Water has a scatter of wooded islands which can be seen from this trail. It runs through mixed woods along the shore where many typical lakeland birds and plants can be seen ● NY264227 off B5289, 1 mile south of Keswick. **2 3**

5 White Moss Common Nature Walk
Cumbria NT *et al.*
Between Grasmere and Rydal Water is a good opportunity to sample the range of typical lakeland habitats. The lakes, stream and woodland are the main interest but you can see the open fell and pastures. The mix of scenery is outstanding ● NY348065 on A591 about 1 mile south of Grasmere. **2 3**

6 Claife Nature Walk Cumbria NT
Three thousand years ago all but the highest mountains, the bogs and coastal zones of the Lake District were covered in broad-leaved woodland. The acid soils were dominated by beautiful, damp, sessile oak woodland, rich in ferns, mosses and lichens. Redstart, pied flycatcher and wood warbler were some of the special birds in these wildwoods and they still breed by this trail on Lake Windermere ● SD388954 end of B5285 on shores of Windermere. **3**

View from Helvellyn of Red Tarn and Striding Edge

7 Beachwood Cumbria CT
Where the Cumbrian soils are of lime-stone origins, the oak gives way to ash and whitebeam with spindle in the shrub layer. This site is rich in flower-ing plants, all associated with limestone woods and fields including herb-Paris and Solomon's-seal. Beachwood has a superb range of twelve species of ferns. You may find white butterbur and other interesting alien species ● SD452786 near Arnside, on foot $\frac{1}{4}$ mile south-west along shore from promenade. **3**

8 Arnside Knot Nature Walk
Cumbria NT
Very close to Beachwood and on the same soil types, this is a circular trail of rich limestone wildlife enhanced by good moth and butterfly populations and some local red squirrels ● SD451773 at Arnside, 3 miles south-west of Milnthorpe. **3**

9 Roudsea Wood Cumbria NCC
The ideal opportunity to see the differ-ence between the main woodland types of this part of Cumbria, Roudsea pro-vides both acid and limestone wood-land. Peatland, salt-marsh and alluvial valley add further habitats to enjoy on this visit. The ridge of carboniferous limestone supports ash and oak, lime, cherry and yew with an understorey of purging buckthorn, spindle, guelder-rose and whitebeam. Lily-of-the-valley, columbine and orchids grow among the false brome and dog's mercury on the forest floor. In contrast the sessile oakwood on the slates has birch with rowan and hazel and a poorer field layer dominated by wavy hair-grass. The valley mire between the woods has typical fen species and interesting sedges. The raised mire of Roudsea Mosses is peaty with birch, rowan and pine. Red and roe deer are present and there are occasional sightings of otter, red squirrels, adder and common toads and frogs ● SD335825 from Greenodd on A5092, there is a public footpath across the reserve. Permits are required for the other paths, obtainable from NCC, Blackwell, Bowness-on-Windermere, Cumbria LA23 3JR. **3**

10 Bardsea Country Park Cumbria CC
On the north-west shore of Morecambe Bay, an attractive area of oak and ash woodland stands above the shoreline. The shingle and mudflats are part of the country park. It is an interesting coastal woodland, at its best in the spring when passage migrants swell the population of breeding birds ● SD294735, A5087, 2 miles south of Ulverston. **3 5**

11 St Bees Head Cumbria RSPB
The warm red colours of the sandstone cliffs with grassland tumbling over the tops of the weathered rock face make St Bees one of the most attractive of our mainland sea-bird colonies. Pro-jecting well into the Irish Sea and with just enough gorse scrub to shelter mi-grants and breeding land-birds, the species list is exciting. The oceanic wanderers pass by, Manx and sooty shearwaters, red-throated divers, terns, gannets and skuas. Little owl, stone-chat, rock pipit and warblers are among the breeding land-birds. The most im-portant users of the cliffs, though, are the auks: razorbill, guillemot and puffin and, on their only English breeding colony, the black guillemot of northern waters. Kittiwakes and fulmars also nest on the ledges, drifting out on the air currents to feed at sea ● NX962118 off B5345, 4 miles south of Whitehaven. **4**

12 The Irish Sea (from the Isle of Man)
Some 40 miles off the mainland the Isle of Man provides the perfect vantage

View from Arnside Knot of the Kent Estuary

point to observe the wildlife of the Irish Sea. The influence of the ocean is always apparent in the scenery, the weather, the fishing and other industries and perhaps most of all in its birds. Wherever you are there is a constant movement of sea-birds overhead. All around the coast there are breeding colonies of marine species including the island's own Manx shearwater. The rocky cliffs and outcrops are irresistible nesting and resting places for sea-birds – auks, gulls, terns, cormorant and shag. Even the choughs and ravens are here, wheeling with the fulmars and kittiwakes on air currents that take hardly a wingbeat to lift them ● There are vantage points along the entire coastline of the Isle of Man. ▉

13 South Walney Cumbria CT
If you have never seen a large gull colony it is worth a visit to South Walney just to see and hear the spectacle. With one of Europe's largest breeding colonies of herring and lesser black-backed gulls, there is also a reserve of many coastal habitats. There are sand dunes with wet and dry meadows, freshwater marsh, open pools, shingle, salt-marsh and mudflats. It is the most southerly breeding site for eiders on the west coast. Mallard, oystercatcher, ringed plover, shelduck and many landbirds nest in their respective habitats. Thousands of waders and wildfowl winter here. The botanical interest in the reserve is substantial and gravel workings have introduced a fascinating diversity of plants: viper's-bugloss, ploughman's-spikenard and henbane ● SD215620 Walney Island from Barrow-in-Furness follow Promenade, Ocean Road, Carr Lane, 5 miles to coastguard cottages. Nominal entry charge for permit on site. Closed Mondays. ▉ ▉

14 The Ayres Isle of Man CT
On the northern coast of the Isle of Man you will find a sequence of marram and fixed dune systems with a rich dune flora and a unique lichen community. A small colony of the delightful little terns and birds on the nearby heathland add to the interest of the

Ayres ● SC438039 take Ballaghennie road north from A10, 1 mile west of Bride. ▉ ▉

15 Isle of Man (The Fells)
This outcrop of the Caledonian Mountains was cut off from the British mainland by the rising sea-level in much the same way as Ireland. Its physical isolation has resulted in some species of mammals failing to reach and colonise the island. While the superb sweeping moors and fells of Man may look similar to those of the Lake District and the Borders, they lack many of the small mammals and, consequently, their predators. Merlin and peregrine do sweep over these moors for they feed on the moorland birds including meadow pipit and red grouse. But the short-eared owl is only present because it has relied on killing brown rats instead of its normal diet of short-tailed voles, which are absent. In all other respects the great tracts of open country remote from human disturbance suit this owl very well. They also suit a substantial insect population where moths and butterflies of the moors enjoy the relative warmth of the island provided by the Gulf Stream. The birds can bridge the gap to the mainland by flight and a full range of moorland species breed, including curlew, grey wagtail, rock pipit, whinchat, stonechat and wheatear ● Central and southern parts of the Isle of Man. ▉

16 Loughrigg Fell Cumbria NT
A good walk from Ambleside, across the river and up the sides of Loughrigg to see the patchwork of lakeland land uses. Grassland and arable fields merge into the upland fell. Woodland and riverside wildlife will also be seen on this varied route ● NY375047 immediately west of Ambleside. ▉ ▉ ▉

17 Cregneish Isle of Man
In the remotest corner of the island, half a dozen iron-age families farmed 300 acres of windswept, thin, acid soil on the Meayll peninsula. This ancient

Celtic settlement may be 2000 years old. It was a self-contained community grazing a few animals and ploughing what they could to supplement a living from their fishing and farm labouring. Five buildings have been restored for the Manx Open Air Museum and they clearly show the hardship of farming the uplands. Peat cut from the moors was stored and thatched with rushes. The only cloth would have been home-spun wool from the native Manx sheep, the loghtan, which are still grazed here in the summer ● SC185675 south-west of Port Erin. ▉ ▉

18 Scroggs Wood Cumbria WdT
Even here on the edge of England's largest national park there is a need to enjoy wildlife close to hand. On a wide meander of the River Kent this mixed woodland brings the wildlife of the lakeland woods into the urban fringe of Kendal town ● SD509908 south-west outskirts of Kendal. ▉

19 Field End Bridge Cumbria CT
Between the dramatic scenery of the Lakes and the Pennines a small canal passes through attractive lowland countryside. It is rich in both aquatic insects and fish, including pike, perch and roach. Horsetails, sedges, water mint and water-plantain grow along the canalside trail ● SD526850 on minor roads north of A590 at Hincaster. ▉

20 Grizedale Forest Cumbria FC
A huge spread of coniferous forest has transformed the area between Coniston and Windermere into a twentieth-century landscape on a grand scale. Superimposed on the Lakeland scene, the forest has retained many of the native features, including streams, tarns, bogs and small heaths and pastures. Goldcrest and coal tits call from every part. Deer are present and the information centre will explain about the new forest of Grizedale and its changing wildlife ● SD336944 from B5285/6 at Hawkshead south to Satterthwaite on minor roads. ▉

If we could follow the water of the Pickering Beck we would experience a journey in time and place. From its source on Lockton High Moor you can see the vast plateau of the North York Moors National Park finally moulded by the glaciers. The beck flows past the bogs and high grouse moors where relic arctic alpines grow at Levisham Moor. There are semi-natural woods and coniferous plantations before the beck runs out into the level plain of the Vale of Pickering. After joining the Rye and the Derwent, it meanders round the Yorkshire Wolds, through the Vale of York, and eventually joins the great rivers of South Yorkshire.

As the now heavily industrialised waterway heads for the estuary it collects the Trent and even the rivers draining the arable and grasslands of the north Lincolnshire Wolds. Spurn Peninsula curves out into the mouth of the Humber opposite a series of superb coastal reserves from Tetney to Saltfleetby. The Humber has a truly remarkable catchment, with an exciting range of sites to visit.

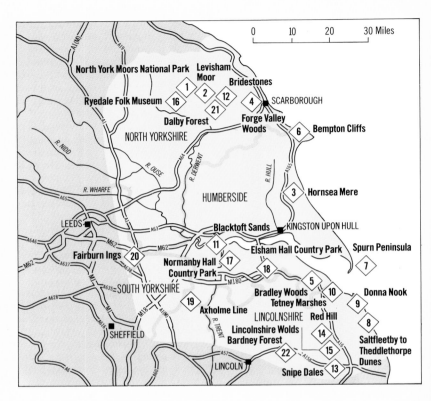

1 North York Moors National Park
Yorks. NPA
The most northerly of the waters feeding the Humber estuary rise on the great plateau of the North York Moors. With its source only 3 miles from the coast, the Derwent chooses to wind for over 80 miles through the Vale of Pickering, round the Yorkshire Wolds to join the Ouse, the Wharfe, the Aire and the Trent discharging into the great estuary of Humberside. The high moors of the National Park are cut by many streams, all joining forces before Malton. Some of these valleys were cut in post-glacial times when Eskdale was a great lake whose waters, trapped by the ice-laden North Sea, spilled over the moors and raced towards the Vale of York. The huge platform of acid sandstone has produced

one of the most distinctive upland areas in Britain. The endless scale of these heather moors is magnificent. They are managed now as grouse moors and for sheep grazing. All the upland species are here and the wetter areas of Egton or Danby High Moors have curlew, dunlin, golden plover and merlin. Along with the regular moorland plants are lesser twayblade and common wintergreen. Where other rocks create varied soils, in the deep-cut valleys of Farndale, Bransdale, Rosedale and Westerdale, rare orchids and even wild daffodil fields occur ● SE725960, Rosedale Abbey gives direct access to the central part of the National Park. **1 2 6**

North York Moors Railway

2 Levisham Moor Yorks. NPA
Embracing all the elements of this fine
National Park, Levisham Moor demonstrates its varied natural history.
Relic arctic alpines survive high on the
moorlands. Specifically, they are the
chickweed wintergreen and dwarf
cornel, both at their southern range
limit and both the last representatives
of the cold, bleak days of arctic influence. Large areas of bracken on the
moor are coloured with heather, bilberry and crowberry. There is a superb
blend of woodlands here too, from thick
oakwoods with alder and willow along
the streams and birch and rowan at
the moorland edge, just the species we
would expect in the wildwood of the
northern upland. Lower down the slopes
lime, maple, guelder-rose and gorse
are found. Watercress and brooklime
edge the streams. Old, rich pastures
are grazed by roe deer with ragged-
robin and cuckooflower growing in the
damp patches ● SE853937 west of
A169, 5 miles north of Pickering. **1** **6**

3 Hornsea Mere Humbs. RSPB
The wildlife of this splendid mere is
impressive. Following glaciation, it has
warmed and cooled over the centuries,
changing dramatically from solid ice
to a lush bank vegetation of wildwood.
Today Hornsea is an outstanding site
for the birdwatcher. The diversity of
habitat and its strategic location only
a mile or so from the sea means that
about 170 species are recorded here
each year, in the reed-beds and fen
and on open water. Winter brings impressive flocks of wildfowl and migrants
feed avidly on a prolific insect population ● TA188471 beside B1242,
12 miles south of Bridlington. **2**

4 Forge Valley Woods Yorks. NCC
Hugging the contours of a steep, narrow
gorge, you can drive the length of the
Forge Valley and see semi-natural woodland all around. Note how the trees
change up the valley sides. Oak dominates near the top, ash and wych-elm
do well on the shelter lower down,
while alder and willow thrive on the
wet soils of the valley floor. A good

understorey of hazel, holly, elder, hawthorn and rowan attracts the breeding
birds. Ferns and mosses are an interesting study. This valley has been wooded
for 6000 years but only recently modified by man. The forge which processed
local ironstone was fuelled by charcoal
timber from the woods ● SE985860
minor road north from East Ayton
which is on A170, 3 miles west of
Scarborough. **3**

5 Bradley Woods Humbs. DC
Spring and early summer are the seasons
to see Bradley Woods at their best,
with the cherry and blackthorn blossom,
orchids and butterflies. There are some
coniferous trees amongst the broad-
leaves but oak, ash and elm, the species
of the Humberside wildwood, dominate ● TA245058 south of A18 beyond the outskirts of Cleethorpes. **3**

6 Bempton Cliffs Humbs. RSPB
As you stand at the precipitous edge of
these spectacular 400-foot-high cliffs,
it is easy to forget you are on the British
mainland. The drama of the sea, the
white cliff faces and the noise of the
birds are overwhelming. Indeed, you
are looking at the only gannetry and
the largest sea-bird colony on the British
mainland. The white chalk cliffs run
for 5 miles, and although the reserve is
often only a few yards wide, 220 species
of plants have been recorded, typically
those of the cliff and chalk. The erosion

of the soft rock has provided narrow
ledges and cracks for 60,000 pairs
of kittiwakes, together with fulmar,
guillemot, razorbill and puffin, with
shag in the caves below. In autumn,
shearwaters, skuas and other oceanic
birds pass by on their endless journeys ●
TA197741 off B1229, 4 miles north-
west of Flamborough Head. **4**

7 Spurn Peninsula Humbs. CT
There can be few other sites in the
British Isles as fragile and yet so important as this thread of shingle and
sand curving out into the mouth of the
Humber. The Spurn we see today is at
least the third one there has been –
each built and each destroyed by the
power of the sea. Our tenuous defences
will not secure this Spurn from its inevitable fate. In the meantime we can
enjoy one of our most outstanding observation sites for migrant birds. Here
we can see spectacular 'falls' of migrants
or individual rarities to add to one of
the most impressive species lists in
Europe ● TA417151 end of B1445,
20 miles south-east of Hull. **4** **5**

8 Saltfleetby to Theddlethorpe Dunes
Lincs. NCC
The shorelines of the Lincolnshire coast
have a very distinctive character even
if their topography is of low-lying dunes
with salt-marsh and mudflats merging
into the sea. The waves have no rocks
to break them and there is a timeless

quality about the coast. Nevertheless, the continuous process of building new land by deposition produces some excellent habitats. Typically, the mudflats are exposed and little vegetation withstands the tidal onslaught. The salt-marsh edge has the sea-plants – glasswort and sea-blite; the innumerable creeks have sea-purslane. Here the waders concentrate – dunlin, redshank, oystercatchers and shelduck add splashes of white plumage to the scene. The dunes themselves rise above the marsh, fixed by marram or dense sea-buckthorn in their early years, of particular interest to migrant thrushes and warblers. There is a dramatic increase in the species range as the dunes age: the oldest, most stable dunes can have fine grassland swards with orchids in profusion. Behind the old dunes the freshwater marshes are out of the tidal reach and though some may still be brackish enough for sea rush to survive, common reed, water dock and skullcap soon take over. The waters are excellent for amphibians. Damselflies and dragonflies prey over the dunes and butterflies tend to seek the shelter of these land-ward habitats ● TF465924 east of A1031 north of Mablethorpe. **5**

9 Donna Nook Lincs. CT
No better reflection of the diversity of habitats can be shown than to say this site supports breeding red-legged partridge, whitethroat, little grebe and ringed plover. Two hundred and fifty other bird species have been recorded. Along the shore in winter there are delightful bouncing flocks of passerines including shorelark, twite and Lapland bunting. Grey and common seals may be seen. Beware the bombing range which has a flag warning system; otherwise this is a superb variety of dunes, mudflats, saltings and sandflats ● TF421998 off A1031 at North Somercotes, 9 miles north-west of Mablethorpe. **5**

10 Tetney Marshes Lincs. RSPB
You will be fascinated by the persistence of the little terns in their efforts to establish a successful breeding colony. Each year the terns nest in scrapes of sand and shingle banks destined to be consumed by the high tides. The wardens

have to raise the eggs and the young on to tideline debris. However, many other species are successful. The reserve has a particularly good flora, including sea-lavender, on the salt-marsh ● TA355035 off A1031 via Tetney and North Cotes villages, 4 miles south of Cleethorpes. **5**

11 Blacktoft Sands Humbs. RSPB
A classical collection of coastal habitats ranging from mudflats to salt-marsh and topped up with a huge reed-bed. One hundred pairs of bearded tits and 400 pairs of reed warblers are in their element with water-rails and the occasional pair of marsh harriers. A new lagoon has been created with islands already occupied by gadwall and teal. In the autumn the water-levels are lowered to increase the feeding areas for waders passing through ● SE843232 on south bank of Humber east of Ousefleet off A161. **5**

12 Bridestones Yorks. CT/NT
Flanked by extensive coniferous plantations, this area of dry moorland with rock outcrops is dominated by heather and bilberry. It is invaded by oak, birch and rowan. Cottongrass reveals the wetter patches. Roe deer, fox and badger are present, no doubt from the forest around ● SE880904 minor roads east of A169 via Low Dalby, 6 miles northeast of Pickering. **6**

13 Snipe Dales Lincs. CT
Grazing has been resumed over large areas of these steep valleys in the Lincolnshire Wolds. Coarser grasses on the higher slopes give way to marshy areas below, with tall ferns and giant horsetail. There was clearly more extensive woodland in the past and its associated flora can still be found in the grass. New plantations have restocked the woodland that has survived. The lowest grassland areas have common spotted-orchid and up to 11 butterfly species ● TF320683 north of A1115, 2 miles from junction with A158 Lincoln to Skegness road. **7**

14 Red Hill Lincs. CT/CC
Probably a remnant of the old Lincolnshire Wold downland the level grassland and the turf on the former quarry area are ablaze in June with lime-loving flowers, kidney vetch, yellow-wort and

Freshwater marsh, Saltfleetby

orchids. The steep red chalk cliff shows the different plants where the site is ungrazed. The rich flora of the lower pastures changes to scrub and rough grassland with fewer flowers ● TF264807 minor roads off A153, 5 miles south-west of Louth.

15 Lincolnshire Wolds Lincs.

Here smooth, rounded hills roll 40 miles through the Lincolnshire countryside in a surprising contrast to the rich peaty fens immediately to the south. But the fields are regular, neat and predominantly arable. Only on the steepest slopes where the plough cannot be hauled is the grassland allowed to establish itself and be maintained by grazing. With a distinctive character, the Wolds are hedged by miles of hawthorn, blackthorn, elder and holly, bringing the depleted woodland wildlife out into the fields. Wherever scrub or woodland can become established the species include oak and ash, beech and sycamore ● From Horncastle north between Market Rasen and Louth.

16 Ryedale Folk Museum Yorks.

Living on the southern slopes of the North York moors, the people of Ryedale knew the management of farms and forests, moorland and mire. Their livelihoods depended on a wide range of skills. In the picturesque village of Hutton-le-Hole a series of eighteenth-century farm buildings is the ideal venue for this collection of buildings, machinery, equipment and paraphernalia of rural life ● SE710900 Hutton-le-Hole north of A170, 1 mile east of Kirkbymoorside.

17 Normanby Hall Country Park Humbs. DC

Amid the intensity of the farming and industry of Humberside an old estate parkland lies close to the River Trent. There is a deer park and sanctuary, several ponds and four nature trails through the old parkland, plus a special trail for disabled people ● SE887169 at Normanby, east of B1430, 4 miles north of Scunthorpe.

18 Elsham Hall Country Park Humbs. EHCP

In the northern part of the Lincolnshire Wolds, nature trails pass through downland and woodland and round artificial lakes. The typical species of new water areas and limestone grasses and woods are readily accessible ● TA029120 off B1206, 4 miles north of Brigg.

19 Axholme Line Humbs. CT

Lime-rich soils on the site of this disused railway line have produced a splendid colonisation of hawthorn, ash, aspen, elder, oak, dog rose and field maple. Birds and butterflies particularly have made full use of the opportunity ● SK773979 off B1396 Blaxton to Haxey Road.

20 Fairburn Ings Yorks. RSPB

Opportunities for wildlife to utilise our developments are never far away. Surrounded by power stations, industry and major roads, a dramatic 2½-mile-long system of subsidence 'flashes' forms an important wetland. Viewed from the adjacent road and paths the shallow pools attract winter wildfowl, breeding and migrating waders and other waterbirds in large numbers. The goldeneye and goosander from the north find shelter and security in these pools which are likely to extend as further subsidence occurs ● SE450275 west of the A1, 2 miles north of Ferrybridge.

21 Dalby Forest Yorks. FC

The extensive forests clothing the hills and moors of the national park's southeast corner are impressive indeed. They contain a fascinating wildlife, especially on the forest floor, where clearings or ride edges bring light to an understorey, shrub and field layers. Mammals include deer, fox and badger. Predators of the air include peregrine, sparrowhawk and kestrel. Small mammals are numerous and birds surprisingly active. Crossbill, siskin, redpoll, chaffinch and coal tit move through the crowns of the evergreens. The forest drive needs to be taken slowly to appreciate the detail ● SE857873 Low Dalby information centre, then to Hackness on forest drives and minor roads.

22 Bardney Forest Lincs. FC

Before the plough had so great an impact on the Lincolnshire landscape extensive broad-leaved forests spread over the lowlands between Lincoln and the Wolds. Bardney Forest today is only a small proportion of that former wildwood and is a new landscape of coniferous plantations, blended with old woodland. As we walk the forest trails the ride edges still show evidence of those ancient woods – oak, lime, wych-elm, dogwood, thorns and wild roses in a tangle beneath the conifers ● TF150735 off B1202, 3 miles south of Wragby.

253

7 WEST OF THE PENNINES

At first glance there appears to be no link between Lancaster and Manchester or between the Wirral and the Forest of Bowland. Blackpool and Chester are very different towns indeed. But they all share the great lowland plains of the Lune, the Ribble and the Mersey, between the Pennines and the Irish Sea. It is a very busy region either side of the M6/M5 corridor and yet solitude and space can be easily found on the fells of Bowland or the shores of Morecambe Bay. There are fine coastal nature reserves on the Ribble salt-marshes, on the Wirral and the dunes near Formby. Wetlands away from the coast and typical of their types include Leighton Moss, Martin Mere, Sandbach Flashes (caused by salt subsidence) and Wayoh Reservoir.

Whether you are studying unusual creatures such as the natterjack toad on Ainsdale Dunes or countless thousands of waders and wildfowl on the Dee estuary, this region provides endless opportunities to understand our natural history. If there seems to be an emphasis on watery places then so there should be, for many of the best lie west of the Pennines.

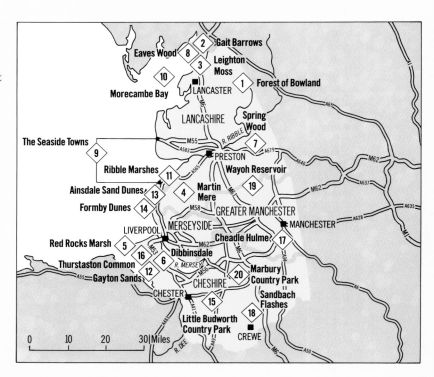

1 Forest of Bowland Lancs.

The loneliest part of this busy region is a wild landscape of sweeping moors, high fells and steep-sided valleys. There is only one road over these hills and you can walk all day meeting only the birds and insects of the uplands. Coniferous forests and reservoirs and the inevitable grouse moors and sheep grazing mark the influence of man. As you stand in the spring sunshine listening to a bubbling curlew consider the place again, in a January blizzard, and the glaciers which moulded these hills will not seem so far away ● Turn off B6478 at Newton for Lancaster. **1** **10**

2 Gait Barrows Lancs. NCC

One of the best examples of limestone pavement, with its fluted slabs of clint and its grikes where water has dissolved narrow fissures in the rocks, is only one of a range of habitats found in this exceptionally rich reserve. The limestone plants have sheltered in the grikes for thousands of years, secure even from grazing animals. The reserve includes wet and dry meadows and a small tarn. The scrub and woods have yew, hazel and juniper among many other species, but the stars of this limestone wonderland are the tutsan, sawwort, northern bedstraw and rare ferns of the pavement ● SD480772 minor roads 2 miles south-east of Arnside, between Arnside, Silverdale and Beetham. **1**

3 Leighton Moss Lancs. RSPB

This man-made fen is not as old as it looks but is considerably richer than we might imagine. Cut off from the sea by an embankment and sluice, it was drained until only about 70 years ago.

Since then the rapid succession of habitats has spread reed-beds into the open water, fen-like marsh into the reed-beds and scrub and woodland into the marsh. Reserve management is essential to maintain the balance of these aquatic habitats and to keep the range of interest for which the reserve is outstanding. Birdlife is abundant and includes resident wildfowl, wader migrants, visiting predators and breeding birds of the water's edge, including bittern and bearded tits. Surprisingly, red deer are present as well as otter, mink and smaller mammals. Eels and fish attract the herons. The information centre will explain how annual cutting encourages the diversity of plants in the reed-beds ● SD478751 on minor roads north-west of Carnforth. **2**

254

4 Martin Mere Lancs. WT
Breeding in the cold northern latitudes of Russia, Iceland or Scandinavia enables many species of birds to exploit a valuable, if temporary, source of food and shelter, without the problems of intense competition. But they cannot survive the rigours of arctic winters and they have to migrate south, thousands at a time, to shelter on the milder wetlands of the British Isles. Extensive marshland, water meadows and open water on this mere provide one of the most spectacular concentrations of wintering birds. There is a special magic in watching the return of Bewick's and whooper swans, pink-footed geese and wigeon. Teal, pintail, mallard, gadwall and many other ducks reach high numbers. Waders change with the seasons too, depending on whether they are breeding, visiting or wintering ● SD428145 on minor roads north of Ormskirk via Burscough Bridge. **2**

5 Red Rocks Marsh Merseyside CT
At the very end of the Wirral and overlooking the mouth of the Dee estuary is a compact wetland habitat comprising freshwater and brackish marshland, with dunes and lime-rich grassland nearby. Stabilised by lyme-grass and marram, the foredune has several sea plant species including sea-holly. These merge into grasslands which contain orchids, quaking-grass and kidney vetch with wild asparagus and parsley-piert on the drier areas. Common reed dominates club-rush, gipsywort and yellow iris in the reed-marsh. Clumps of alder and grey willow offer shelter to migrant birds ● SJ204884 on A540 beyond West Kirby. **2**

6 Dibbinsdale Merseyside DC/CT
The woods lining the valley sides of this delightful reserve are probably relics of the ancient woodland of the Wirral. Ash and wych-elm dominate and pro-vide an excellent reserve for woodland birds. Most of the tree specialists breed here including nuthatch, treecreeper, great spotted woodpecker and tawny owl. You will also enjoy meadows, reed-beds and grassland on this site ● SJ345827 south of Bebington on the Wirral. **3 7**

7 Spring Wood Lancs. CC
A tall closed canopy of mixed broad-leaved trees provides first-class cover for the locally unusual wood warbler and a host of other woodland birds. A trail helps to explain the ecology of the woodland, at its best with the spring chorus of songbirds ● SD740364 on A671 near junction with A59, 3½ miles south of Clitheroe, 5 miles north of Accrington. **3**

8 Eaves Wood Lancs. NT
Red squirrels are very localised in this area but do frequent the wood. Worth

Leighton Moss, with mallard and heron

a visit simply as a good example of limestone woodland, it is a hillside covered in oak, ash, lime, beech and yew over a typical understorey of buckthorn, privet and spindle ● SD467762 on minor roads south of Arnside. **3**

9 The Seaside Towns Lancs.
It may be that your only link with the sea is your annual holiday at one of the Lancashire resorts. As you enjoy the walks along the sea front you can always discover something about the wildlife of the sea. There is a constant movement of sea-birds, especially gulls, fulmar, terns and cormorants flying low over the waves. Each tide will deliver a new batch of specimens for you to examine, shells, egg cases, seaweed and sometimes dead fish or mammals from the ocean. The shrimpers of Morecambe and the fishing vessels in all their guises will indicate where the creatures of the sea may be swimming ● Morecambe, Blackpool, Southport and Lytham St Annes resort areas. **4**

10 Morecambe Bay Lancs. RSPB
If you find it hard to imagine what a quarter of the total British winter population of bar-tailed godwit, knot, dunlin, oystercatchers and turnstones might look like, then you will have to come to Morecambe Bay and see them. They are there with large numbers of other wader species together with thousands of wildfowl. Without doubt the greatest concentration of wintering shore-birds, their movements up and down the bay in accordance with the tides is one of birdwatching's most thrilling sights. You can read in Ch. 5 how, during the ice ages, the land to the north and south of the bay rose and fell with the balance of water and ice, alternately exposing and drowning new coastlines ● SD468666, A5105 north of Morecambe. **4 5**

11 Ribble Marshes Lancs. NCC
Flat expanses of salt-marsh and mudflats at the mouth of the Ribble provide an impressive and colourful show of typical plants. There are spectacular flocks of waders in spring and autumn, while during the winter, large flocks of wildfowl roost on the mudflats and feed on the salt-marsh. This also provides a largely undisturbed habitat for waders, gulls, terns and finches ● SD360210 view from coastal road Southport north to Crossens. **5**

12 Gayton Sands Cheshire RSPB
The advance of the salt-marsh on to the mudflats is accelerated by the rapid colonisation of cord-grass. To ensure their continued spread the salt-marsh plants seed profusely and attract flocks of finches to feed on this harvest of the shore. Shelduck and pintail favour this site particularly and, as you may expect with the reserve surrounded by the estuary of the Dee, vast numbers of other wildfowl and waders winter here. Foxes and weasels chase the large numbers of small mammals and short-eared owls; hen harrier and merlin check this changing shoreline regularly ● SJ273786, between Heswall and Neston off the A540. **5**

13 Ainsdale Sand Dunes
Merseyside NCC
A mixture of alien and native woodland species occupies this extensive area of sand dunes. Inland are pinewoods planted earlier this century and management is now creating a mixed woodland with different ages of trees. The wet slacks in the sand dunes are the home of the rare natterjack toads and many species of insects and plants. The dunes were planted with sea-buckthorn in the 1890s and, although they stabilised the sand and their orange berries attract many thrush species and other birds in the autumn and winter, they also smother native plant life and are therefore controlled. Watch out for the rare dune and pendulous helleborines ● SD290105 coastal dunes south of Ainsdale, 2 miles south of Southport. Permits required except for public footpath. **5**

14 Formby Dunes Merseyside NT
Sharing many of the same features of the nearby Ainsdale Dunes, these include commercial asparagus fields and a special area set aside for the red squirrels. These continental animals were introduced many years ago but are a popular and familiar attraction. Natterjacks are here too, and well worth the search ● SD275083 coastal dunes west of Formby. **5**

Flock of waders, Morecambe Bay

15 Little Budworth Country Park
Cheshire CC

Here on the great Cheshire plain in an area of rich agricultural land lies a spread of glacial sands which supports a quite different range of habitats. The drier heath soils are associated with the typical heathland cover of heather, gorse and bracken. The heath is invaded by birch woodland, always the first tree to establish on the heaths with its abundant seed production. In damper places, sphagnum moss has filled the depressions of the bogs, and cotton-grass and cranberry vary the plant species present. Insects are outstanding here and an autumn visit will reveal why this heath is well known for its fungi. Tree pipit and redpoll are two of the heathland specialists ● SJ590655 on minor roads east of the A49 at Cotebrook. **6**

16 Thurstaston Common
Cheshire NT/DC

An exposure of the rocks known as the upper mottled sandstones are exposed here on the Wirral producing an area of acid heathland. Scrub is invading a heather and bracken heath. The rich insect life is most noticeable in the late summer ● SJ244853 off A540, 2 miles south-east of West Kirby. **6**

17 Cheadle Hulme
Greater Manchester DC

Hedgerow plants and animals are the stars of this delightful nature trail. The main structure of the species-rich hedge consists of alder, elder, hawthorn, hazel, holly, oak, rowan and willow. They form the support for climbers including hop, honeysuckle and wild rose. The hedge is thick and offers excellent cover for a number of birds of the farmland and ideal nesting sites for blackbird, chiffchaff, willow warbler, wren and robin. The trail also introduces you to the open pasture and the ecology of grasslands ● SJ875855 south of Cheadle in the borough of Stockport. **7 8**

18 Sandbach Flashes Cheshire CT

As the salt in the rocks below ground has been washed out by natural solution and by brine pumping for commercial salt production, so the voids have collapsed and the land at the surface subsided. For over 100 years such subsidence has been a problem in Cheshire but it can also create 'flashes' of low-lying wetland. This string of pools and marshes is not open to visitors but can be clearly overlooked from rights of way and minor roads. The habitats you will see include open water, lime beds, mud, sedge and reed-beds, woodland and meadows. Obviously, the salinity of the pools is high so curiosities such as the sea aster and lesser sea-spurrey grow with the more typical freshwater plants. The breeding birds include little grebes, reed and sedge warblers. Passage migrants can include rarities, and wildfowl winter on the waters ● SJ725595 on minor roads south-west of Sandbach, 3 miles north of Crewe. **10 2**

19 Wayoh Reservoir Lancs. CT

So many of our reservoirs have little interest for wildlife with few opportunities for water's-edge vegetation or surrounding habitats to develop. However, as you look across this splendid hill reservoir to the viaduct, you will see a panorama of open water, marsh, grassland, scrub and woodland. Marsh-marigold and marsh valerian, horsetails and ferns add their distinctive characters to an excellent flora. Great-crested grebe breed on the reservoir, where tufted and pochard ducks dive in winter. Seven species of warblers have bred on the reserve ● SD733168 north-east of B6391 near Entwistle Station. **10 2**

20 Marbury Country Park
Cheshire CC/CT

The combination of public access to the countryside and the need to protect special wildlife areas from unreasonable disturbance is well balanced in this country park which is adjacent to Budworth mere. The park offers woodland walks with leaflet guidance. A hide has been constructed to overlook the adjacent Marbury reed-bed, avoiding the need for visitors to enter the reserve to enjoy the water, reed-beds and wet woodlands. Coot, moorhen and great crested grebe can easily be seen going about their daily lives paying no regard to the visitors 'next door' ● SJ651763 access via country park near Comberbach, 2½ miles north of Northwich. **10**

8 CAMBRIA

You will find no greater contrast than between the rugged cwms of the Snowdonian peaks and the flat expanse of the Dee estuary's mud and silt. But this part of Wales has its own identity simply because it is the giant rock pile of the Cambrian mountains standing on a narrow coastal plain. The mountains are clear and fresh and wet as witnessed by the superb growth of lichen, moss and fern in the ancient oakwoods of Coed Dinorwig and Coedydd Maentwrog. From Lake Vyrnwy to the Llangollen Canal water is an integral part of Cambria's regional character and is the source of great rivers such as the Dee, the Wye and the Severn.

The coastal sites at Ynys Hir and South Stack are rich in birdlife; Cors Caron is one of the finest wetlands of its type. As you travel around the Cambrians you will see some of the most dramatic and beautiful wildlife in the British Isles.

1 Snowdonia National Park
Gwynedd NPA

Imagine, for a moment, that you could see the mountains through the eyes of a merlin – that instead of an arduous climb you could sweep gracefully over some of the most dramatic scenery in the British Isles. With the speed of this falcon's low-level flight, the scale and beauty of wild mountain tops, sheer cliffs, tumbling screes and the knife-edge ridges of the cwms would spin and roll beneath you. The spectacular corrie lakes and the glistening white torrents of the waterfalls would be impressive indeed. The glaciers scraped and smoothed, crushed and fractured the rocks into these shapes and features. As the merlin drops on to the cold, north-facing peaks it settles among relic plants of the mountain tundra. The arctic alpine plants include the Snowdon lily, found nowhere else in the British Isles and associated abroad with permanent snow-fields. Alpine species of

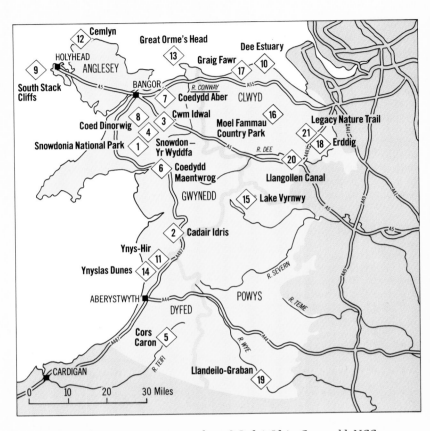

saxifrage, meadow-rue, mouse-ear and cinquefoil have occupied their niches in these mountains since the last glaciation. As the climate warmed and the light-grey, almost lifeless tundra soils slowly built up their organic material, other plants moved up the slopes. Tough, stunted colonisers of birch and pine together with grass and heather were followed 5000 years later by wet oak forests with a rich fauna. Between the mountain tops and the farmland of the valleys and lowlands are vast expanses of grass moorland with heather and bracken in which the merlin and its main prey, the meadow pipit, breed. Raven and wheatears are also found here. The park comprises 838 square miles and includes sites 2, 3 and 4 below ● SH720580 north and west of Capel Curig. ■

2 Cadair Idris Gwynedd NCC
If you want to see glacial relic landscape features and wildlife at their best climb from the Afon Fawnog to the fine corrie of Cwm Cau. With cliffs rising 1000 feet from the Llyn Cau corrie lake to the summit of Penygadair, the power of the glaciers becomes apparent. Ravens wheel round on the air currents which rise up the cliff faces, too steep to be grazed. There on the Cadair Idris, having been undisturbed for thousands of years, are moss campion, globeflower, Welsh poppy and purple saxifrage. The isolation and exposure of Britain's high mountain habitats is one of the most demanding environments for plants and yet one of the most enduring ● SH730114 off B4405, 8 miles along A487 south of Dolgellau. ■

3 Cwm Idwal Gwynedd NCC
There could be no better way to understand the character of these mountains than to follow the Cwm Idwal nature trail around the first Welsh national nature reserve. Explained and set before you in panoramic views are the formation of cwms and corrie lakes, together with the structure and complexity of these unique rocks. In total contrast, the trail also directs your attention to the lives of individual plants, how they survive, why they are there, and why their conservation is important to the story of Snowdonia ● SH640590 off A5, 6 miles west of Capel Curig. **1**

4 Snowdon – Yr Wyddfa
Gwynedd NCC
Even if you do not climb to the summit of Yr Wyddfa it is worthwhile walking the Miners' Track from Pen-y-Pass to Llyn Llydaw. Constructed to serve the copper mines of the nineteenth century, this route tells us much about Snowdon's history and wildlife, for example,

how the sheep pastures of the lower land are like a lawn of mat-grass but how the older grasslands which are not grazed are richer and more colourful. Towards the lake appear small bogs coloured with sphagnum moss and bog asphodel. Insectivorous plants such as the sundew and butterwort are poised to consume passing insects to supplement their poor diet from the soil. The bright red bills and legs of the choughs are visible as they perform aerobatics above this wild mountain landscape ● SH630530 off A4086 at Llanberis Pass. **1**

5 Cors Caron Dyfed NCC
If you find the process of change from water to raised bog difficult to understand, then this site will reveal nature's techniques. Originally a shallow lake trapped by a moraine in the Teifi valley, the flood plain mire spread over the valley floor. Plants and organic material filled the water to produce a rain-fed mire above the river level. The river

divides the bog, which is clearly visible by its cover of purple moor-grass, heather, cottongrass and deergrass, from the rising land either side of the valley. Sphagnum moss inevitably covers the highest points, where adder, lizard and slow-worm may occasionally be tracked by polecat. The wetter areas where winter floods occur may have water voles and otters to observe. The variety of habitats, including willow scrub, attracts many breeding and wintering birds. Water-rail, willow tits and wintering hen harriers are typical of this very important wetland ● SN696632 between A485 and B4343, north of Tregaron. **2**

Llyn Cau from Cadair Idris

6 Coedydd Maentwrog Gwynedd NCC
The oaks in the high woodland of Coed Llyn Mair are covered with lichens, mosses and ivy with ferns all around. This is one of a group of three woods, forming one reserve and representing the natural oakwoods of Wales – wet, shady places where pied flycatchers and mottled umber moths are part of a rich insect and bird fauna. In pockets too wet for even the oaks to grow are rushes and willows. Clearings are dominated by bracken or purple moor-grass showing how very close we are to the uplands ● SH652414 on B4410, 3 miles west of Ffestiniog. **3**

7 Coedydd Aber Gwynedd NCC
Although it is clear that man has been present in the Aber Valley since Iron-Age times, these ancient oakwoods have survived the clearance of surrounding forests, probably because they were too steep and inaccessible. As the trail leads up to the Aber Falls so the composition of the woodland changes with varying site conditions. Alder and goat-willow are in the open, wet patches; ash, elm and hazel on the lower slopes; and rugged rowan, birch and twisted oaks on the high, steep cliffs by the falls. Typically the woods are rich in lichens, mosses and ferns. Redstart, pied flycatcher and warblers are all present ● SH662720 turn off A55 in Aber, 8 miles from Conwy. **3**

8 Coed Dinorwig Gwynedd CC
While most of the Welsh hill oakwoods have been grazed, this ancient oak forest on the slopes of Padarn Country Park was fenced. It shows clearly how attractive the natural flora of the wildwood must have been. A curious mixture of species from the wood, the heath and the moorland communities form a tangled undergrowth ranging from bramble to wood-rush and from hazel to parsley fern. Native hunters include buzzard, sparrowhawk and polecat ● SH586603 Padarn Country Park, 6 miles east of Caernarfon. **3**

9 South Stack Cliffs Gwynedd RSPB
As you look down on the sea over 300 feet below, you will not fail to be impressed by the spectacle of sea-bird colonies on these famous cliffs. Every tiny ledge is packed with a family of hungry guillemots, razorbills, puffins, kittiwakes or fulmars. The parents make constant journeys to and from the sea to bring food to the young so precariously balanced above the waves. From these delicate perches the young auks must eventually make their maiden flight down to the waves where they will live until they return to nest on the stacks ● SH205823, 3 miles west of Holyhead, Anglesey. **4**

10 Dee Estuary Clwyd various
The estuary started with the meltwaters from the glaciers depositing material washed down from the Cheshire Plain. As the climate warmed, the sea-level rose and drowned the river mouth to start another process of deposition. The silts and sands of this massive estuary system attract so many waders in autumn and winter that counting them seems pointless. But why do tens of thousands of these delightful birds of the water's edge come to the Dee? Incomprehensible numbers of tiny crustaceans and worms are packed into the estuarine silts and muds. The waders are especially adapted to find and eat them. In summer as many as 200 grey seals may congregate and other sea

mammals are seen – dolphin, porpoise and killer whales. But the drama is in the autumn flocks of waders as they rise like billowing smoke clouds to fly the tide line in search of a secure resting place ● SH125847 the entire estuary can be good but Point of Ayr is a reliable observation point. North of A548, 4 miles east of Prestatyn. **4** **5**

11 Ynys-Hir Dyfed RSPB
While the woods and moorland of the reserve are bird habitats of considerable importance, the estuary and salt-marsh of Ynys-Hir are special. Forming a flat coastal plain in a beautiful mountainous landscape, they attract, among other wintering ducks, wigeon, teal, red-breasted merganser and goldeneye. The Greenland white-fronted geese visit the salt-marsh and hen harriers and peregrine falcons check for unwary prey ● SN683963 off A487 in Furnace village. **5**

12 Cemlyn Gwynedd CT
Winter storms and spring tides add a colourful variety of stones to the shingle bar of this storm beach. This harsh environment drenched with winter salt

spray and baked in the summer sun is colonised by specialised plants such as strong, fleshy sea-kale, sea-beet, scurvy-grass and thrift. Behind the shingle bank a brackish pool attracts winter wildfowl and shelduck breed in old rabbit burrows in the dunes ● SH336932 minor roads west of A5025, 6 miles west of Amlwch, Anglesey. **5**

13 Great Orme's Head Gwynedd DC
The fine North Wales coastline has its share of rugged cliff scenery. Here on the peninsula beyond Llandudno, the cliffs support a varied flora with such lime-loving plants as common rock-rose, dropwort and quaking-grass growing alongside coastal wild flowers which include sea-pink, spring squill and wild cabbage. Colonies of kittiwakes, guille-mots and razorbills share the sea cliffs with jackdaws, ravens and rock pipits. During the winter months, the head-land plays host to snow buntings and chough, and red-throated divers may be seen close inshore ● SH780832 off A546 beyond Llandudno. **5**

14 Ynyslas Dunes Dyfed NCC
The greatest threat to this fragile system of dunes is from the 300,000 visitors who come to enjoy this part of the Dyfi estuary as part of their summer holiday. The flora and fauna of the dunes and slacks are well worth a visit during the week. But the reserve has much more to offer the inquisitive naturalist with estuary birds and a sunken forest ● SN610940 off B4353, 8 miles north of Aberystwyth. **5**

15 Lake Vyrnwy Powys RSPB
Part of the most extensive heather moor in Wales and complemented by thou-sands of acres of grass moorland and mire, the moors are grazed by many hundreds of mountain sheep and are periodically burnt to improve the heather. Red grouse, curlew and whin-chat breed on this extensive managed moorland. Coniferous forest adjacent has red squirrel and polecat. Newts and frogs are found in the mire pools and several fritillary species in the broad-leaved woodland ● SH985215, B4393 from Llanfyllin. **6**

16 Moel Fammau Country Park Clwyd CC
High rolling heather grouse moor con-jures a picture which Moel Fammau will fit very well. It is a superb example of a widespread and important habitat of the uplands. Heather, bilberry and bracken are the familiar plants but there are delightful new ones to discover too, including marsh pennywort and cross-leaved heath ● SJ171611 north of A494, 4 miles from Ruthin. **6**

17 Graig Fawr Clwyd NT
Overlooking the Vale of Clwyd this great limestone hill has the shallow turf of lime-loving plants which is a treasure in any region. Small scabious, lady's bedstraw and harebell are plentiful. Hoary rock-rose grows in thick mats on the steeper, western face. The com-mon blue butterfly thrives in this, its favourite habitat ● SJ064802 A547 south from Prestatyn. **7**

18 Erddig Clwyd NT
At the agricultural museum, on the fascinating Erddig estate, an exhibition demonstrates the changes in agricul-tural practices over the last two or three hundred years. Combined with the meticulous reconstruction and pres-entation of the house, outbuildings and contents this gives us one of the clearest pictures of eighteenth- and nineteenth-century rural life. Erddig introduces us to some of the local characters whose work slowly changed the country-side ● SJ326482 off A525, 2 miles south of Wrexham. **8 9**

19 Llandeilo-Graban Powys CT
Meadowland, marsh and woodland are the varied habitats we can see from this old railway line overlooking the River Wye. Watch for slow-worm and common lizard on the slopes and butter-flies in the open spaces ● SO090438 to 112419, B4594 off A470, 7 miles south-east of Builth Wells. **10**

20 Llangollen Canal Clwyd CC
A very good example of how the more usual plants and animals can colonise an area and quickly create an interest-ing and attractive habitat. The rare and the spectacular are not needed to enjoy the delights of nature's improve-ments to our engineering works. Peer into the watery world of the canal to see snails and leeches and a host of insect larvae, including dragonfly and great diving beetle. Bream, carp and rudd are three of seven species of fish that swim in the murky waters ● SJ198433 immediately north and east of Llangollen. **10**

21 Legacy Nature Trail Clwyd CEGB/NWNT
The mounds were constructed to help screen the substation and blend this piece of twentieth-century technology into an attractive landscape. There is now a nature trail specifically laid out to demonstrate the colonisation of man-made habitats. Marsh and grassland have been deliberately introduced to diversify the habitats available ● SJ295483 off the A483 immediately south-west of Wrexham. **10**

Cyrniau moorland above Lake Vyrnwy

Between the rugged splendour of the Cambrians and the industrial development of the Midlands spread soft, rich lowlands with reminders of the adjacent landscapes. The Malverns and the Long Mynd reflect the ancient uplands of Wales. There are splashes of industry in the Shropshire countryside where disused canals and quarries record 300 years of industry. The timber of the royal forests of Dean and Wyre were exploited for construction and charcoal burning, whereas the present-day plantations of Chaddesley and Wentwood will supply some of our modern needs for timber.

The region is warm and sheltered and the farmland very productive. The Vale of Evesham is distinctive and contrasts sharply with heathlands at Hartlebury Common and the Devil's Spittleful. The rivers all have a story to tell, but none so dramatic as the winding gorge of the Wye. Despite only a narrow neck of industrialised coastline this region, the lowland catchments of the Severn and the Wye, contains Peterstone Wentlooge with its marvellous range of shoreline habitats on the estuary.

1 Long Mynd Shropshire NT
This softly rounded mass of rocks has continued to be changed through many geological eras, culminating in the crushing weight of the Pleistocene ice. The glaciers rubbed the hills to a whale-backed plateau still over 1500 feet above sea-level. The post-glacial pine-woods gave way to a natural cover of broad-leaves but man soon cleared the Mynd and used it for sheep grazing. In the worst of the winter months the streams are again recharged with melt-water, to cut ever deeper, winding valleys down the slopes. These clear, fresh waters are rich in insect life and attract the dipper which will breed on these uplands with the ring ousel and wheatear. The former mountain habitats have all but gone, leaving an exten-

sive grouse moor with a regular mowing programme to encourage the heather and reduce the bracken ● SO425945 west of Church Stretton on A49, 12 miles south of Shrewsbury. ▪ ▪

2 Wye Valley Gwent
No other river in England or Wales retains its natural character as dramatically as the Wye. From its source in the Cambrian mountains to the Severn estuary, it winds through narrow gorges with spectacular wooded cliffs. Originally on a slow and wandering course over a level plateau, the river then had to excavate a deeper channel to compensate for a fall in sea-level. Rejuvenated by the massive volume of melt-water from the Welsh glaciers the river retained its meander-

ing course but cut deep into the rocks like a young stream. So the autumn landscape of the Wye Valley can be stunning. The colourful woods and clear, clean waters provide exceptional habitats for wildlife. The individuality of the Wye is typified by the rare and delicate upright spurge which occurs nowhere else in the British Isles ● The entire valley from Builth Wells to Chepstow is well served by public roads. ▪ ▪

3 Colemere Countryside Leisure Area Shropshire CC
Elsewhere, across the plain and north of Shrewsbury, the glaciers had spread great volumes of sand, gravel and clays from the hills and valleys they scoured. The depressions in these mounds filled

with melt-water and in turn the succession of vegetation either built up
the pools to make bogs or fringed the
lakes with a wealth of aquatic plants.
Here at Colemere the open water remains with woods and meadows down
to the water's edge. Water-birds are
always present but at migration times
there are also passage terns and
waders ● SJ434328 on minor roads
off A528, 14 miles north-west of
Shrewsbury. **1** **2**

4 Brown Moss Shropshire CC
The influence of man's drainage and
peat cutting has extended the natural
changes in this former bog to create an
area of dry, acid heath around a series
of pools. Nevertheless, thirty species of
birds breed here and uncommon wetland plants include floating water-
plantain, floating club-rush, water-
violet and orange foxtail ● SJ564394
on minor roads less than 2 miles south-
east of Whitchurch. **2**

5 Feckenham Wylde Moor
Hereford and Worcester CT
This 28-acre fen marsh has extensive
beds of reeds, rush and sedge, together
with grazed and mown wet meadows.
A new lake adds to the wetland habitats. A hide is open to the public and
snipe are usually to be seen as they
breed and winter here ● SP012603,
B4090, 8 miles east of Droitwich. **2**

6 Forest of Dean Glos. FC
In the quiet arboreal calm of England's
first national forest park you can reflect
on the character that makes each of
our woodlands distinctive. You will
sense the passage of time in the age of
the trees in the different parts of the
forest. You can follow the mixture of
species as you pass from one part to
another over changing soils. You will
see the drastic influences of man's management in the Saxon clearances and
the medieval coppicing. Alien species
were introduced to increase the volume
of timber which the forest is capable of
growing. Above all, you can enjoy the
wildlife. From the oaks, limes, elm and
cherry of the wildwood to the spruce
and larch of recent decades, there are
homes for half the British butterfly
species, including brown argus, grayling and pearl-bordered fritillary. The
Dean is most important as the representative of the wildwood for our familiar native woodland wildlife.

But it has its share of the uncommon
too: there are hawfinch, crossbill and
tree pipits. The exotic martagon lily
and the ancient woodland lichens are
specialities ● SO615080 Parkend is a
useful starting point on the B4234 or
B4431. **3**

7 Wyre Forest
Hereford and Worcester NCC/FC
With its distinctive appearance and
variety of woodland types the Wyre
brings the wildlife of the uplands close
to the West Midlands conurbation. In
places it is like the damp oak coppices
of Wales but elsewhere the woods resemble the native forest of the Midland
clays. Remnants of ancient oak woodland are set among modern plantations
and the fast-flowing Dowles Brook is a
great attraction. In the older parts, the
woodland flora is mixed and colourful,
the invertebrate populations are exceptional and the range of moth species
alone could provide a lifetime's study
here. Woodpeckers, woodcock and owls
are present with redstarts, tits, warblers
and many other woodland birds. The
mammals, too, have survived the forest's changes and all the usual species
can be found together with the rarer
dormouse. The continuity of woodland
cover, once protected by royal forest
laws, has provided one of our most
precious lowland woods ● SO759766
north-west of Bewdley, 4 miles from
Kidderminster. 🔳

Dowles Brook, Wyre Forest

8 Nunnery Wood
Hereford and Worcester CC
Nightingales are among the songbirds
of this ancient wood and you can hear
their liquid notes on quiet May even-
ings, when woodcocks rode their territorial boundaries. The mixed wood of
ash, oak, aspen, hawthorn and hazel is
managed traditionally as coppice with
standards and has occupied the site for
at least 900 years. There are several
fine examples of the wild service tree.
● SO877543 off A422, 2 miles east of
Worcester. 🔳

9 The Knapp and Papermill
Hereford and Worcester CT
The habitats of this delightful reserve
include woodland, orchard, meadow
and brook which demonstrate very
clearly the effects of management on
the natural woodland cover as well as
many of the traditional techniques.
While the crack willow by the water
are pollarded, the alder and ash there
are coppiced. The wooded slopes of the
valley have areas of oak, lime and wild
service tree, which have been coppiced,
and fine stands of oak and ash over
coppiced hazel. In the dampness of the
lower land are ferns, orchids, butterbur
and comfrey. On the drier banks are
cowslip and primrose. The site is occupied by uncommon silver cloud and
wave-backed moths, 30 species of
butterfly have been recorded and
20 mammal species enjoy the shelter
of this woodland scene ● SO748522
on minor roads near Alfrick off A4103,
3½ miles west of Worcester. 🔳

10 Goldcliff and Coldharbour
Gwent CT
Long recognised as a major flight path
for our millions of migrating birds, the
Severn Estuary invariably carries good
numbers of all birds of travelling species.
Here on an estuary foreshore, waders
and wildfowl congregate in the autumn
and winter as they move south ahead
of the cold ● ST385825 via minor
roads south of Newport. 🔳

11 Peterstone Wentlooge Gwent CT
You will appreciate how the sea wall
has created a diversity of habitats by
controlling the influence of salt water
on the new land. The mudflats and
salt-marsh are excellent, attracting
dunlin and knot among many other
waders. Unusual winter visitors include
long-tailed duck and common scoter
but the sight of a dashing peregrine or
a short-eared owl slowly quartering
the reserve will never fail to delight.
Behind the sea wall are grassland and
scrub, adding shelter and food sources
for smaller birds passing through ●
ST278807, B4239 midway between
Newport and Cardiff. 🔳

12 The Devil's Spittleful
Hereford and Worcester CT
Occasional fires have resulted in a varied
age structure of ling on this spread of
lowland heath. Areas of open heather
intermingle with birch woodland and
hawthorn scrub creating a mosaic
which supports a wide variety of heathland plants and animals ● SO810747
on A456 between Bewdley and
Kidderminster. 🔳

13 Hartlebury Common
Hereford and Worcester CC
An important lowland acid heath with
scrub woodland, bogs and pools giving
all the character of the heathland community. Broom and gorse form ideal
perches for the stonechat and whinchat. Shepherd's cress, buck's-horn and
white harebell are to be found among
the commoner heathland plants. The
movement of windblown sand has been
arrested by the colonisation of the 'inland' dunes by vegetation, since myxomatosis reduced the number of grazing
rabbits ● SO820705 off A449,
4 miles south of Kidderminster. 🔳

14 Malvern Hills
Hereford and Worcester
Do not be tempted to view the Malverns
only from the farmland below. The
best way to sense the character of this
intricate mass of ancient rocks is to
walk across and over it and to look

down from its summits on to the mosaic of habitats. The influence of the grazing animals is a transition from grassland to scrub or woodland. Woods run up the shallow valleys and between the mounds. The slopes and cliffs are scattered with gorse and broom. Even the exposed rock patches have stonecrops, mosses, lichens and ferns ● SO768454 immediately south-west of Great Malvern on A449. **6**

15 Earls Hill Shropshire CT
The dependence of habitats on particular land uses and of the history of their changes is extremely well demonstrated on this steep-sided bluff jutting out of the Shropshire Plain. The iron-age hill fort is evidence of the early occupation of man. He cleared the forest, no doubt initially to defend the fort and build its structures. Then cattle and sheep would be introduced, perhaps 2000 years ago, and wherever they could reach they would nibble out the seedling trees. So a pattern would develop of short-turfed, close-grazed grassland with its prostrate plants and of crags, crevices and ledges where woodland grew because the animals could not reach them. No doubt the grazing pressure has varied over the centuries and scrub

has invaded, as it is doing now, but on being cut back the grasses will return ● SJ409048 south of A488 near Pontesbury, 7 miles south-west of Shrewsbury. **7**

16 Vale of Evesham
Hereford and Worcester
There is no other agricultural landscape quite like that of the Vale of Evesham. Historians now believe this area has been intensively farmed since Roman times and the variety of crops and the layout of the fields gives a most attractive and distinctive landscape. The famous orchards of the Vale are a marvellous sight in spring blossom. This landscape and its long traditions has also gained its own wildlife associations. Birds and insects in orchards may not always be welcome but they can never be completely excluded ● An extensive area between the A46 and the M5 south of Evesham. **8**

17 Acton Scott Farm Shropshire
A complete working farm using nineteenth-century arable techniques on a traditional four-course rotation. Eighteenth-century buildings and a fine collection of the traditional breeds of farm animals, including working shire

horses, are among the attractions. Open from April to October, every afternoon and some mornings ● SO435895 at Marshbrook on B4370 off A49 near Church Stretton. **8**

18 Lancaut Glos. CT
In a typically spectacular curve of the Wye, Lancaut Reserve embraces natural and man-made habitats of great contrast: from the deep tidal waters and the mud and salt-marsh of the valley floor, up steep gorge sides where woodland contains all the species of the wildwood, to the little chapel and the Offa's Dyke at the top of the cliffs where ancient man has left his marks. The river terrace has been quarried and colonised by limestone grassland with many of its delightful flowering plants: St John's-wort, yellow-wort, hairy violet and lesser calamint. The open limestone ledges do not enjoy the same full sun but the naturalised wallflowers give them the appearance of window-boxes on the cliff ● ST539967 on B4228 north of Woodcroft, 1 mile or so north of Chepstow. **10**

19 Wentwood Forest Gwent FC
An ideal opportunity to compare the wildlife of the ancient broad-leaved woods of oak and beech to the twentieth-century plantations of larch. As you wind through the trails, the forest provides a mixture of tree species and ages which offer a range of habitats from the open clearings for nightjar to the mature conifers for crossbills. Amphibians do well in the pools. Raven, buzzard and sparrowhawk are three of the predators breeding here ● ST436936 off A449, 4 miles north-east of Newport. **10 3**

20 Chaddesley Woods
Hereford and Worcester NCC
The combination of wildwood species including small-leaved lime, wild service-tree, hazel, oak and birch indicate that parts of Chaddesley are of ancient origin. Elsewhere, there are recent conifer plantations. The importance of this particular reserve is how its management demonstrates that the pursuit of commercial forestry need not necessarily be contrary to the aims of nature conservation ● SO914736 off A448, 6 miles south-east of Kidderminster. **10 3**

The Malvern Hills, with Worcestershire Beacon

10 THE ENGLISH MIDLANDS

You might have expected that, in the wake of industrial innovation and expansion, traces of the former landscapes would be obliterated and animals and plants of the wildwood and heath would be absent. The forests and heaths of Sherwood, Rockingham, Cannock and Charnwood are indispensable refuges for wildlife and essential escapes for urban man.

The fox is the symbol of Midland wildlife; it was around the Crags of Creswell in post-glacial times. It is resourceful enough to use the urban wetlands of Martin's Pond and the cemetery of Merriale. It hunts the heaths of Budby and the shores of Rutland Water; it is hunted itself over the woods and fields of north Leicestershire. The countryside of the Quorn hunt is a fine example of enclosure landscapes. The open fields at Laxton, though, give us a clear impression of the Midland farmland and its wildlife of 600 years ago.

Compare the rushing glacial streams of the Coombes and Manifold Valley to the impressive new water parks on the Trent and Tame. You will then have the essence of the Midlands' variety.

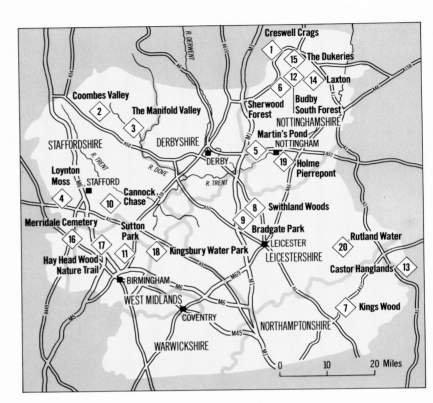

1 Creswell Crags Notts. CC

There is an element of surprise in discovering these ivy-clad crags confined in a narrow gorge among an open Midland landscape. The lake is man-made but the waters which cut through the hill also excavated deep caves. Evidence left by stone-age hunters illustrates the wild animals of Britain after the Ice Age. The interpretive centre explains the history of man and beast. Looking out of these cold caves you can still experience the feeling of security which the early hunters must have shared ● SK538744 on B6042 off A616 at Creswell (Derbys.). **1**

2 Coombes Valley Staffs. RSPB

Charged with the gushing melt-water of post-glacial thaws, the stream cut

and plunged down its steep-sided valley soon to be covered in oak woodland. The character of the reserve today still holds these important elements – the uplands, the brook and the woodland. There are beech, oak, ash and birch with a superb range of woodland and grassland plants. Insect populations are high; reptiles include common lizards and adders. The birds are the highlight of this rich display. Redstarts and tree pipits of the oakwoods and grey wagtails and dippers of the upland stream are examples of the full list of 130 species, half of which breed here ● SK005530 on minor road to Apesford off A523, 4 miles south of Leek. **1** **2** **3**

3 The Manifold Valley Staffs. NT/CC

In summer, the river in the Manifold disappears down 'swallet' holes in the limestone and the bed dries out. In winter, though, the volume of water carries on over the holes and follows a dramatic fall past meadow, limestone grassland, woodland slopes and craggy cliffs. A range of limestone plants which enjoy damp or dry conditions find some part of the valley to their liking. Mountain currant drapes the rocks, kingfishers and dippers feed on the clear water and the damper patches display water avens, comfrey and valerian ● SK100543 on minor roads above Ilam, 4 miles north-west of Ashbourne (Derbys.). **2**

4 Loynton Moss Staffs. CT

The continuous process of change is clearly demonstrated in the progress of Loynton Moss from water to woodland.

Quite recently the centre of this glacial depression was open water but common reed has advanced across the entire water area. Part of the wetland is like a fen and contains unusual plants, including yellow loosestrife and greater spearwort. The sphagnum mosses, which originally filled the depressions around, support broad buckler-fern. Elsewhere old grassland is being invaded by bramble and bracken. As the new lands dry out so the oak and birch woodland dominates yet another stage in the succession ● SJ791246, A519, 1 mile south-west of Woodseaves. **2**

5 Martin's Pond Notts. DC/CT
Well within the built-up area of Greater Nottingham, this pond with marsh and scrub habitats is remarkably rich in wildlife. A delightful walk takes you past the pond and the reserve through bulrushes and willow scrub, open water and marsh. The interest is spread evenly between colourful and lush plant growth, breeding and wintering birds, insects, amphibians and mammals ● SK526402 off the A609, Ilkeston Road in Wollaton, Notts. **2**

6 Sherwood Forest Notts. CC
If you stand beneath the 'blasted oaks' it is not difficult to imagine the forest of medieval times when some of these ancient giants were mere seedlings in the bracken. Protected by forest laws these woods of oak and birch high forest were never cleared though they were often stripped of their best-quality timber. Assarts would have been cleared and farmed before reverting back to heath, then forest. Since the spread of the two oak species (both of which are present in the same proportion), the continuity of forest cover has endowed this legendary place with an invertebrate population of international significance. Fungi too are outstanding. An early autumn visit will show you an ancient, dry oak forest in all its regal splendour ● SK627677 on B6034 $\frac{1}{2}$ mile north of Edwinstowe and adjacent site 12 below. **3**

7 Kings Wood Northants. DC/CT
Another ancient Midland forest had no outlaw to perpetuate its name and Rockingham Forest has been forgotten. Yet it was extensive in area and rich in wildlife as we can witness from the

evidence of Kings Wood. Ash and many old oaks stand over hazel with impressive displays of bluebell, wood sorrel and sanicle. Orchids show in early spring and the forest is one of the best in the area for lichens ● SP864874 off A6003 south of Corby. **3**

8 Swithland Woods Leics. BPT
The variety of soil types must have given Charnwood a wider range of native trees. Indeed, the remnant of that ancient forest has many of the wildwood species still present. Oak, ash and small-leaved lime form the high forest but hazel, birch and alder are here too. Regular coppicing was abandoned 100 years ago. The plants of the forest floor have found sufficient light to survive and range from grasses to bluebells and yellow pimpernel to pendulous sedge. A true mixed woodland with its roots in the wildwood of 2000 years ago ● SK538129 off B5330, 3 miles west of Rothley and adjacent site 9 below. **3**

9 Bradgate Park Leics. BPT
Dramatic Charnwood heathland on the land overlooking the ancient Swithland Wood and the recent Cropston Reservoir. As we escape to an expanse of heath with grassland and bracken we can see close views of grazing deer. Many trees are scattered over the hill-

sides. The reservoir holds good numbers of wintering wildfowl; wigeon and teal round the edges, with goldeneye and tufted duck on the deeper water ● SK523116 off B5330, 3 miles west of Rothley and adjacent site 8 above. **6 10**

10 Cannock Chase Staffs. CC
Look carefully across the heathland landscape and you will see all the features which you need to build the history of Cannock. Scattered oak and birch are the remnants of the wildwood. The chase was protected by forest laws, then depleted by felling for charcoal burning in the ironworks of the West Midlands. Deer and rabbit can still be seen and it was these animals, together with sheep, that prevented the regeneration of the forest trees and so created the heathland of today. Along the skylines are twentieth-century forestry plantations. The valley mires have northern plants at their southern limit (marsh hawk's-beard) and southern plants (southern marsh-orchid) at their northern limit. They also have round-leaved sundews, cranberries and grass-of-Parnassus. The most distinguished characters of Cannock, though, are the nightjars and the deer – many fallow but small numbers of red and muntjac too ● SJ971160 follow the signs on to minor roads south-west from Rugeley. **6**

Fallow deer in Cannock Chase

11 Sutton Park W. Midlands DC
Somehow this vast heath has escaped
the spread of urban development to
form a popular open space and a fine
example of natural features surviving
intensive public use. The oak-holly-
birch-rowan woods are clearly of
ancient origin. Grassland, bracken,
bilberry and heather heaths have been
invaded by birch. Wetter patches dis-
courage public trampling and alder
carr, purple moor-grass, cottongrass
and sphagnum mosses mark the wetland. Moths and other insects are less
disturbed by the public access than the
birds, though there are many fewer
species in the conifer plantations ●
SP103963 west of Sutton Coldfield in
West Midlands conurbation. **6**

12 Budby South Forest Notts. MOD
Immediately adjacent to the best part
of the ancient Sherwood Forest, this
extensive heath provides further illustration of the tenuous nature of heathland. Invasion by pine, birch and oak
is vigorous in places, fine grassheath
and bracken areas remain elsewhere.
The pattern is controlled by land use
and grazing of wild animals. The site
has an outstanding invertebrate population. Redstarts, tree pipits and other
oakwood birds move out into the heath
where nightjar churr and woodcocks
rode in the evening ● SK610690 used
in part for military training, public footpaths and waymarked trails across
from site 6 above. **6**

13 Castor Hanglands
Cambs. Northants. Trust/NCC
Your visit to this national nature reserve
would be justified to see any one of
four main habitats: woodland, grassland, scrub or wetland. But the grassland is of special interest. Common
grazing ceased in the 1930s when mixed
scrub immediately invaded, only to be
cleared by the Ministry of Defence during
the Second World War when it was
used as a bombing range. Parts are
now cut for hay, swiped or grazed in
different combinations. This variety of
management is carefully compiled to
produce the best range of flora and
fauna. Many birds and insects benefit
particularly from the coarser, longer
grass areas. The reserve offers a remarkable habitat range ● TF118023,
take Helpston Road north of A47 at
Ailsworth, 4 miles west of
Peterborough. **7**

14 Laxton Notts.
Transport yourself back in time to the
arable farmland of 600 years ago, or
more. The last remaining fully oper-
ational open-field system started by the
Saxons still covers this village. Three
magnificent open fields roll over the
Midland clays with sykes, ridges, baulks
and commons still intact. But do not
expect too much wildlife on these open
fields where the strips are most clearly
visible in the early spring. Hare and
skylark are two of very few species at
home in the open. Once the animals

and plants of the ancient parish woods
would have spilled out on to the farmland. They have been sadly depleted
and the hedges along the ancient back
lanes and parish boundaries are the
only compensation with buckthorn,
maple, bryony and long-tailed tits, the
hedgerow specialists. The language of
toft and croft, court leet and penfold is
still relevant in Laxton. As well as its
national historic importance, Ch. 8 explains how Laxton still retains the true
character of a working community ●
SK725670, 4 miles east of Ollerton,
the village is signposted from A616
and A6075, general access on foot. **8**

15 The Dukeries Notts. NT/CC
So much of the north-east section of
Sherwood Forest was enclosed to form
private estates that the concentration
of magnificent parkland bears the popular name of 'The Dukeries'. They are
splendid examples of the English Landscape Movement's fashion to create
informal and romantic settings to the
ducal homes of the eighteenth century.
They provide a range of mixed woodland, farmland, heathland and lakes.
The rivers were dammed to create landscape features which now hold important winter wildfowl stocks. The
woodlands are particularly rich in birdlife. Ancient oaks, reminding us of the
former forest, have been retained together with their invaluable invertebrate populations ● SK615730 between the A60 and A614, Clumber
and Rufford Parks have straightforward
public access. **9**

16 Merridale Cemetery
W. Midlands DC
This old-established and well-wooded
cemetery provides a curious illustration
of wildlife adjusting to man's environment. The trees range from native to
exotic, planted or colonised and attract
the delightful spotted flycatcher. The
nuthatch calls will eventually give away
their presence too. Compare the birds
and insects here to those of a small
garden nearby and see the potential of
wildlife gardening ● SO899979 on the
western outskirts of Wolverhampton. **9**

17 Hay Head Wood Nature Trail
W. Midlands DC
Old mine workings and a canal basin provide considerable wildlife habitat along this short trail in Walsall. Look for alder, hawthorn and ramsons in the quarries and bright yellow marsh-marigold in the wetland ● SP 041990 off A454 in Walsall. ⏸

18 Kingsbury Water Park
Warwicks. CC
Part of this very large water park complex is a nature reserve with open water, reed-beds and willow swamp based on flooded gravel workings. The areas of alder and willow carr produce a wide cross-section of woodland birds. In spring, the songs of nine species of warblers may be heard, including blackcap, lesser whitethroat and grass-hopper warblers ● SP204958 off A51, 4 miles south of Tamworth. ⏸ ▪

19 Holme Pierrepont Notts. CC
An ambitious programme of gravel extraction and land reclamation has produced the National Water Sports Centre, an Olympic-sized rowing course, a country park and nature reserve. The attraction to water-birds is increased by the presence of further flooded gravel lagoons on the opposite bank of the Trent at Colwick. The winter gull roost numbers thousands of birds and wandering skuas have chased terns down the course. Little ringed plovers may be found regularly in the summer when common sandpipers dip and call along the shores of the pits ● SK615390 off the A52 immediately east of West Bridgford on the outskirts of Nottingham. ⏸

20 Rutland Water Leics. CT/AWA
You will enjoy a site planned and designed for wildlife as part of the awe-inspiring enterprise of creating Britain's second largest man-made lake. The sheer scale of Rutland Water reminds us, and apparently the birds too, of the sea. Cormorants, gulls and other sea-birds are common. Around the edge, the treatment and management of the shore provide ideal conditions for wetland and water species of all kinds. On the migration routes of the Nene and Welland the reservoir is already of national significance to wildfowl. Large flocks of ruddy duck are to be seen among twenty other regular ducks, swan and geese species. For an inland water, spring and autumn passage is outstanding and comfortably observed from a number of well-sited hides. This new landscape will continue to grow in stature and is already one of Britain's outstanding water areas ● SK897049 off A6003, 2 miles south of Oakham. ⏸ ▪

Open fields at Laxton

11 EAST ANGLIA

Since bronze-age man worked the flints of Grimes Graves, the area we now call East Anglia has always had a most distinctive character. To win the richest dark soils in the country, men have battled to drain the Fens, destroying almost all of the varied wildlife they once supported. We have expended considerable energy on a task which, if we had left well alone, nature would have completed for us. Chapter 2 explains how much of the fen, marsh and swamp would, without our intervention, now be high and dry. Instead we are committed to perpetual pumping to preserve our agricultural land.

In so doing, though, we have created new wetlands, as on the Ouse Washes, with new wildlife associations. The coasts too are always changing, yet they are still of international wildlife significance. The beauty of the Norfolk estates, the intimate Suffolk lanes and the mysterious solitude of dawn on the Fens are, uniquely, East Anglian.

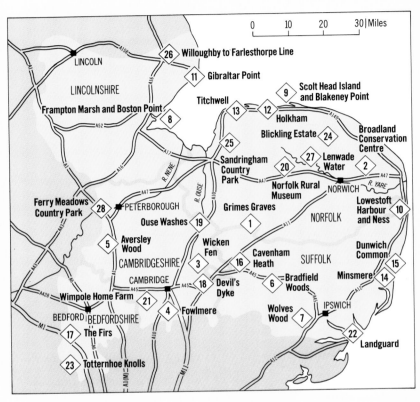

1 Grimes Graves Norfolk DOE
Descending the shafts of the largest flint mines in Europe transports us to the world of 2500BC. Stone-age, then bronze-age men used red deer antlers and the bones of the wild aurochs to pick flints from the chalky rocks. The men made their first tools here, including axes to cut down the forest around ● TL818898 off B1108, 7 miles north-west of Thetford. **1**

2 Broadland Conservation Centre
Norfolk CT
The story of the Norfolk Broads is explained in this centre overlooking Ranworth Broad. It is approached by a duckboarded trail through typical broadland scenes, including wet woodland and fen. The milk parsley is the foodplant of the swallowtail butterfly larvae ● TM355155 off B1140, 10 miles north-east of Norwich, April–Oct. closed Mondays. **2**

3 Wicken Fen Cambs. NT
This superb example of relic fenland contains all the habitats associated with the succession of changes through reed-bed, sedges, alder buckthorn thickets, mixed scrub and wet woodland. The management of each stage has produced a beautifully rich flora and a high population of birds and invertebrates linked with the fens. One of the oldest reserves in Britain, it provides a rare opportunity to view the fenland habitats once common in East Anglia ●
TL563705 off the A1123, 8 miles north-west of Newmarket. **2** **10**

4 Fowlmere Cambs. RSPB
These derelict watercress beds are now one of the finest reed-beds in the region. A hundred pairs of reed warblers add to a splendid spring chorus of songbirds. Water forget-me-not is one of the water-loving plants which grow in profusion here. Ducks and waders shelter during the winter with species of birds not usually associated with aquatic habitats, including corn bunting and thrushes ● TL407462 off the B1368, 8 miles south of Cambridge. **2**

5 Aversley Wood Beds./Hunts. WdT
The structure of this beautiful ancient woodland includes mature ash/oak/maple with less common trees, and dense thickets of blackthorn (providing a home for the very rare black hairstreak butterfly) ● TL160817 on minor roads between B660 and A1. **3**

6 Bradfield Woods Suffolk CT
One of the finest examples of traditional woodland management, this ancient wood shows the stages of coppicing and pollarding. Access is restricted to the pathways but a visit, following the essential leaflet which is available, is a practical introduction to woodland history and to the site with the best range of plant life in East Anglia ● TL935581 minor roads east of the A134, 4 miles south-east of Bury St Edmunds. **3**

7 Wolves Wood Suffolk RSPB
Another outstanding example of traditional management encouraging a fine woodland flora and fauna. The soils are wet clays and ponds diversify the natural history interest of this attractive oak/ash/maple woodland. A hornbeam coppice is an unusual feature ● TM054436 north of the A1071, 8 miles west of Ipswich. **3**

8 Frampton Marsh and Boston Point Lincs. CT
If you want to view the massive expanses of the Wash and its coastal mudflats and salt-marshes, the long walk to Frampton Reserve and Boston Point is rewarding. Where sky, sea or shore meet or merge is difficult to pinpoint in this dramatic seascape. There is a continuous movement of gulls across the area. Waders will rest and feed here on migration and winter wildfowl provide encouragement for those who will brave the exposure ● TF390385, 4 miles south-east of Boston. Beware tides. **4 5**

9 Scolt Head Island and Blakeney Point Norfolk NCC/NT
In a wild and open landscape of their own making, these sites belong to the sea. The shingle banks are covered by sand and then successions of dune vegetation. Accessible by boat they are worthwhile visiting, not simply for their birdlife but also to witness the power of the sea and the wind in creating and destroying our land ● TF805465 and TG001464 north of A149, by boat or a long walk. Beware tides. **4 5**

10 Lowestoft Harbour and Ness Suffolk
Both are uninspiring man-made features but they bring together the life of the sea and the shore. All sorts of fishing

vessels reflect the range of marine life we hunt off the east coast. The winter flocks of grebes, gulls and sea-ducks are supplemented by rarer sea visitors ● TM550940 Lowestoft town, the Ness is ¼ mile north of harbour. **4 5**

11 Gibraltar Point Lincs. CT
The stretch of coastline out to Gibraltar Point provides one of the best places in Britain to see the accumulation of new land from the sea. The progression from tidelines and windblown sand to dunes clothed in dense shrubs can be followed, with each stage marked by its distinctive plants and animals. The marram grass and sea-buckthorn play vital roles in the seaward extension of dry land. A nationally outstanding list of migrant and resident bird species includes those normally associated with woodland and heath as well as the coast and the sea.

The natural history of this part of the coast is explained by the information centre's exhibitions ● TF556581, 3 miles south of Skegness, follow signs to Seacroft. **5**

12 Holkham Norfolk NCC
For over 20 miles most of the land adjacent to the north Norfolk coast, from Holme to Cley, is under management as a nature reserve. We have selected Holkham and Titchwell (*see* 13 below) because they combine the typical habitats of international significance. Holkham has dunes (stabilised by Corsican pine), salt-marsh, sandflats, mudflats and farmland. It has all the special plants of these habitats including marsh helleborine and orchid species. The bird and invertebrate life is outstanding ● TF892447 north of A149, 2 miles west of Wells. **5**

13 Titchwell Norfolk RSPB
You will always find Titchwell a delightful and rewarding visit. To the Holkham
habitats above can be added brackish
water lagoons, freshwater marshes,
scrub and reed-beds. Birds, invertebrates and amphibians abound. An
exciting day for the expert, it also provides interest and information for the
casual visitor too. The bittern booming
across the reed-beds and the marsh
harrier overhead are as unmistakably
East Anglian as the Norfolk dialect •
TF750436 on A149, 6 miles east of
Hunstanton. **5**

14 Minsmere Suffolk RSPB
This must be one of the world's most
famous nature reserves, yet there is so
much more to Minsmere than the story
of the avocets. It would rank among
the best of the British sites even without
these delicate and beautiful waders.
Coastal flora includes the enormous
marsh sow-thistle and hemp-agrimony.
The entire site is a naturalist's paradise • TM473672 off B1122, 6 miles
north-east of Saxmundham. Limited
opening owing to reserve's considerable popularity. **5**

15 Dunwich Common Suffolk NT
Near to Minsmere, this coastal heathland tells a long story of the Suffolk
natural history. These 'sandlings' are
remnants of once extensive sheep-
grazing heaths with an exceptionally
fine collection of grass species owing to
the distribution of wetter areas. There
are low sandy cliffs down to the pebble
beach where shingle plants, like the
sea pea and yellow horned-poppy, add
further colour and botanical interest
to the site • TM476685 off B1125,
7 miles north-east of Saxmundham. **6**

16 Cavenham Heath Suffolk NCC
This is the most dramatic of the remaining Breckland Heaths. The plants have
to survive acidic and dry conditions,
binding a thin, sandy soil. Historically,
the Brecklands have been farmed with
difficulty. Their heaths and forests are
incongruous landscapes in a region of
otherwise intensively-farmed land. An
impressive range of plants, birds, butterflies and moths can be found. Look for
the resident herd of roe deer and watch
for the adders, too • TL757727 off
A1101, 8 miles north-west of Bury
St Edmunds. **6**

17 The Firs Beds./Hunts. CC
Heaths also occur out on the Green-
sands of Bedfordshire. The Firs has all
the facets of heathland habitats with
a mixture of heather, broom, gorse,
grasses and bracken. In the wetter
patches watch out for gipsywort, and
marsh violet and a further range of
attractive plants • TL028376 off A530
west of Ampthill. **6**

18 Devil's Dyke Cambs. CT/CC
Survivors from the lost Cambridgeshire
Downs clothe the banks of this iron-
age military earthwork. For 7 miles
the chalk flora ranges from grassland
to scrub, and includes the pasque flower,
spring-sedge and bloody crane's-bill
forming a colourful reminder of the richness of the chalk downland now under
arable cultivation • TL570660 to
654585 accesses from B1102, B1061
and A11 between Reach and
Stetchworth. **7**

19 Ouse Washes
Cambs. RSPB/WT/CT
Created in the seventeenth century to
store the surplus winter floodwaters of
the River Great Ouse, the Washes are a

major contribution to the maintenance of the arable land of the fens. The grasslands and ditches are carefully nurtured to encourage their nationally important ornithological and botanical interest. In summer, when the water-level is down, the cattle are surrounded by breeding ruff and black-tailed godwits. But you will see the Washes at their most spectacular in the wintry evening light, when waving skeins of Bewick's swans fly over the banks to splash down among the tens of thousands of wintering wildfowl, roosting and feeding on the flooded grasslands ● TL500880 on B1411 or TL470860 off B1093, east of Manea. **7** **8**

20 Norfolk Rural Museum Norfolk
Arable farming has been the life-blood of East Anglia for hundreds of years. With some of the most productive farmland in the world, every step in the development of agriculture has been witnessed in this region. Some of the most important stages originated here. This museum shows vividly the life and times of the Norfolk farmers over the centuries, their surroundings and their animals ● TF960150, B1146, 3 miles north of East Dereham. **8**

21 Wimpole Home Farm Cambs. NT
Dated 1794, the Home Farm of the superb Wimpole Hall was ahead of its time: a model to demonstrate the newest ideas in farming. The magnificent Great Barn has been restored as a base for an excellent agricultural museum – 350 acres of parkland are grazed with rare breeds of livestock to create a good overall impression of the estate scene 200 years ago ● TL336510, A603, 8 miles south-west of Cambridge. **8**

22 Landguard Suffolk CT/CC
This is a fascinating reserve with a fine pebble beach backed by a broadly level shingle plain and then a wooded bank with Landguard Fort watching over Harwich Harbour entrance. While the plain has delightfully subtle vegetation changes in its many shallow depressions, it is the migrants for which the site is famous. Once we waited and watched for enemies, now we search for the arrival of butterflies and birds from another continent ● TM285319, A45 from Felixstowe via private road to Dock Viewing area. **9** **5**

23 Totternhoe Knolls
Beds./Hunts. CT/CC
The story of the Knolls reflects the changing influence of man's use of the site since he built a Norman castle on the highest point. The gentle chalk-hills were cleared of woodland and grazed by sheep for centuries. Then the layers of harder Totternhoe Stone were quarried leaving a topography of hills and holes, now with a thin turf and a beautiful range of chalkland plants. Orchid species and clustered bellflower are among the less common flowers on the grasslands. The scrub contains ash, privet and spindle; the woodland is dominated by beech. Many of the downland butterflies and moths are present ● SP986216 via B489, 2 miles west of Dunstable. **9** **7**

24 Blickling Estate Norfolk NT
This is a splendid Norfolk estate with a beautiful house and rolling masses of yew hedging at the entrance. The gardens have evolved over hundreds of years with a careful blend of colourful formality, unusual specimen trees and shrubs, and grand avenues. Even the extensive rhododendrons are not as dull and formal as many of their Victorian contemporaries. Wild flowers grow in the woods and birds are everywhere ● TG178286 north of B1354, 10 miles south of Cromer. **9**

25 Sandringham Country Park
Norfolk SE
This famous estate has a most attractive Country Park where the nineteenth-century estate woodlands provide homes for a range of fauna. Squirrels, redpolls, jays and nuthatches are some of the arboreal creatures you can find

regularly, but the resident flocks of crossbills are elusive. The patches of heathland attract breeding nightjars. Follow marked trails to enjoy the quieter areas and see the full range of woodland habitats ● TF689287 turn east off A149, 2 miles south of Dersingham. **9**

26 Willoughby to Farlesthorpe Line
Lincs. CT
A section of derelict railway line has been transformed into an attractive nature reserve. A wealth of meadow plants line the grassy track. The scrub which invaded after the line closed now accommodates breeding and wintering songbirds ● TF467720 to 475736 off B1196, 3 miles south of Alford. **9**

27 Lenwade Water Norfolk CT
This reserve derived from flooded gravel workings attracts those plants and animals which typically colonise new areas of open water, together with some plants associated with the fens. The gravel pit specialists are here too: great crested grebe, reed warbler and sand martin ● TG110184 off A1067, 10 miles north-west of Norwich. **9** **2**

28 Ferry Meadows Country Park
Beds./Hunts. PbDC
Part of the new Nene Valley Regional Park, Ferry Meadows is an exciting new landscape. Flooded gravel workings supplement the enjoyment of woodlands and river meadows and provide a wider range of habitats. The lakes support a range of gravel pit plants, invertebrates, amphibians and a variety of waders and waterfowl – 185 different species of birds have been recorded in the park ● TL145975, north of A605, 5 miles west of Peterborough. **10**

Wildfowl on the Ouse Washes

What is it that unites the wild sandstone landscape of the Brecon Beacons and the beauty of the Pembrokeshire Coast? What links the complex habitats at Oxwich, on the Gower, with the breathtaking gannetry on Grassholm? It is not geology or soils, climate or vegetation, because this region has an extremely diverse collection of different habitats. It is the sense of place which sets this region apart. It is an intangible feature of every site, felt most strongly by the local people and respected by the visitor.

The following selection is intended to show how this part of South Wales is at once romantic and dramatic. The memories of your visits to sites such as Taf Fechan and Castle Woods will evoke the senses of wonder and delight which you felt when you first saw them. They may travel the oceans but the seals of Ramsey Island and the petrels and shearwaters of Skomer are as Welsh as the ravens at Blaenrhondda.

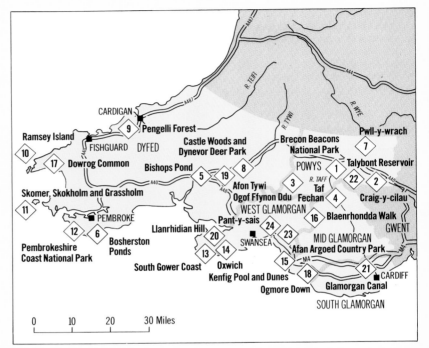

1 Brecon Beacons National Park
Powys/Dyfed/
Gwent/Mid Glam. NPA
From the highest peaks of this wild landscape, you can see the results of massive forces of heat and ice which have modelled the old red sandstones. The glaciers created corrie lakes and scraped the edges of sheer mountain sides. The rivers which swelled as the ice melted cut steep gorges, now wooded, where the grazing sheep and ponies cannot reach them. On the inaccessible ledges of the cliffs grow relics of Brecon's former vegetation: globeflower, purple and mossy saxifrage and great woodrush on the lower slopes. Elsewhere, the moors of heather and bilberry have been transformed to smooth sweeps of grassland. This dramatic landscape is accessible by car with many roads over the National Park, from which the montane animals and plants can be seen. The Brecon Beacons are re-

nowned for their upland birds; watch for the flashing white rumps of the wheatears, and for ring ousel, raven and the rare merlin ● SO050290 roads from Brecon in all directions. ◼

2 Craig-y-cilau Powys NCC
The sweep of chalk white cliffs at Craig-y-cilau gives away the change to limestone rocks and a unique flora. Five exceptionally rare whitebeams with elm, oak, yew and beech are scattered over the steep slopes above a bog. Here in a glacial depression is a small raised bog with round-leaved sundew at the edges. The gushing melt-waters cut out a cave-system beneath the crags which are used for hibernation by lesser horseshoe bats ● SO188159 minor roads off A4077, 6 miles west of Abergavenny. ◼

3 Ogof Ffynon Ddu Powys NCC
The caves are even more spectacular at Ogof Ffynon Ddu (please note a permit is required to enter them). Elsewhere on this site are relic plants surviving in the 'grikes' or narrow slits between the stones of the limestone pavement (you can even see which way the glaciers moved). Secure from grazing sheep are green spleenwort, lily-of-the-valley and mountain melick ● SN867155 off A4067, 15 miles north of Neath. ◼

4 Taf Fechan Glam. DC
In this steep valley is a delightful collection of habitats derived from the influences of water, and then man. Flowing over acidic grits and softer limestones, the ice was followed by a torrential river cutting a deep section through the rocks. Where they are hard and wet grow liverworts, mosses and ferns. At the water's edge are sedges and figworts. After the limestone quarries were abandoned hawthorn, fairy flax and wild thyme took over. The

valley bottom ranges from alder swamp to wet meadows. The water is full of insect larvae feeding brown trout, dippers and wagtails ● SO045097 at Cefn-coed-y-cymmer on A470, 1 mile north-west of Merthyr Tydfil. **2** **10**

5 Bishops Pond Dyfed CT
An ox-bow lake severed from the main flow, this pond marks the former path of the wandering Afon Tywi. Fringed with reed-sweet grass, the pool is dominated by yellow water-lilies in summer. Bewick's swans occasionally join small numbers of wildfowl in winter ● SN446212 off B4300 east of Carmarthen. Access via Country Park adjoining the Carmarthen Museum at Abergwili; 1 mile east of Carmarthen. **2**

6 Bosherston Ponds Dyfed NT
One of the region's few large areas of open freshwater was created as recently as 1790 to 1840, when three narrow limestone valleys were dammed. The drowned valleys are edged with yellow iris, reed-beds and water mint, together with extensive beds of white water-lilies and stonewort. Fed by now submerged springs, these clear waters support a variety of aquatic insects and birds such as the reed warbler. Otters and wintering wildfowl add further interest to a reserve which ranges from wooded limestone slopes through thorn scrub to sand dunes and sea cliffs ● SR966948 south of B4319 via Bosherston or Stackpole, 4 miles south of Pembroke. **2** **10**

7 Pwll-y-wrach Powys CT
Here you will find woodland which is very like the former natural cover of the steep river valleys of the Brecon Beacons. The upper slopes of sandstone are dominated by tall oak with a good understorey lower down on the harder shelf of limestone. By the waterfall there is ash and spindle. Part of the area is now being coppiced and this attracts speckled wood, comma and fritillary butterflies. The carpet of woodland flowers beneath the oak is best in the spring ● SO163327 on minor roads, 1 mile south-east of Talgarth. **3**

8 Castle Woods and Dynevor Deer Park Dyfed CT
This is one of the most exciting woodlands in South Wales and is on a limestone bluff above the Afon Tywi. The woodland is primarily oak and wych-elm, the latter decimated by disease. The shrub and ground cover is outstanding, with cherry, holly, spindle, dog-violet and the parasitic toothwort. Lichen communities are of importance and include the rare lungwort. Overlooked by the romantic castle of Dynevor, the fine, old parkland has herds of fallow deer. The mature trees attract woodpeckers, redstarts and pied flycatchers. In winter the water meadows draw large numbers of ducks.

Lichens are a speciality ● SN627220 off A40 through the town park at Llandeilo. **3**

9 Pengelli Forest Dyfed CT
Seventy years ago these woods were clear-felled for charcoal and mining timber. The trees have regrown from coppice stools to form an attractive habitat with a most distinctive flora and fauna. Polecats, badgers, frogs, lizards and slow-worms are among the inhabitants of this maturing forest, which remains the largest block of primary oak woodland in the area. It is an example of how the continuity of woodlands can survive the axe if the axe is not followed by the plough ● SN124395 off minor roads from A487, 10 miles east of Fishguard. **3**

10 Ramsey Island Dyfed
Of all the ocean mammals the grey seal is the most appealing and the one which affords us the best opportunity to study at close range. On the northern tip of St Bride's Bay and standing the full force of the Atlantic gales, this inshore island has the most important colonies of chough and grey seals in Wales ● SM700235, daily boats from St Justinian's, June to September. **4**

11 Skomer, Skokholm and Grassholm Dyfed CT/RSPB
Three of the most spectacular sea-bird colonies on the British coast, these islands will eventually draw every bird-watcher to view the spectacle. On Grassholm – an almost bare rock in the Atlantic – there are 28,000 pairs of noisy, aggressive gannets fighting to protect their mini territories. The puffins tunnelled the old peat here so thoroughly it collapsed and all but a few have moved away.

Skokholm is larger, more accessible and closer to land with some interesting vegetation. The most maritime of all our sea-birds nest here and so we have the perfect opportunity to see them – Manx shearwater, storm petrel, puffin, guillemot and razorbill.

Skomer is the largest of the three and battered into its present dramatic shape by waves, wind and ice. Waves cut a platform on a tide line now nearly 200 feet above sea-level. Then glaciers moving down the Irish Sea deposited strange boulders from northern Eng-

The Brecon Beacons

Skomer Island: greater black-backed gull among thrift

land. Erosion continues today: Midland Island has been more recently severed and soon the striking isthmus known as the Neck will be detached from Skomer.

The thunder of waves and screams of the sea-birds should not distract the visitor entirely from a good range of heath and moorland plant communities including yellow-eyed-grass, presumably introduced from America by a migrant bird. To the breeding bird list for the islands can be added kittiwake and fulmar, gulls, wheatear, peregrine falcon and many others. The 100,000 pairs of nocturnal Manx shearwaters could go unnoticed by the day visitor. The Skomer vole is bigger, lighter in colour and has a different skull shape to its mainland relative, the bank vole. There is a large marine nature reserve beneath the waves of the inland waters around Skomer and Marloes peninsula.

All three islands form an important part of the Pembrokeshire Coast National Park (*see* 12 below) and may be visited during the summer but strict control is operated on numbers, and sailings need to be arranged in advance ● Adverse weather can preclude any access at short notice. 🄴

12 Pembrokeshire Coast National Park
Dyfed NPA
The smallest of our National Parks is all the more appealing because its wide range of habitats are to be found in such a concentrated area. The coastal scenery ranks among the finest in the British Isles and the bays and drowned valleys have rafts of scoters, other sea-ducks and auks. The estuaries offer sheltered accommodation for west-coast migrant insects and birds, and the dunes, farmland and cliffs seen from the coastal path provide enjoyable and fascinating walks at any time of year – particularly in spring when the coastal flora is at its best ● Pembrokeshire coastal path from Cardigan to Carmarthen Bay. 🄵

13 South Gower Coast
Glam. CT/NCC/NT
If you can visit the Gower when it is free of the crowds of holiday-makers, you will find a wild landscape of natural beauty with a great deal of wildlife interest. The cliffs and shallow limestone grasslands have a comprehensive list of plant species including small restharrow and goldilocks aster. Incapable of spreading, even in suitable habitats, these plants must be the survivors which weathered the glaciers on these ice-free cliffs but which could not spread, like the other plants, when the grip of the Ice Age was released. The coastal sites are of exceptional interest for their flora and fauna ● SS470840 at Port Eynon (A4118) then east to Mumbles Head and north to Whiteford Point. 🄵 🄰

14 Oxwich Glam. NCC
If you want to follow the natural progression of almost all the coastal plant communities from the tidal zone to the cliff top then Oxwich is the site to visit. A trail leads you from the sea-holly and saltwort of the sandy beach, through marram-grass dunes and calcium-rich, damp hollows with common centaury and dune gentian. On the more stable slopes bracken grows where rain has washed out the calcium – wild privet and carline thistle prosper where it hasn't. Before the woodland trail is a grass sward with clover and then the scrub of hawthorn and gorse maturing to tall oak and ash woods before the rising land levels off to cliff-top grassland. This wonderland of habitat progression supports an equally varied fauna of reptiles, mammals and birds ● SS501865 immediately south of A4118 on Gower Peninsula, 9 miles west of Swansea. 🄵 🄶 🄷

15 Kenfig Pool and Dunes Glam. CC
The fact that 500 flowering plants have been recorded on this reserve is sufficient to indicate its importance and richness. There is a full range of dune vegetation types. A clean reed-fringed pool provides a comprehensive range of wetland habitats too, from open water to willow and birch woodland. A botanist's delight, this site will reward those looking for birds and insects too. It tells its own story of how the habitats are constantly developing and the wildlife is changing within them ● SS802815 Kenfig village, 3 miles north of Porthcawl on minor roads. 🄵

16 Blaenrhondda Walk Glam. CC/FC
Wide sweeps of moorland at the head of the most famous industrial valleys in the world with heather, bilberry and the delightful yellow tormentil. Pipits, wheatears and wagtails cheer this upland walk ● SN922021 at Blaenrhondda, 2 miles north of Treorchy off A4061. 🄶

17 Dowrog Common Dyfed CT
The pattern of different plants growing in the varying soils and wet and dry conditions is very apparent on this lowland heath with pools. The wealth of flowering plants include a number of scarcer species and the pools provide an excellent habitat for dragonflies and

the rare marsh fritillary. The wintering birds are regularly joined by wildfowl and hen harrier ● SM769268 minor road from A487 crosses the common 2 miles north-east of St David's and provides a good vantage point. **6**

18 Ogmore Down Glam. CT
The Downs are valuable remnants of much more extensive grasslands destroyed by quarries. Where the soil is thin, the lime-loving plants grow in colourful profusion, controlled by grazing. In the deeper soils the lime has been partly washed away and a fascinating mixture of limestone and acidic plants grow together: rock-rose with tormentil, or lady's bedstraw with cross-leaved heath. Glow-worms can be found, feeding on the plentiful supply of snails which love the shell-building limestone soils ● SS897762 west of B4265, park in St Bride's Major, 3 miles south of Bridgend. **7**

19 Afon Tywi Dyfed
This region of coastal cliffs and heaths, of exposed moors and mountainsides, supports a relatively small proportion of arable land. If you follow the Afon Tywi up its valley you will see the ploughland along the coastal plains change to small fields clinging to the lower valley slopes and eventually disappear as the Beacons are approached. Relying heavily on their animals, the farmers have always supplemented their produce from the sea and the rivers. Here on the Tywi they still launch coracles to net the salmon and trout. Notice how the fields change shape and size as the valley grows steeper and higher and the land becomes too poor to plough at all ● SN420200 following A40 from Carmarthen to Llandovery then minor roads into the hills. **8**

20 Llanrhidian Hill Glam. CT
The disused limestone quarries made a tough start for the colonising scrub and grassland plants but elder, hawthorn and ash have succeeded with grassland species. Stonechat and linnet

occupy the shrubby cover ● SS497922 off B4295 near Llanrhidian on the Gower. **10**

21 Glamorgan Canal Glam. DC
Powerful forces are clearly at work as nature covers the canal and railway cutting we have left behind. Arrowhead and yellow loosestrife grow in the marsh and canal. There is strong woodland colonisation, enough to attract woodpeckers, siskin and redpoll ● ST143803 in Cardiff city. **10**

22 Talybont Reservoir Powys CT/NPA
A long, deep reservoir high in the Brecon Beacons and lying in a steep-sided valley. The shores vary from muddy cliffs to flat areas ideal for greenshank, green sandpiper and many other waders too. The greatest attraction for the visitor to this man-made landscape feature is the huge flocks of wintering wildfowl: dabbling ducks, mallard, wigeon and teal around the edge; diving duck, including tufted and goldeneye, in the deeper waters ● SO098190 turn off B4558 at Talybont, 5 miles south-east of Brecon. **10**

23 Afan Argoed Country Park Glam. CC
Coniferous forests cover a significant part of this region and the pine and larch forests on the steep valley slopes of Afan Argoed are typical of these quiet, evergreen woods. Pockets of much older woodland occur in the plantations which hold many of the plant and animal species which do well in the shade ● SS821951 off A4107, 6 miles north-east of Port Talbot. **10**

24 Pant-y-sais Glam. DC
Sandwiched between the Tennant canal and the B4290 road and crossed by a railway lies a striking example of twentieth-century nature conservation. Close to the massive oil refineries and the modern industrial landscape of Neath is a narrow strip of rich fen. Reeds, bulrush and royal fern on the fen, white water-lilies on the canal and scrub on the towpath. From trees to aquatic plants this site offers an important sanctuary for a wide range of plants and their associated insects ● SS713939 between Neath and Swansea off the B4290. **10**

Gower coastline

13 THE CHILTERNS AND COTSWOLDS

Perhaps your favourite impressions of these hill ranges in southern England are of their villages, some of the most picturesque in the country. Perhaps, though, you remember the gentle hills of chalk and limestone, dry valleys, beechwoods and rolling downland. The colourful downland turfs and rich woodlands are full of song and the activitites of birds and butterflies.

Exceptionally rare plants have drawn botanists to the Avon Gorge for a century and more, and it is still the plants and their associated insects which attract naturalists to the Cotswolds and Chilterns today. There are other fascinating sites to explore, including a magnificent park at Blenheim, the world's greatest wildfowl collection at Slimbridge, outstanding coastal habitats at Brean Down and new wetlands at the Cotswold Water Park and Stony Stratford.

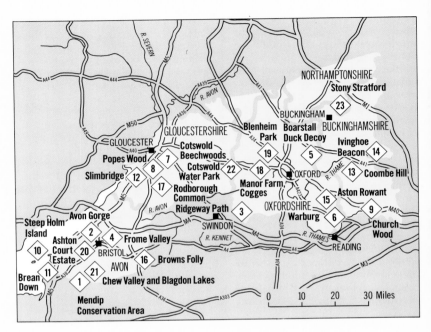

1 Mendip Conservation Area
Avon/Somerset CT
No one can fail to be impressed by the richness and diversity of this group of three reserves. The dramatic geology of the quarries spans thousands of years when the caves in Long Wood were occupied by hyena and woolly rhinoceros. The wood is dominated by ash and contains a superb display of ferns on the rocky slopes. Velvet Bottom is pitted by the lead workings from pre-Roman times to the 1880s and now forms ungrazed grassland ideal for butterflies. The woodland on the Black Rock ranges from native broad-leaved stands to modern coniferous plantations ● ST482545 off B3135 near Cheddar, for the Black Rock reserve. **1**

2 Avon Gorge Avon NCC
This deep, narrow gorge has long been famous for its unique botanical interest. The carboniferous limestones are exposed on steep cliffs and the woods have an international botanical importance. The Bristol whitebeam is found nowhere else in the world. There are many other exceptionally rare species, including Bristol rock-cress and some rare sedges. These plants have evolved in the isolation of the gorge, relatively secure from the changes around. Man's influence has been present but was limited to the iron-age hill fort and woodland management, including the coppicing of hazel which continues today ● ST553731 off A369 at Clifton Bridge. **1**

3 Ridgeway Path
Oxon. and Bucks. C Com
This ancient trackway follows the line of chalk hills giving splendid views across the plain of Aylesbury. It passes Aston Rowant reserve (see 15 below) and ends at Ivinghoe Beacon (see 14 below). It is a relic of the earliest days of travel when the rolling chalk hills were cleared and farmed and trading links established with the south. In spring and early summer you can enjoy the spectacle of the chalkland flowers and butterflies in a man-made habitat held in a time-capsule for thousands of years ● SU259833 from south-east of Swindon to SP770013 the Chilterns near Princes Risborough. **1** **7**

4 Frome Valley Avon BNS
Within the Bristol city boundary this trail, beside a fast-flowing river, provides an opportunity to see waterside plants, animals and birds. An occasional king-fisher or heron may be seen fishing, or a delightful grey wagtail chasing insects. Look for arrowhead and river water-crowfoot among the water-plants ● ST622765 approx. 3 miles north-east of Bristol city centre. **2**

5 Boarstall Duck Decoy
Bucks. CT/NT
One of the few remaining working decoys in Britain where in winter you can watch the dog enticing the wildfowl

278

into ever narrower channels of the netted enclosure. The ducks eventually can be ringed and released. Apart from the decoy demonstrations, there is a fine mixed woodland to enjoy. Demonstrations are held twice daily at weekends and Bank Holidays, or as published by The National Trust ● SP623151 west of B4011, 8 miles north-west of Thame. **2**

6 Warburg Oxon. CT
For its size and diversity the woodland habitat of Warburg is outstanding. You will find open chalk grassland, old meadows, banks and scrub, but the woodland dominates. The tall trees include beech, yew, sycamore, and sweet chestnut and conifers. The understorey shrubs and trees range from dogwood, privet, spindle, field maple and wayfaring tree. Woodcock, wood warbler and willow tit are three examples from the wood's long list of breeding birds and the moths have some fascinating names: maple prominent, scarce footman, clay triple lines and map-winged swift moths ● SU720880 off A423 near Bix, 3 miles north-west of Henley-on-Thames. **3**

7 Cotswold Beechwoods Glos. NCC
If you would like to see how the Cotswolds looked before their thin limestone soils were cleared and farmed, then this string of woodlands on the steeper slopes will provide the answer. Although they were coppiced once, present-day management tends to re-create the natural woodland of 5000 years ago. This is beech high forest with a rich flora associated with limestone. Amongst the carpet of brambles, ivy, dog's mercury, sanicle and wood spurge are the rarer bird's-nest orchids and the common wintergreen ● Buckholt Wood SO894131 off A46, 6 miles south of Cheltenham. **3**

8 Popes Wood Glos. CT
Another mature beech woodland which will dispel the idea that beechwoods have uninteresting ground cover. Here too, the structure of the wood has a wealth of interest. Green hellebores, spurge-laurels and orchid species are present. The cover provides for a good range of woodland songbirds ● SO875128 off A46, 7 miles south of Cheltenham. **3**

Cotswold beechwood with ground flora

279

9 Church Wood Bucks. RSPB
Where two of the region's main rock types merge near the surface, the resulting woodlands are very varied. Church Wood has a mixture of the beech, hornbeam and yew on the chalk with oak and birch on the more acidic flinty clays. Two hundred plants and 80 species of birds tell their own story about the richness of wildlife here. White admiral and purple and white-letter hairstreak butterflies enjoy the woody clearings and rides. The dense cover of shrub species attract the nesting warblers ● SU973873 off A355, 2 miles south of junction 2 M40. **3**

10 Steep Holm Island Avon KAMT
You can visit this offshore island sanctuary by boat from Weston-super-Mare and find the most remarkable range of wildlife species. Cormorants, gulls and other sea-birds breed here, with slow-worms, hedgehogs and muntjac deer.

An incongruous mixture of creatures from the land and the sea, which is complemented by the plants including the rare wild peony and wild leeks ● Offshore by boat from Weston-super-Mare, from April to October. **4**

11 Brean Down Avon NT
An extension to the Mendip Hills jutting out into the southern estuary, Brean Down is a massive ridge of limestone. You will find the south slope is steeper, with jackdaws, kestrels and rock pipits on rocky ledges, while the north side of the ridge slopes gradually to the estuary with its mudflats and salt-marsh. Peak migration times bring thousands of birds to the reserve and nearby coastline ● ST296586 off A370 south of Weston-super-Mare. **5**

12 Slimbridge Glos. WT
The world's most comprehensive collection of wildfowl also ranks as one of the region's most important estuary sites. Vast expanses of mudflats, salt-marsh, grazing meadows and lagoons can be viewed. They hold nationally important populations of waders as well as geese and ducks. The largest winter flocks of Bewick's swans and white-fronted geese in Britain can assemble on this part of the Severn Estuary at Slimbridge. Migration and population studies carried out from here are explained at the Trust's centre ● SO723048 off A38, 7 miles west of Stroud. **5 7**

13 Coombe Hill Nature Trail Bucks. NT
In a region centred on the chalk and limestone soils, acidic heaths are uncommon but form an important contrast to the lime-loving species elsewhere. Along this nature trail you will see the difference between the chalk slopes with juniper, yew and whitebeam and the clay with flints on the hill-

Winter wildfowl at Slimbridge

tops where broom, gorse and heather flourish. The walk to the top is rewarded by panoramic views to the Cotswolds and the Berkshire downs ● SP853063 west of A413, 6 miles south of Aylesbury. **6**

14 Ivinghoe Beacon Bucks. NT
The views from these hills attract many visitors and the chalky slopes are well trodden. Nevertheless, there are quieter areas where steeper slopes, thinner soils and fewer feet allow the typical chalkland flowers to survive; kidney and horseshoe vetches, bird's-foot-trefoil, milkwort with yellow rattle and orchids. Grazing is used in order to keep the grasslands clear of the invading scrub, where trampling feet do not suppress its growth ● SP961168 off B489, 5 miles south of Leighton Buzzard. **7**

15 Aston Rowant Oxon. NCC
Despite being severed by the construction of the M40 motorway, this national nature reserve retains its importance as the finest example of the vegetation of the Chilterns. Over one-third of the reserve is covered with the superb ancient downland turf including the rare Chiltern gentian and pale toadflax. Insects are exceptional too with dark green fritillaries and rarer skippers. Beech woodland and scrub widen the reserve's appeal, particularly for the birds ● SU741967 north of A40, 6 miles south-west of Princes Risborough. **7**

16 Browns Folly Avon CT
You can sit on the terraces of limestone downland and see over the canopy of mixed woodland around. Browns Folly is an isolated building standing on a massive rock high above the Avon. From here was once quarried the famous stone of Bath but the woodland and grassland now cover the old quarries. Woolly thistle and agrimony are found in the grassy spaces ● ST798664 off the A363, 3 miles northwest of Bradford on Avon. **7**

17 Rodborough Common Glos. NT
On this plateau of characteristic Cotswold downland we find a fascinating distribution of lime-loving grassland plants. On the thinner soils of the steep slopes occur scabious, harebell, rockrose and eyebright. On the level land with deeper soils the different grazing patterns result in both short and long grass growth and yellow rattle, greater knapweed and kidney vetch are common. There is the usual range of butterflies and moths associated with downlands. The site is famous for its orchid displays ● SO852035 off A419 near Stroud. **7**

18 Manor Farm, Cogges Oxon.
In a range of Cotswold stone farm buildings you can see the workings of an Edwardian Oxfordshire farm. Local breeds of livestock include the Oxford down sheep, the Oxford sandy and black pigs. A history trail leads to a deserted village and to the remains of ancient field systems around Cogges ● SP370095 off A40 near Witney. **8**

19 Blenheim Park Oxon. DOM
It is clear from the many ancient oaks in the park that some of the site's existing features were incorporated into the Duke's grand designs for this most dramatic parkland creation. A fine example of how the wildlife occupied the new opportunities of amenity planting in the eighteenth century and earlier. A nature trail leads around the park, woodlands and lake. The variety of birds is outstanding ● SP442168 off A34 at Woodstock. **9**

20 Ashton Court Estate Avon BNS
Attractive parkland spreads over both acid and lime-rich soils. In a small area we can compare the vegetation of the two: the bracken and birch typical of the acid heath, or the plants associated with the limestone scrub or grassland– the common rock-rose and green hellebore. Both habitats attract good insect populations but quite different species. The variety of the woodland is further increased by the presence of exotic species and there are many native trees and shrubs. The nature walk round

this old parkland may provide close views of fallow deer and sunny summer days can be excellent for seeing butterflies ● ST554726 off A370 on western outskirts of Bristol. **9**

21 Chew Valley and Blagdon Lakes Avon BWC
These very large reservoirs have mainly natural banks which attract nesting water-birds including gadwall, mallard and shelduck. The rapid spread of the ruddy duck since its escape into the wild has been assisted by the availability of such large man-made open water sites. The reservoirs also provide wintering grounds for wildfowl and waders and feeding areas for tired migrants ● ST570615 north of A368, 14 miles west of Bath. **10 2**

22 Cotswold Water Park Glos. CT
When we see nature reserves in the making we can feel the sense of optimism and excitement as we witness the creation of valuable new habitats. The full effects of the loss of wetland in the Thames Valley will never be known to us. The range of plants and animals we may have found here 2000 or 5000 years ago can never be appreciated fully. After excavating the valley terraces for their gravel we have left a series of shallow, lime-rich pools of fresh water. These may persuade some of the native species of the marshes to return. An ever-increasing range of plants and animals live here and many more species of birds call on their travels. As the vegetation of the pools matures it provides marvellous opportunities for us to study the colonisation of new habitats ● SP215007 off A361, $\frac{1}{2}$ mile north of Lechlade. **10 2**

23 Stony Stratford Bucks. CT
The river valley water conservation area was established in 1980 specifically as a new nature reserve following the extraction of sand and gravel for the construction of the new A5. Primarily, it provides breeding grounds for waders but open water and islands are also available. The establishment of a good aquatic vegetation cover has been assisted by transferring water-plants from the nearby canal. Wildfowl, redshank, ringed plover and kingfisher all use this new site ● SP785412 off A5 west of Milton Keynes. **10**

It is interesting to consider the impact of one of the greatest cities in the world spreading out over the heaths, forests, marshes and downs. But even as London sprawled, pockets of countryside were left. Greatly modified by their urban surroundings, Epping Forest, Regent's Park and Wimbledon Common are valuable reminders of the former scene. Now the cycle of urban development has come full circle. On the derelict banks of canals at Camley Street and St Pancras, conservationists are creating new urban habitats.

Despite being so densely populated, the south-east has a complex pattern of many types of countryside, accessible to the visitor and liberally distributed across its landscapes. You may choose the popular Box Hill–a splendid downland site–or you may prefer the fascination of Kentish wetlands at Stodmarsh. Thursley (a Surrey heath), Lyddon (Kent downland) and The Men's (ancient Sussex woodland) are other representatives of these special retreats now protected so we can enjoy the countryside and its wildlife.

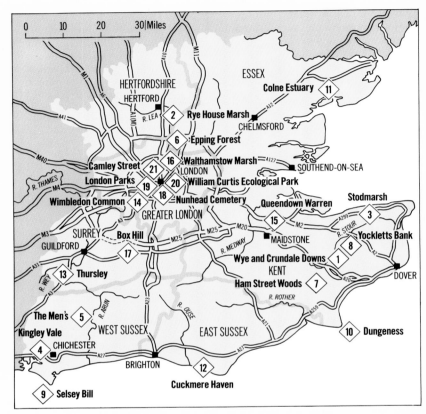

1 Wye and Crundale Downs
Kent NCC
If you stand on the edge of Coomb Head and look down the steep-sided valley of the Devil's Kneading Trough you will see a dramatic sweep of lush grassland and farmland beyond. But 12,000 years ago this same site was a frozen waste. You are standing on a thin layer of soil over a massive thickness of chalk. Even the soft chalks are harder rocks than the clays of the Weald around and have withstood the erosion of wind and rain and scraping glaciers. About 10,000 years ago, at the end of the Ice Age, the surface of these chalky hills was shattered by the constant freezing and thawing of the tundra soils as the influence of the ice diminished. During the thaws, gushing melt-water from the ice and snow on

the Downs where you are standing pushed the broken earth down to the plain below. Thus the dry valley, or Coomb, you can see was created. Plants took a foothold in the shallow soils. Grazing animals, first wild deer and then sheep and cattle, trampled out the narrow 'terracettes' on the sides of the Kneading Trough. These animals prevented the invasion of woodland and scrub (they have not continuously grazed on the adjacent Pickersdane scrub), and the specialist grassland plants could thrive, including sheep's-fescue, hoary plantain and dwarf thistle. Today the site is outstanding for orchids. Uncommon species include the musk orchid in the short turf, and fly orchid in longer grass ● TR077455 on minor roads 4 miles north-east of Ashford. ■ ▇

2 Rye House Marsh   Herts   RSPB
This marsh is rich in plant species and full of insects on which feed a splendid range of wetland birds. From the warblers in the reed-beds to the swallows and swifts catching the insects in flight, the intricate food chains are beautifully illustrated by the variety of bird species, each having adapted to its own food source. Hides provide excellent viewing and your birdwatching will be made more exciting by the terns which stay to breed and migrants which briefly pass through. The marsh also provides winter quarters for water-rail, snipe and ducks ● TL386100 by the river Lee at Hoddesdon off the A10. ▇

3 Stodmarsh   Kent NCC
The wetlands of the Stour Valley had all but disappeared through drainage

schemes when subsidence, due to underground coal workings, recreated the marshland of the past. Lagoons and reed-beds are full of reed and bul-rush, dykes have bogbean and spear-wort and elsewhere are typical plant communities of the bank and wet scrub. The rare bittern, bearded tit, Cetti's and Savi's warblers are here. In winter the watery habitats attract dabbling ducks. There is a long list of migrant birds regularly using the marsh as a resting and feeding station. Flooded meadows with mare's-tail and sea club-rush provide food for wildfowl ● TR222607 walk along the Lampen wall or the river wall. On minor roads 5 miles north-east of Canterbury. **2**

4 Kingley Vale Sussex NCC
In the beautiful chalk valley of Kingley Vale is one of the finest yew woodlands in Europe. There is no better place to see what a mature yew-wood looks like. It is a strange and magical place. For over 500 years these ancient, twisted trees have slowly welded a canopy of dark green foliage, so dense and cool it has excluded all but a handful of plants beneath. On the slopes are younger trees, only 50 to 250 years old, with ash where the yew have slipped from the hill to create a gap. Elsewhere the woodland cover of the reserve changes to oak and ash, with holly, buckthorn, spindle and dogwood ● SU824088 near West Stoke off A286, 4 miles north-west of Chichester. **3**

5 The Men's Sussex CT
You will find that the Men's group of woodlands are remarkable by any standards. They are, to most visitors, a beautiful and emotive image of true woodland. They are also of immense historical importance and you will not be in them for long before you realise they have a wealth of wildlife interest too. This combination is not by chance. It is through man's continuous influence on the native woodland which must have been here 3000 years ago. Trees in the Men's had to be pollarded or left to grow as high forest because grazing animals would have destroyed the traditional coppice growth of other Sussex woods. More than any other, the Men's looks like the native wildwood of Sussex. The full range of woodland plants and animals are therefore able to find a home. Deer and fungi are outstanding but the entire woodland ecology is of importance ● TQ024236 on A272, 3 miles east of Petworth. **3**

6 Epping Forest
Essex City of London Corporation
The 5000 acres or so of Epping today are the remnants of an ancient woodland which spread over almost the whole of Essex and beyond. This was a grazing wood where animals continuously foraged the forest floor and browsed the trees. The small-leaved lime was once the dominant native tree but the less palatable oak and beech better survived the grazing. Pollarding was the principal form of management since the Middle Ages but was abandoned about a century ago, since then the growth from the ancient trunks has spread uncontrolled, creating peculiar shapes and a thicker canopy over the wood. The site is of national significance for invertebrates but the breeding herds of roe and fallow deer have left ● TQ412981 on A104 between Chingford and Epping. Forest museum at Queen Elizabeth's Hunting Lodge, Rangers Road, Chingford. **3**

7 Ham Street Woods Kent NCC
On the southern edge of the Weald clay where it slopes down to the flat expanse of Romney Marsh you will find a large area of damp oak woodlands managed under the traditional coppice with standards system. The diversity of woodland habitats provide for a superb range of woodland birds, from the tits in the high crowns of the trees to wrens and dunnocks on the forest floor ● TR010340, 1 mile north of Ham Street village on A2070, 4 miles south of Ashford. **3**

8 Yockletts Bank Kent CT
If you want to see chalk woodland and its grassy glades at their best this site is a classic. Ash, oak, beech and hornbeam grow over shrubs which include dog-wood, maple and the wayfaring tree. These are crowned by a superb display of common spotted, early purple, fly and pyramidal orchids and other spring flowers. Badgers and nightingales represent two species of the many mammals and birds on the reserve ● TR125467 on minor roads east of B2068, 8 miles south of Canterbury. **3 7**

9 Selsey Bill Sussex
Projecting out into the English Channel this area has been swamped by develop-ment yet still holds its place as a favourite haunt of sea-bird watchers. The oceanic species pass by and the divers and grebes which resort to the sea in winter gather in flocks off the Bill ● SX860925 at the end of B2145, 8 miles south of Chichester. **4**

Reed-beds at Stodmarsh

10 Dungeness Kent RSPB
Probably the largest shingle ridge in
Europe, the scale of this massive heap
of stones dumped by the sea is awe-
inspiring. Within is an intricate range
of habitats from small pools to pockets
of grassland. Altogether it is one of the
most exciting birdwatching sites in the
country. It is migration that makes
Dungeness spectacular, as it is the first
landfall for birds such as the wryneck
and bluethroat or clouded yellow
butterflies ● TR063196 minor roads
to Dungeness, 4 miles south-east of
Lydd. ▣

11 Colne Estuary
Essex   NCC/CT *et al.*
The wide spreads of colour over the
salt-marsh remind us that these coastal
estuaries can be both beautiful and
interesting for their plants as well as
their birds. Sea-blite, sea-beet and sea
wormwood indicate the maritime origins
of the plants. The tidal mudflats are
less picturesque but attract the brent
geese and thousands of waders ●
TM085154 off B1027 through St Osyth
to sea wall and creek. ▣

12 Cuckmere Haven Sussex CC/DC
The Cuckmere Valley itself is attractive
downland but from the Haven to Beachy
Head is some of the best chalk coast in
the country. The famous Seven Sisters
extend the scene west to Seaford. The
cliffs are like spectacular chalk walls.
The whole area is defined as the Seven
Sisters Heritage Coast and is renowned
for its chalk downland plants, including
such rarities as the burnt orchid and
early spider-orchid. Fulmar nest on the
cliffs, and terns and ringed plovers on
the shore ● TV518995 south of A259
between Eastbourne and Seaford. ▣

13 Thursley Surrey NCC
There is a special story of man and
wildlife on Thursley. The mists of time
still roll across one of the most important lowland heath and bog sites in
southern England. They must have
shrouded the first farmers who felled
the wildwood, covered the exhausted
farmland as it reverted to heath and
then concealed a continuing history of
human enterprise: peat digging, iron
working, grazing, burning, wildfowling,
military training and, finally, conserving this valuable site. There is a

quite outstanding range of plants and
animals in the heath, pools, scrub and
bog. You can experience for yourself
the true character of rich and ancient
heathland ● SU915400 is the access
gate on the A3, 2½ miles south-west of
Milford. ▣

14 Wimbledon Common
Greater London   Wimbledon and
Putney Common Conservators
Of immense value, owing to its accessi-
bility, this heath is also very interesting

because of its range of habitats. Higher,
gravelly areas are grass with gorse and
birch scrub; oakwoods and hornbeams
do well on the clay slopes and bogbean
and sundew are found in the two valley
bogs. Reptiles are always a surprise
to find – lizard and grass snake are
present ● London SW19. ▣

15 Queendown Warren Kent CT
From its origins as a commercial rabbit
warren over 700 years ago, the continuous grazing and nibbling of the

Bell heather on Thursley Heath

284

grass has provided the short turf suited to rock-rose, wild thyme and marjoram. Occasionally a beech seedling survived the grazing, or was deliberately planted and these stand over the pastures. The scrub and wood indicate where grazing once stopped. Chalkhill blue butterflies and grasshoppers are not difficult to find in summer ● TQ827629, 2 miles north-west of A249 about 5 miles west of Sittingbourne. **7**

16 Walthamstow Marsh
Greater London LVA
One of the last remnants of long-established grassland in the Lee valley, these fields are typical wet meadows. Sedges and reeds are among a surprising variety of 350 species of plants recorded here ● London E5. **7**

17 Box Hill Surrey NT
Box Hill is first and foremost a marvellous open space for everyone to enjoy. It also happens to be a very good example of chalk downland and woodland. There are several woodland types but the most notable is full of box and yew. The scrub on the edges of the woods contains whitebeam, dogwood and wayfaring tree while the wild cherry adds a splash of colour in the spring. The open downland, created by centuries of animal grazing, has a full range of chalkland butterflies and contains nearly 400 species of plants including many types of orchid. Intensive public access has not destroyed the wildlife value of this splendid natural playground ● TQ179513, 1 mile north-east of Dorking on A24. **7** **3**

18 Nunhead Cemetery
Greater London DC
You can find little gems of nature hidden all over the city but this small reserve in a cemetery is truly curious. Dominated by the prolific growth of the sycamore which thrives in these tough

urban spaces, over 100 other plants have started their process of colonisation. Watch for butterflies and, in the evening, foxes ● Linden Grove, Peckham, London SE15. **9**

19 London Parks Greater London
For Londoners, Regent's Park and others like it are indispensable. The hand-fed chaffinches, squirrels and pigeons are only the more obvious tip of a much larger proportion of species relying on man's urban environment. Each park is different, with its own character and its own distinctive blend of wildlife. Resident or migrant visitors, native or introduced species, however well-adjusted the animals may be, they will eventually need to seek the water, shelter, security or food supply of the urban parklands. The range of habitats and species is surprising; we have underestimated how nature can adjust to even our harshest environment in the centre of our greatest city ● Central London: Hyde, Regent's, Richmond and St James's Parks. **9**

20 William Curtis Ecological Park
Greater London
The cycle of habitats has come full circle. As the city expanded, the site was developed for housing at the expense of woodland and wetland. In time the houses were demolished and on the derelict lorry park which followed was established an important

and pioneering project. The park was planted with trees and shrubs, including alders and willows. A pond was dug to attract water-birds and insects. Toads, frogs and slow-worms are among the remarkable inhabitants. The black redstart, the most urban of all our birds, is here too ● 16 Vine Lane, Tooley Street, London SE1. **10**

21 Camley Street
Greater London LWT
Sometimes the natural colonisation of derelict land can form the basis of a new future for the wildlife of the city. On a piece of derelict land adjacent to the canal in Camden, the Camley Street Natural Park has been created. It is a wildlife refuge and a place where people can go to enjoy nature in the city centre. The pond supports aquatic plants and amphibians while reed-beds and marsh provide breeding areas for birds and food for dragonflies. Meadow plants support butterflies and bees in the summer months, while many species of birds can feed from the scrub surrounding the whole park. Alder and willow complement the buddleia which existed here prior to the construction of the park ● Camley Street, London NW1. **10**

Nunhead cemetery

From the high, rolling downs to the Somerset levels there is a richness of colour and activity, a variety of habitats and a finely balanced enjoyment of the rare and the familiar. Throughout this region the antiquity of man's presence and the evidence he has left behind are strikingly clear. From the iron-age tracks of Wiltshire to the motorway in Berkshire the passage of man and his influence on the wildlife around him is apparent. The entire region is like a living museum and a very impressive one too. Who could fail to admire the phenomena of Chesil Bank or the Needles, or wonder at the natural history of the New Forest? Who could not share Gilbert White's enthusiasm for the beechwoods, or Thomas Hardy's respect for the heaths? Most of this region lies in the area which Hardy called Wessex and we could not think of a better name for this romantic region.

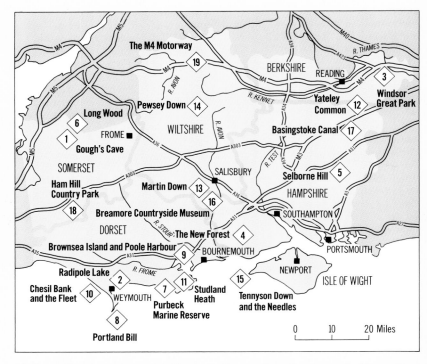

1 Gough's Cave Somerset
We can learn much from human occupation of this cave about the animals of the post-glacial era. A necklace of fox's teeth and the bones of horses, bears and wolves, which the occupants had eaten, are clues to the past. Occupied during the retreat of the glaciers 12,000 to 8000 BC, Gough's Cave must have been a warm and secure shelter in an icy landscape ● ST475545 off B3135, 8 miles north-west of Wells. ■

2 Radipole Lake Dorset RSPB
Changes in wetland habitats can be surprisingly fast and take place for many different reasons. This freshwater lake and reed-bed was part of the tidal estuary of the River Wey only 60 years ago. Then sluices prevented the inundation by salt water and the ecology quickly changed. Now managed as a valuable feeding and resting place for migrant birds. Reed-beds have colonised since 1945. The airborne migrants in-

clude swallows, martins and swifts. The reed-beds have attracted breeding bearded tits and Cetti's and sedge warblers. You will probably notice the number of garden plants, buddleia and bramble among the waterside vegetation –they arrived with the building rubble from the housing areas in Weymouth which was used to make the paths ● SY676796 in the centre of Weymouth town. ■

3 Windsor Great Park Berks. CEC
There are very few opportunities for us to experience the character and feeling of a particularly ancient woodland. The oldest stands of open high oak forest, with their grand old trees, dignified even in decay, give us a dramatic

impression of one type of wildwood in Britain. Even here the woodlands have been protected and managed as royal hunting park, estate woodland and productive forests. Nevertheless, the continuity of oak forest cover and the presence of the ancient trees have ensured the survival of hundreds of species of animals and plants that rely on the oak forest. Invertebrate populations are of national significance and it is worth searching for some of the spiders and beetles (2000 species are present), as well as the 30 butterfly species and 4 species of deer. Birds include hobbies, nightjars and woodpeckers ● SU953735 south of Windsor. ■

4 The New Forest Hants FC. et al.
Each part of the New Forest is a rich historical record with a very special woodland ecology. As a whole it is one of Europe's most extensive and most important ancient lowland forests. For 2000 years the woodland has been

adapted to suit the needs of man. It has been used as a source of food or fuel, material for building homes or ships or for early industries. The forestry cycles of management have been completed time and again over generations but still the sense of a natural woodland prevails. Once a wildwood of oak, hazel, lime and elm, the New Forest now has superb mature beech and oak woodland with many other species present. The grazing beneath limits the ground cover and, not surprisingly, holly forms one of the main shrub layers. Elsewhere, the variety of soil and drainage conditions gives a mixture of other plant associations with the trees. Roe and fallow deer are present in good numbers with a few red and sika. The lawns, damp open clearings of grass and moss, are special places at dawn when the birds and animals of the forest cautiously work their way into the open while undisturbed. There are many areas of heathland, too, and these complement the insect and bird populations of the forest. All three British sundews are here in the heaths. The wettest 'lawns' and valley bottoms in the forest have marshland habitats which attract redshank and snipe. Other New Forest birds include the nightjar, stonechat, hen harrier, hobby, merlin and many more. The appearance of the area today is the result of man's sometimes ruthless exploitation of New Forest timber but the continuity of habitats through history allows us to enjoy a very beautiful place, with a most distinctive character and natural history ● SU300080, A337 and minor roads out from Lyndhurst and Brockenhurst. **3** **6**

Selborne from the beech hanger

5 Selborne Hill Hants. NT
The familiarity of this superb woodland combination must have inspired one of our greatest natural historians. Gilbert White studied the habitats of Selborne and first observed many of the relationships we now take for granted. Selborne Hanger is a very steep wood of tall beech with a rich understorey and ground cover. The plateau of Selborne Common includes grass and heath as well as oak and beech woodland, first pollarded then coppiced ● SU735337, B3006, 3 miles south-east of Alton. **3**

6 Long Wood Somerset CT
Above the Cheddar Gorge, Long Wood occupies the head of a steep limestone valley. The wood was originally of ash and oak with an understorey of hazel and a rich ground flora. The wood was clear-felled in the 1930s and planted with beech, which is shading out the native plants. The beech is being removed to re-establish the oak and ash of the ancient wood ● ST488551, B3135 east of Cheddar. **3**

New Forest ponies

Crab, Purbeck Marine Reserve

7 Purbeck Marine Reserve Dorset CT
This was the first marine reserve to be
established on the British mainland
and shows the value of this area of
Kimmeridge Bay. Clear, shallow waters
allow us to glimpse the life of the sea
beyond the tidal zone. The interpret-
ative centre helps to reveal a colourful
and fascinating world of plants and
creatures that we rarely see ●
SY909788 on Isle of Purbeck via
minor roads off A351. **4**

8 Portland Bill Dorset
Projecting far into the English Channel,
the Bill grants an exciting day's birdwatching throughout the year. At peak
migration times in spring and autumn
the birds of the ocean pass by on their
seemingly endless journeys. There are
ducks, divers and waders, terns harried
by the skuas, and shearwaters, auks
and scoters which are so accustomed
to the sea they seek land only for nesting
sites. Rarities can be expected ●
SY680685 beyond Weymouth off
A354 to the Bill. **4**

9 Brownsea Island and Poole Harbour
Dorset CT/NT
This intriguing gravel island stands in
the complex estuary and harbour of
Poole, now heavily used for sport and
recreation. However, there is still room
for the birds which have always fre-
quented the bays and the reserve on
the island itself is important with freshwater pools and reed-beds. The many
sea-birds are joined by herons from
one of our largest heronries and the
woods provide a secure stronghold
for the red squirrel ● SZ032877 by
boat from Poole Quay or Sandbanks
Ferry. **5**

10 Chesil Bank and the Fleet Dorset
SgE
You can wonder at the spectacle of
Chesil Bank, one of Europe's five largest
shingle banks, and the Fleet–a brackish
water lagoon–at any time of the year.
The herd of mute swans has fed
on the eelgrass and algae of the
Abbotsbury Swannery for centuries.
In winter they are joined by teal, brent
geese, goldeneye, mergansers and
thousands of wigeon ● SY568840 off
B3157 Abbotsbury to Weymouth. **5**

11 Studland Heath Dorset NCC/NT
This heath is where you can find all six
British reptiles in a series of dunes and
heaths with pools and slacks. Lesser
dodder is a parasite growing on heather
and gorse on the drier ridges. Elsewhere,
in damper places, are round-leaved
sundew and bog myrtle with cottongrass. The heath is a site for dragonflies and many other insects. Beware
the extreme fire risk ● SX034836 off
B3351, Studland on the Isle of
Purbeck. **6**

12 Yateley Common Hants CC
If you want to see the variety of heathland habitats within a short, popular
walk, this country park offers a delightful nature trail through wet and dry
heaths with pools. Gorse, broom, birch
and pine form good scrub cover for the
birds. Heather and purple moor-grass
give way to sphagnum and acid bog
plants or to rich marshland in the pools.
Bulrush, yellow iris and water-lilies are
easily recognised but look also for the
less familiar plants and the butterflies
(including silver-studded blues) ●
SU822597 at Yateley, 4 miles north-
west of Frimley. **6**

13 Martin Down Hants. NCC
By manipulating the grazing patterns
of the sheep, a mosaic of short and long
grassland can be created. Uncontrolled
scrub growth would otherwise spread
rapidly, as shown by the five types
already present on the reserve, including
chalk scrub species of ash, buckthorn,
privet and spindle. Dogwood grows

where the downs were ploughed during
the Second World War, and elder is
strongly associated with the disturbed
soils of the earthworks. Butterflies are
outstanding with rare silver-spotted
skippers and adonis blues, hairstreaks
and fritillaries ● SU058192, A354,
10 miles south-west of Salisbury. **7**

14 Pewsey Down Wilts. NCC
To see this expansive sweep of short-
grazed chalk downland is a memorable
experience indeed. High on the slopes
there is a spring carpet of flowers in
the ancient turf, known to be one of
the longest grazed of the few large
downland sites now left. Chalk milkwort, bastard-toadflax and field fleawort
are survivors from the ancient pastures.
Pewsey Downs are free of the invading
scrub because of the continuity of
grazing management. Many individual
plants, especially burnt and bee orchids,
are stunning but it is the overall
impression of this ideal example of
downland which will remain ●
SU115635 on minor roads between
Marlborough and Devizes. **7**

15 Tennyson Down and the Needles
Isle of Wight NT
It is the atmospheric location of this
important range of downland and scrub
habitats that makes it both interesting
and dramatic. The sheer chalk white
cliffs drop 480 feet to the sea below.
Even the shortest grassland herbs suffer
from the exposure but short-stemmed
harebells and dwarf thistles are well-
adapted. The scrub is rich in shrub
species with unusual combinations–
including gorse, blackthorn and privet–
growing together ● SU324855 the
B3322 to the most westerly point of
the Isle of Wight. **7**

16 Breamore Countryside Museum
Hants.
We must often look to the tools and
equipment associated with the countryside crafts to reveal how the operations
of farming the land have changed the
countryside. Here the historical development of farming tools and machinery
is complemented with developments in
transport and power and the collection
of livestock. All help to build a picture
of the changing countryside. Open
April to September ● SU155175 off
A338, 8 miles south of Salisbury. **8**

17 Basingstoke Canal Hants. CC
The towpath walk along this reopened canal gives us a very different picture of the region. Here is an enclosed and intimate landscape with species ranging from the aquatic plants of the canal to the birds and animals of the farmland and woods. A different world to that of the high open downs or the cliffs and estuaries of the coast ● SU719514 between Basingstoke and Aldershot. ⑩

18 Ham Hill Country Park
Somerset DC
You will find the disused limestone quarries well concealed by a vigorous colonisation of plants and animals.

Where man has abandoned the land and left spoil heaps and rock faces, a surprising variety of wildlife has moved in ● ST478167 off A303 between Ilchester and Ilminster. ⑩

19 The M4 Motorway
Berks./Wilts. DTP
A dramatic landscape of large-scale road construction gently winds its way through an open arable farmland. These noisy strips of grassland carry high populations of voles and shrews, mice and invertebrates—all attractive prey for kestrels which are frequently seen hovering over the verges as we speed by—less conspicuous are the weasels and stoats which pursue the small mammals of this grassland, and the omnivorous hedgehog which occasionally wanders on to the highway. At night, the same verges are patrolled by short-eared owls and barn owls, glimpsed fleetingly in the headlights of your car ● The M4 over the Downs east of Swindon. ⑩

View from Pewsey Down

The forces of the wild Atlantic impress themselves on some of the most dramatic coastal scenery in the British Isles. This peninsula of hard rocks is exposed to the sea and yet in the lush, green, sunken lanes of Devon, you may feel as safe and sheltered as anywhere. There are wonderful wildlife contrasts within this region's differing habitats. It provides a richness and interest of its own. On the estuaries we find wild, open spaces; in the rock pools there are intimate details to enjoy. The delicate and rare butterflies in the Devonshire woodlands and the seemingly indestructible sea-birds battered by the ocean gales tell their own story of the south-west.

The beauty of the scenery and the special nature of the wildlife will never fail to draw its visitors, annually seeking their own experience of this part of wild Britain.

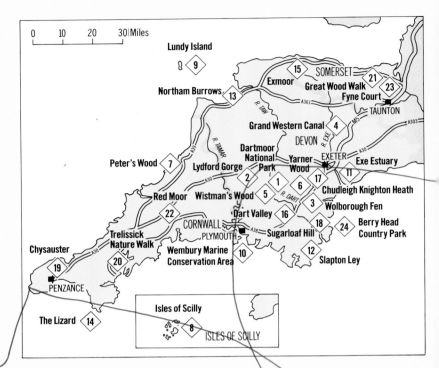

1 Dartmoor National Park
Devon NPA
Climb the granite tors of Dartmoor and you will see how the hand of man has so completely changed even this wild and remote landscape. You will see how screes called 'clitters' have been formed when huge boulders were split from the granite tors by ice. The woodlands which once covered the hills are now only small relics surviving on the clitters which have remained free of grazing ponies, sheep and cattle. The small farms concentrate in the sheltered valleys with the fields on the slopes and the open land on the moors. At Grimspound we can see a timely reminder that thousands of years ago early farmers lived up here on the moors, retreating to the lower land as the climate cooled and poor soils became exhausted. The infamous mires and bogs are relics, too, of ancient wetlands refilled by the heavy rainfall ● Grimspound SX705815 off B3212, 7 miles north-east of Two Bridges. **1**

Ponies on Dartmoor

2 Lydford Gorge Devon NT
The gorge is a dramatic illustration of the powerful forces which created the character of the south-west. This famous ravine scooped out by the River Lyd is 1½ miles long. It is a series of pools and falls leading to the 90-foot-high White Lady Waterfall. The steep, rocky cliffs of the gorge are covered in beautiful oak woodland ● SX509846 west of A386, 6 miles south of Okehampton. **1 2**

3 Wolborough Fen Devon CT
A rare example of fen, Wolborough is a small area of wet birch and willow carr with reeds, offering specialist accommodation for the birds and insects of the fen ● SX866703, 1 mile south-west of Newton Abbot. **2**

4 Grand Western Canal Devon CC
In contrast to the torrents of the rivers in spate, the Old Tiverton canal is a slow water rich in plant and animal

life. A linear park follows the canal banks ● From SS963124 near Tiverton to ST074195 near Wellington. **2** **10**

5 Wistman's Wood Devon NCC
This is an ancient wood on the rain-soaked slopes of Dartmoor, high among great boulders strewn across the hillside. Wistman's ancient oaks are ghostly shapes in the ever-present shroud of mist. Their gnarled appearance and stunted shapes result from the terrible exposure to wind and rain. Yet the air is so clean their trunks and branches are covered with beautiful lichens and mosses ● SX612772 on the moors 1½ miles north of Two Bridges. **3**

6 Yarner Wood Devon NCC
In complete contrast to Wistman's Wood the oaks of Yarner Wood lie in a sheltered valley, partly on disused farmland. It is a very attractive wood indeed with pied flycatchers and wood warblers, and a wealth of fungi and invertebrate species. You will not fail to be intrigued by the nest constructions of the wood ants. An integral part of this woodland

ecology, there may be 800 nests occupied by 200 million ants ● SX785788 on B3344, 2 miles northwest of Bovey Tracey. **3**

7 Peter's Wood Cornwall CT
Many of the narrow, steep river valleys of the north Cornwall coast provide shelter for small pockets of woodland. Too steep to farm, they have been little used by man and parts of Peter's Wood are of ancient origin. The plants, for example, great wood-rush and hard fern, indicate wet, acidic conditions. A wide range of plants is established, including the unusual royal fern and Tunbridge filmy-fern. There are sufficient invertebrates to provide food for three different resident bat species and the river itself attracts dippers ● SX113910 off B3263 near Boscastle. **3**

8 Isles of Scilly Cornwall DOC/NCC
The story of the sea is encapsulated in these beautiful isles. Only 5 of the islands are inhabited although another 40 have land vegetation above a variable sea-level. Once joined to Cornwall and

wooded with oak and hazel the central plateau was drowned by a 300-foot rise in sea-level and only the rim of the land mass now stands above the waves as a group of islands. The Atlantic dominates the scene, the air is clean, the waters clear. As a landfall for migrating birds the islands are famous, but the sea itself is rich with colourful marine life including corals, sea snails and sea anemones. The elegant feather-star is a deep-water creature but here in the Scillies can be found in the shallows ● By air or by ferry from Penzance. **4**

9 Lundy Island Devon LT/NT
By the time the boat reaches Lundy from the mainland you will have been drawn to the character of this granite outcrop: the smell of the sea, the starkness of the cliffs and the sounds of thousands of sea-birds nesting on the tiniest ledges overhead. There are dramatic views of the wave-lashed rocks and amazing aerobatics of the birds. All these will leave you with a lasting impression of one of Britain's

Lundy Island

291

most interesting sea-bird colonies. But that is only half the story. Below the waves is a fascinating world of wildlife associated with the ocean as well as the coast. In the relatively warmer currents of this Marine Nature Reserve grow beautiful corals and sea anemones, with sea slugs normally associated with the Mediterranean ● SS143437 by helicopter from Hartland Point, or boat from Ilfracombe. **4 5**

10 Wembury Marine Conservation Area Devon WMCAAG
This fascinating rocky shore provides an opportunity for studying the richness of the shallows below the level of low tide, as well as the tidal rocks and pools. Wembury Point is a useful location for watching waders and migrating birds ● SX507484 off minor roads south of Plymouth. **4 5**

11 Exe Estuary Devon Various
You should try to visit this huge estuary in the winter as well as the summer for it is then that the wildfowl are at their most spectacular. Large flocks of brent geese, mallard, shelduck teal and wigeon are found on the shore, while the sea has rafts of sea-duck including eiders and scoters. Autumn, too, is worthwhile as the flocks of waders comb the estuary. The longshore drift creates sandflats, mudflats and salt-marsh across a wide expanse which can be overlooked from footpaths on both shores ● SX980785 south of Exeter, footpaths from SX973845 north of Powderham and SX992836 south of Lympstone. **5**

12 Slapton Ley Devon FSC
A superb complex of habitats provides an intimate and memorable study of the richness of the wildlife of the southwest. Shore dock and sea radish grow in the shingle; the lake is full of plant and animal life and the reed-beds and fen of the Higher Ley provide shelter for a superb range of butterflies and birds. The Ley forms a valuable winter retreat for the sea-birds from Start Bay ● SX826431, A379 east from Kingsbridge, entrance to the woodlands by permit only. **5 2**

13 Northam Burrows Devon CC
If you want to compare all of the major habitats of the shoreline in one area, they are here at the mouth of the rivers Taw and Torridge. You will find rock pools with crabs; sandy beaches and mud with sandwort and sea spurge; and sand dunes with blue and brown butterfly species. Out on the estuary are curlew, ringed plover and shelduck ● SS444298 from Northam, 2 miles north of Bideford. **5**

14 The Lizard Cornwall various
The rare and complicated rock formations of this most southerly peninsula create unusual habitats ranging from coastal cliffs to heathland. The cliffs at Predannack face the full force of the Atlantic westerlies. Plants survive the exposure only in stunted forms (oxeye daisy, knapweed and scabious), or by growing flat: prostrate forms of broom, privet and juniper can be found. Cornish heath is restricted to this county but is readily found here. Other unusual plants include dwarf and pygmy rushes. Spring squill and dog-violets provide colourful seasonal displays ● SW701140, A3083 south from Helston. **5 6**

15 Exmoor Somerset and Devon NPA
On the high moors of this National Park you can see how man has changed the landscape and the wildlife of this area. How far did the woodlands spread before farming and clearance limited them to a few steep hillsides? How long ago did the hilltops become heath and moor, peat bog and mire? Exmoor is England's last stronghold of wild red deer and the Exmoor pony is the breed which is closest in form to the primitive wild horse most commonly found in north-west Europe in prehistoric times. Exmoor's interest and beauty is all the more profound because of its variety of scenery, including farmland, woodland, cliff and shore, moor and heath and the variety of wildlife associated with these areas ● Drive across the moor from Ilfracombe to Exbridge. **6**

16 Dart Valley Devon NPA/CT
From the rain-soaked bogs of the uplands, the Dartmoor rivers flow through steep-sided, often wooded valleys and through heaths of gorse and grasses. The combination of woodlands and streams near to these extensive heaths results in a distinctive species list of birds. In this typical valley are the dipper and grey wagtail, buzzard, redstart, whinchat and ringed ousel. The beautiful old stone bridges blend man's progress into a timeless landscape where fox and badger hunt the banks, and salmon and brown trout breed in the river ● SX672733, take B3357 to Dartmeet and follow the valley. **6**

17 Chudleigh Knighton Heath Devon CT
An important example of lowland heath in the south-west, this site has dry and wet heathland with small ponds. Invertebrates do well in the scrub and woodland habitats and on the heath attract a range of songbirds, including nightingales ● SX838776 west of the A38, 10 miles south-west of Exeter. **6**

18 Sugarloaf Hill Devon Torbay C
A good example of coastal grassland is persevering on the slopes and shallow cliffs of Sugarloaf Hill. The site includes an active railway line and is close to the holiday resorts and an interesting rocky shore ● SX895583 on the coast south of Paignton. **7**

19 Chysauster Cornwall
The substantial remains of this iron-age village give us a real impression of the first settlements based on arable farming. Cultivating small arable fields and garden plots next to the eight dry-walled houses, the early Celtic farmers occupied the site from about 2100 to 1700 years ago ● SW460355, 4 miles north of Penzance. **8**

20 Trelissick Nature Walk Cornwall NT
You will enjoy this beautiful woodland and parkland walk for pastoral scenery, woodland and coast. The trail will take you to a viewpoint overlooking the man-made parkland on the slopes of the River Fal. It is an impressive example of dramatic landscape enhancement and wildlife interest ● SW837396, B3289, 4 miles south of Truro. **9**

21 Great Wood Walk Somerset CT
The recent landscapes of the Quantocks include parkland and coniferous forest. Red deer are present and you may find coal tits and goldcrests, two of the specialist birds of the conifers ● ST165360 east of the A358, 9 miles north-west of Taunton. **9** **10**

22 Red Moor Cornwall CT
This delightful mosaic of habitats combines wetland, heath scrub and woodland like pieces in a jigsaw. The former working of alluvial tin has created a compact reserve demonstrating how a range of species from lichens and heather to linnets and spiders has moved in where man moved out ● SX077622 off B3269, 4 miles south of Bodmin. **10**

23 Fyne Court Somerset CT/NT
The county trust headquarters offers a fine display of the wildlife habitats of the Quantocks, some of which are being restored and managed within the grounds. Woodland, lake and ponds, together with an old quarry, provide the basis of habitats to be developed in the future for studying and enjoyment ● ST223321 minor roads 6 miles north of Taunton. **10** **9**

24 Berry Head Country Park
Devon Torbay C.
Near the popular seaside resorts of Torbay this remarkable nature reserve doubles as a country park for the enjoyment of visitors. The value of this superb range of habitats is increased by its dual role. The headland is topped with scrub and heathland of bracken, gorse and heather. The strikingly-coloured stonechat males are seen on the tops of the bushes and the headland forms a landfall for migrant passerines including black redstarts. Further interest for the birdwatcher is provided by the cliff-nesting guillemots and razorbills, fulmars and kittiwakes which breed in very few other places on our south coasts. The birds can be viewed from the Head's vantage point above the waves ● SX943564 east of Brixham. **10** **5**

The River Dart

The wild, bare mountains of Donegal, Mayo and Galway are the oldest in Ireland. They are lashed by wind and rain and their soils are thin and poor. Except where shell sands blow in from the sea or where estuaries have laid their silts, there is little sustenance for farming. As you travel between the freshwater loughs you will see how blanket bog reigns supreme in these hills and on the lowlands, creating the largest wilderness in Ireland.

But there is a distinctive beauty in these remote landscapes and everywhere wildlife has found the niches to flourish. Small, mossy oakwoods are scattered through Donegal; moors, rivers, heaths and grasslands can be found in many places. Above all, the coast is as dramatic as it is romantic. Whether you are on great sea-bird cliffs, or in the clear waters of Aillebrack, you will understand how the life of the sea and the land are inextricably woven in this less familiar part of Ireland.

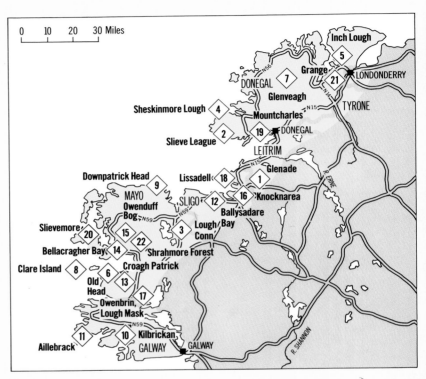

1 Glenade
Sligo/Leitrim Mountains P/C
Glaciers scraped a trough-like valley here in the Sligo/Leitrim mountains. At the base of the cliff walls are gigantic screes, mostly grass-covered today, but occasional scars show that erosion is still taking place. Alpine plants have clung to the cliffs for over 10,000 years and the calls of ravens echo from the rock walls. The wetness and the shade promote mosses and ferns: see if you can match the record of finding 20 different ferns. Ring ousel perch on the rocks and screes ● G8046 from south-west side of Glenade Lough, off T54. **1**

2 Slieve League Donegal C
From the top of one of Europe's finest cliffs you will see how the violent pounding of the Atlantic waves has eaten away the solid rock. Ice, too, has eroded the plunging cliffs of Slieve League

where an 1800-foot mountain meets the sea. Two ice-cut corries may once have existed here: one was broken into by the sea as its level rose; the landward one still exists with tiny Lough Agh at its base. The ridge between them, called 'one man's path', is not for the faint-hearted. The Lough Agh cliffs shelter alpine and arctic plants whereas the sea slopes are covered in maritime grassland grazed by sheep and watched by choughs ● G5578 from Carrick to Teelin Road. **1 5**

3 Lough Conn Mayo P
If you sit quietly beside the lake in the early morning you may see the Irish mountain hares loping around the shoreline. Low shores of rocks, sand or bog surround most of this lake. The ground rises at the south end into ice-smooth rocky knobs with heathery islands offshore, the nesting sites of common scoters. Northern bedstraw

and burnet are noticeable plants among the stones; juniper and aspen grow around fragments of ancient woodland. On boggy parts of the shore the pine stumps of 4000 years ago are being revealed from their peaty preservative. Look out for buckthorn and the brimstone butterflies that feed on it ● G2010 lakeside roads, especially at Terrybaun, Cloghans and Garrycloonagh. **1 2**

4 Sheskinmore Lough Donegal P/IWC
An excellent site for your early-morning fox watch as the dunes are full of rabbits. This coastal lake has an excellent aquatic plant list including two American species that occur on both

sides of the Atlantic, the slender naiad and the pipewort. Six types of waders nest, including snipe, lapwing and dunlin. In winter a large flock of barnacle geese feeds on the sandhills and Greenland white-fronted geese come to roost on the lake ● G6897 footpath from the Ardara to Rosbeg road on the north side of the lough. **2**

5 Inch Lough Donegal P/F
This shallow, brackish lake beside the fiord of Lough Swilly is renowned for its wildfowl, even in summer when mute swans nest in an island colony.

Whooper swans make their first landfall from Iceland in the autumn, feeding with grey geese on the reclaimed fields near by. But in the winter up to ten sorts of duck occur on the lough, occasionally flying out to Blanket Nook when disturbed ● C3422 at Ford below Speenoge (T74) or on causeways at either end. **2**

6 Old Head Mayo FWS
On a headland in Clew Bay you will find the most exciting form of Atlantic oakwood. The trees are small but they are festooned with sheets of lichens,

mosses and liverworts. Together with the abundant ferns they make walking through the wood an amazing experience. The resemblance to the tropics is more than coincidental for a few of the species are more at home in the Azores, the Canaries or the Caribbean ● L8382 off T39, 2 miles east of Louisburgh. **3**

7 Glenveagh Donegal OPW
Ireland's largest National Park sits astride this long, glaciated valley set in the heart of Donegal. A remnant of ancient woodland shelters between the high hills. It consists of oak, birch and holly with several other trees, including two species of cherry, crab apple and hazel. You may notice rhododendron which was introduced with the red deer when man thought he could improve on the species provided by nature ● C0121 from north-east end of Lough Beagh (L82). **3**

8 Clare Island Mayo C
Head towards the north-west side of Clare Island if you want to see magnificent cliffs with large sea-bird colonies. Guillemots, razorbills, fulmars and kittiwakes briefly abandon their oceanic wanderings to breed. There is an extraordinary density of choughs which have found the perfect combination of short pasture and cliff crevices. A few gannets occur too, the start of Ireland's fourth gannetry. But there is so much more on this island. The site of a biological survey in 1910 which increased the known Irish fauna by a quarter, Clare Island is always worth a visit ● L6686 by boat from Roonagh Quay west of Louisburgh. **4**

9 Downpatrick Head Mayo C
The powerful attacks of the sea on the land have produced dramatic visual and sound effects as the waves thunder into caves and blow-holes. The Head drops sheer into the sea where long-tailed ducks dive in the cold winter waves. Only 200 feet offshore is a sea-stack crowded with birds and topped by the ancient fort of Doonbristy. The calls of kittiwakes and guillemots ring out from the cliffs, and grey seals may rise out of the sea almost anywhere. The seals and birds are liable to be fatally caught in drift nets, set offshore for salmon ● G1242 from coast road north of Ballycastle. **4** **5**

Slieve League cliffs

10 Kilbrickan Connemara F
Marine zoologists find the sheltered bays
and clear waters of this coast ideal for
underwater photography. Seals and
otters enjoy them too. The zones of
different wracks lie clear on the shore
above the forest of kelp that dries out
only on the lowest tides. Search among
the sheets of orange seaweed or in the
rock pools for shells of all shapes and
sizes. Some of the larger ones are ten-
anted by hermit crabs. The top shells
show a shine of mother-of-pearl; the
winkles are like traditional snails; the
limpets cone-like. Watch out for that
tiny gem, the blue-rayed limpet with
streaks of brilliant blue on its young
shells ● L9135 from L102 along
shores especially west side. **4** **5**

11 Aillebrack Galway Bay C/P
As you walk along Aillebrack, the
spotted rock, keep watching the sea for
a sighting of the bottle-nosed dolphins
which can be found here all year round.
The so-called coral to the north is
a special seaweed which has become
bleached along the shore and is a pinkish

colour when it grows on the seabed.
Wherever it occurs it makes the water
much clearer, to the delight of snor-
kellers and divers. Coral sand from this
strange plant and shells of all sorts are
driven against the rocky shore to make
this an area of contrast. The machair
vegetation, a low turf made colourful
with flowers of bedstraws, thyme and
kidney vetch, grades into heath and
lake, each with many other plants of
interest. The white beaches change
their shape from year to year as they
absorb the full force of the Atlantic. In
summer they are seldom without the
harsh call of terns ● L5944 westwards
from Ballyconneely, following signs to
Connemara golf club. **4** **5**

12 Ballysadare Bay Sligo F
The sand-choked estuary of the Unshin
River shows good variety rather than
large numbers in its shore-birds. At
Streamstown, on the south shore,
godwits and greenshanks stalk the
shallows, herons fish constantly and
wigeon and teal fly in and out. But
look out into the bay to see the hulks of

common seals, seemingly washed up
on the outer sandbanks where they
relax in safety ● G6231 from shore
roads N59 and L132. **5**

13 Croagh Patrick Mayo C
This is the place for you to view the
strange, drowned, drumlin landscape
of Clew Bay. The walk is also rewarding
because you can enjoy fine moorland
habitat on the clean, cone-shaped
mountainsides. These slopes are better
drained than most and heathers grow
well in the shallow peat. The winds,
the sheep and occasional fires restrict
tree growth to the rough ground below.
But the birches here continue their
inbuilt attempt to spread, sometimes
succeeding and sometimes falling
back ● L9080 southwards from
Murrisk (T39). **6**

14 Bellacragher Bay Mayo P/F
Birch scrub and heath surround the
head of this sheltered bay, famous for its
stand of the rare Mediterranean heath.
The plant grows six feet high here and
its pink flowers in April, along with the

gorse, make a memorable sight. It is one of the handful of southern plants that reached Ireland along the fringes of western Europe when sea-level was reduced. On the warm slopes nearby, stonechats perch on the bush tops, wheatears and skylarks nest and a hovering kestrel often appears seeking the small animals of the heath ● L8196 off L141 and T71. **6**

15 Owenduff Bog Mayo P/C
If you want to experience the wild beauty of a really extensive blanket bog then you must go to where the Owenduff River descends from Nephin Beg. This is part of the Bog of Erris, an enormous wilderness, now partly cut for fuel. The peat covers everything, the forests and farmland of long ago, rocks, streams and slopes. Here in the peat we find European plants that normally grow in richer fens and marshes, a quirk of nature not yet properly explained. As you take in the remote scale of this great wetland enjoy its detail too. There are sundew and asphodel on the bog surface and the scent of bog myrtle ● F8607 eastwards on laneways from T71. **6**

16 Knocknarea Sligo C/P
Climb through the limestone grassland on this hill to appreciate a superb view of the Sligo landscape. These were some of the earliest grasslands and animals have grazed here for thousands of years. They have left trees only in the glen on the south side. The summit is covered by bog and crowned by Queen Maeve's Tomb, a megalithic monument ● G6234 from Culleenduff (L132). **7**

17 Owenbrin, Lough Mask
Connemara C/P
Acres of unfertilised open grassland spread over the delta of Owenbrin River, on the shores of Lough Mask. The river channels change continually in their sandy ways and open water alternates with marsh, pasture and bog. You can see how plants such as chamomile, allseed and corn mint change with these different habitats. Curlew, lapwing and lesser black-backed gulls frequent the area. During spring and early summer the voices of skylarks and dunlins add to the chorus of other lakeside birds ● M0560 from road north of bridge. **7**

18 Lissadell Sligo FWS
If you pass this field only in summer and see its grazing cows there will be no hint of its outstanding importance as a goose field in winter. For a long time it was the only place where you could guarantee seeing barnacle geese on the mainland of Ireland, although Donegal now has such an area too. At Lissadell the geese were first recorded in this field in the 1890s. Numbers built up, especially after protection, and now sometimes reach 1000 ● G6444 from main avenue at Lissadell House. **7**

19 Mountcharles Donegal Bay
This is a small-scale landscape with tiny fields, twisting roads and splendid hedges. The road along the north shore of Donegal Bay is lined by hedges of fuchsia which you will often see in western Ireland. Other hedges have elder, willows and hawthorn. The older houses are sheltered by clumps of sycamores, planted in a brave attempt to calm the frequent gales. A low sun may catch the gleam of a patch of primroses, a foxglove or some montbretia naturalised in the roadside bank ● G8277 from T72. **8**

20 Slievemore Mayo Coast C
Slievemore is a deserted village on Achill Island with a sad story to tell about extensive areas on the mainland too. It was abandoned during the famine when the potato crop totally failed. No longer cultivated, the fields nevertheless show clearly the scale and intensity of farming in the early nineteenth century. Cultivation ridges, which were remade each

year, run from the stream to a height of 300 feet on the mountain and each would have carried the dense growth of potatoes. The crop had to be cooked well causing an incessant search for sticks and turf for fuel. This must have resulted in a major impact on the Irish countryside, populated as it was then by almost three times as many people as now ● F6307 from road on west side of Keel Lough. **8**

21 Grange Tyrone P/RSPB
The reclaimed fields by the River Foyle are large and flat, two of the main features that attract wild swans and geese. There is abundant food in the form of grass, winter barley and potatoes. Whooper and Bewick's swans occur here in large numbers. Both species are beautiful birds, the sight or sound of which is memorable, as they fly against the rising land of Tyrone, or across the river to Donegal. In winter both greylag and white-fronted geese also visit the area and waders fly up and down the tidal river ● C3606 west from A5. **8** **9**

22 Shrahmore Forest Mayo FWS
Set in a wide valley in the Nephin Beg Range Shrahmore forest is one of the largest tracts of coniferous forest in the west. It transformed former bogland and heath, completely altering animal and plant life. Gone are the meadow pipits and grouse of open moorland, but robins, blackbirds, wrens and goldcrests have invaded the new wood ● F9706 northwards from Newport (T71 by Lough Furnace). **10**

Barnacle geese, Lissadell

18 NORTH-EAST IRELAND

The countryside of north-east Ireland shows many distinctive glacial features which create a unique and recognisable landscape. Made up partly of a lake-filled lowland, the region has also the great inland sea of Lough Neagh. There are higher hills on the lava flows of the Antrim plateau and in the Mournes but it is the lowland features which excel. Drumlins, those innumerable rounded hills of glacial origin, undulate the land from Clew Bay to Strangford Lough.

The loughs and winding rivers form important freshwater habitats across the region. Occasionally the hills are wooded with splendid ash and oak forests as well as the modern coniferous plantations. The Antrim coast and the marine life of the North Sea channel are outstanding. The coastal region is linked by a famous raised beach which marks the coastline of the post-glacial sea. Complete with its own cliff, it is specially noticeable around Lough Foyle and on the Antrim coast where you can drive along the former shoreline on the present-day coast road.

1 Mourne Mountains Down
High in the Mournes the evidence of the Ice Age is clear to see. Corries have been notched into the north and east slopes of several mountains. The loose stones and sand slipped off the ridges during freezing and thawing. But larger rocks and boulders remained where they were and now form sculptured tors, in the shape of pillars and pinnacles. You can see them on Slieve Bingian, Slieve Bearnagh or Slieve Commedagh. The Mournes are the home of the mountain raptors – merlin, peregrine and kestrel ● J3428 from Bloody Bridge in the east or Silent Valley in the south. ◼

2 Strangford Lough Down P/S/NT
You will find the county of Down and the shores of Strangford Lough are good

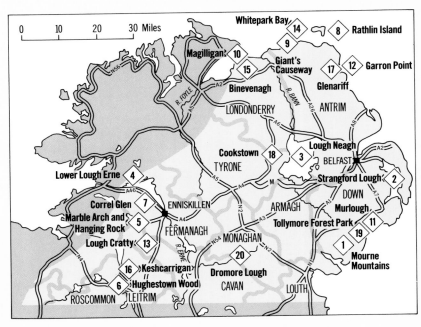

places to see drumlins. They are characteristically Irish hills that produce a 'basket of eggs' landscape with roads winding between the piles of glacial debris. We have not fully understood how they were created by the ice-sheets but they have an attractive cover of varied agricultural land with small fields and high hedges. They run to the shores of the lough where 400 million tons of water flow in and out through the Narrows with every tide, leaving mudflats full of food for shore-birds. It is one of the best places to see brent geese in winter, as 14,000 feed here when they arrive from the far north. Shelduck, wigeon, knot and dunlin also come in huge numbers. In summer, listen for the calls of terns as several species breed on the islands, and watch for the common seals ● J5461 from A22 to Reagh I, Ringhaddy, from A25 to Castle Ward. ◼ ◼

3 Lough Neagh
Antrim/Tyrone/Armagh
If you walk the lonely shores of this giant lake you will not fail to be impressed by its wildlife. Spreading like an inland sea, the full scale of 150 square miles of Lough Neagh is hard to appreciate from the low-lying shores. This must always have been a natural paradise. Great fens and bogs at the southern end are now dissected by drainage ditches and the bushy western side is perhaps easier to explore. If you find somewhere that cattle have not grazed, the tall loosestrifes, both yellow and purple, the marsh ragwort and the mints will come into their own. Clay beds at Toome were formed from the skeletons of millions of freshwater algae that once lived in the lake. Today the algae are different but they still support abundant animals and birds.

Each year an unbelievable 20 million young eels reach the Lough after their long-distance migration from the Sargasso Sea. The Lough Neagh pollan is a special race, related to a marine species but now isolated and breeding in the

fresh water of the lake. As explained in Chapter 2, this relic fish and the few maritime plants that grow around the shore suggest that, just after the Ice Age, the sea had access to Lough Neagh. Great-crested grebes prey on the fish and the Raughlin peninsula has a huge colony of these beautiful birds with their captivating displays. In winter the number of diving ducks that come to the lake make it the third most important wildfowl site in Europe. The presence of 60,000 ducks tells us much about the richness of this vast lake water ● J0475 from shore roads at Derryadd, Derrycrow, Killycolpy, Bartins Bay, Shane's Castle etc. **2**

4 Lower Lough Erne Fermanagh S
The wooded shores and drumlin islands of Lough Erne provide breeding sites for a host of waterfowl. Around Castle Caldwell common scoter, merganser and grebes frequent the islands. Even terns find suitable ground. The flora is varied and in the shade some plants grow tall. There are forests of hemp-agrimony and groves of meadowsweet.

All round the lake, the garden warbler shows its Irish habit of nesting only beside water. It adds its voice to a splendid bird chorus in early summer. Watch out for sandwich terns, here unusually breeding inland ● H0260 from A47 and other roads at Blaney and Killadeas. **2**

5 Marble Arch and Hanging Rock Fermanagh S/P
The best ash woodland in Ireland occurs on the limestone hills overlooking Lough Macnean. Billowing trees climb layer upon layer up the cliffs. In the light shade below, the growth of other plants is spectacular. Primroses, bluebells, yellow pimpernels and helleborines are frequent and, among the shrubs, the characteristic guelder-rose and spindle are obvious. Ferns and mosses are here in plenty ● H1234 from south side of Blacklion to Florence Court Road. **3**

6 Hughestown Wood
Shannon Valley P
Set on a low hill by the Shannon, this small wood gives us an idea of the character of the vast oakwoods that once covered the drumlin country. Oaks thrive in the wet clay soils, as do alders, ashes, elms and birches. All species here are natives; the shrubs and the tangled ground flora flourishing in the winter-wet conditions. Lichens grow high in the canopy and they still cover many fallen branches ● G9001 from T3, east of bridge. **3**

7 Correl Glen
Carrick Lake, Fermanagh S
A mossy oakwood survives in this river valley above Carrick Lake. Though it is small you will find a great variety of vegetation on its cliffs and screes. The sessile oak is dominant with other natives of birch and rowan. Wood-rush covers much of the forest floor but ferns are common and include the delicate filmy-ferns that need constant moisture in the air ● H0754 at bridge above Carrick Lake. **3**

8 Rathlin Island North Channel S/P
The rugged coastal scenery of grey and white cliffs is covered with sea-birds in spring and summer. Few people can be unmoved by the sight of thousands of auks on the stacks of the Kebble National Nature Reserve at the west end. Guillemots, razorbills and puffins occur in abundance as well as those twilight visitors, the Manx shearwaters. But do not forget the flora. Tree-mallow, rose-root and lovage grow on the cliff tops along with thrift, spring squills and spurrey. One of the buzzard's Irish strongholds, it is as exciting for the botanist as for the birdwatcher ● D0950 by boat from Ballycastle, then on foot. **4**

9 Giant's Causeway North Channel NT
Could the giant have walked the causeway to Fingal's Cave in the Outer Hebrides before the sea-level rose? We assume these fascinating rock formations continue beneath the waves and are evident only at each end of his path. For now, though, the cliff-walk east of the causeway takes us above the roar of the breaking waves. From here you are high enough to see groups of eider duck and oystercatchers as well as the ceaseless traffic of fulmars, cormorants and gulls on the high seas. Down on the shore the straight-edged rock pools have many types of seaweeds and, if you wait to see them, crabs, rock fish and shrimps ● C9444 from B146 at Causeway Head. **4**

10 Magilligan Londonderry F/C
This very long beach backed by ridges of sandhills includes outstanding examples of all types of dune habitat. From the sea rocket of the strandline, through the ridges of marram grass, then the damp depressions between them and the grassland behind, you can follow the history of the dunes in their growth above the sea. The marshy places are perhaps the most interesting and they are augmented by straight streams flowing from the lowland behind ● C6937 westwards from Benone Strand, on A2. **5**

11 Murlough Down S
Sea-buckthorn is plentiful here and the masses of winter-moth caterpillars which feed on its leaves in turn provide food for a large number of resident and passage migrant birds. The Murlough National Nature Reserve includes both sand dunes and mudflats. The dunes have many of the typical plants like creeping willow and carline thistle but they also carry heathland communities because of a lack of lime in the older soils. Mosses and heathers occur, giving a surprising mixture of plants. Old soils beneath the dunes are exposed in places and bear traces of the earliest inhabitants ● J4035 from A2 at Dundrum. **5**

12 Garron Point Antrim Coast P/C
At 1000 feet above the coast road you can find a wet blanket bog where the call of the curlew and perhaps the golden plover add to the sense of isolation. Moor-grass and heather dominate the drier sites; the wetter areas have rushes and pondweed. The flora is of considerable interest, many sedges occur near springs with butterworts and sundews, cranberry and spearwort ● D2823 from Gortin above Carnlough or directly from A2. **6**

13 Lough Cratty Leitrim C
The Lough Cratty bog lies on a shoulder of Cuilcagh Mountain. On relatively flat ground it has developed a good thickness of peat. Sphagnum mosses of several colours are abundant and you will find their soft cushions can be up to 5 feet in diameter. The curious purple liverwort is similarly widespread on this wild bog, hardly touched by peat cutting or fire. The peat encloses small lakes which are the home of midge larvae, beetles and a few dragonflies ● H1527 from narrow road ½ mile north of Swanlinbar. **6**

14 Whitepark Bay Antrim Coast NT
The big sandy beach and the white chalk cliffs form a startling contrast with the dark cliffs of Antrim. Flint and bronze tools have been found in abundance indicating the grassland here must be some of the oldest in the country. The sward is bright with flowers in spring and early summer. The white grass-of-Parnassus will catch your eye, as will the blue meadow crane's-bill, here in the centre of its small Irish range ● D0143 from A2. **7**

15 Binevenagh Londonderry FS/C
Binevenagh is crowned with heath grassland which runs right to the edge of the cliffs above Magilligan (see site 10). Harebells grow widely among the grass and the only large plants are giant thistles which seem to stalk their way across the land. The cliffs house remnants of an alpine flora as well as a few maritime plants. Fulmars often soar on the updraft, although it is several miles from the sea ● C6931 from A2 at Magilligan station (field centre), up road to reservoir. **7**

The Giant's Causeway

16 Keshcarrigan Leitrim P
These drumlin lands of south Leitrim were once densely populated. Countless deserted cottages now tell of the decline that started in the 1850s. Small fields with tall hedges cover the countryside. The constant slopes and soil which is heavy and poorly drained deter mechanisation. Small gardens are still cultivated beside the houses but, otherwise, rushy pastures dominate a land which can grow conifers faster than any other part of Europe. Find an ungrazed field somewhere and look at its flora. Devil's-bit, ragged-robin, lousewort, sorrel and three or four orchid species vie for your attention, with clouds of craneflies and grass moths ● H0709 from minor roads between T55 and L3. **7** **8**

17 Glenariff Antrim P/S
Several broad valleys break the edge of the Antrim plateau and agriculture has been quick to take over these fertile pockets, so different from the bleak moorland above. The lower valley has marshy fields and is floored by an old raised beach. Many of the farms are arranged in a ladder pattern to ensure a fair share of this soil, of the better-drained marginal land and of the sloping pastures that rise towards the cliffs. The glen narrows near its head where waterfalls take the river down from 1000 feet through flowery woods ● D2323 from A43. **8**

18 Cookstown Tyrone P
This remarkable country town was laid out in 1750. It has a straight main street 1¼ miles long, flanked by a line of houses with gardens 400 feet deep. Trees border the gardens and bring in the wildlife from the surrounding countryside. Hooded crows, rooks and wood-pigeons are often in town. Stoats, foxes and kestrels are more occasional visitors ● H8177 on the A29. **9**

19 Tollymore Forest Park
Mourne Mountains, Down FS
Based on a fragment of old woodland in a valley of the northern Mournes, Tollymore is a mixed forest of great beauty. Many of the conifer stands are well grown, attractive and reaching ma-turity. The cascading river has dippers and grey wagtails. Above them chiff-chaffs, blackcaps and blackbirds fill the air with song. Wood-pigeons, goldcrests and coal tits have typically invaded the new plantations where siskins call and long-eared owls hunt ● J3532 from B180. **10**

20 Dromore Lough Monaghan FW
Only a fringe of willows separates the coniferous woodlands from the water of Inner, Dromore and Drumlona Loughs. The forests give the scenery a Scandinavian feeling which is strengthened when you meet squirrels, deer and even pine martens. Substantial numbers of teal and mallard occur around the edge and in winter 500 wildfowl are often present ● H6117 forest roads from L48. **10**

Mixed woodland of Tollymore Forest Park

The central plain of Ireland is formed by the most extensive area of limestone countryside in Europe. This rolling lowland has been the heart of Irish agriculture through successive cultures. They left Celtic burial mounds in the Boyne valley and great monastic institutions at Clonmacnoise by the Shannon. The land is littered with eskers, moraines, smoothed pavements and loose rocks, reminding us of the powerful influence of the ice on these soft rocks. The slopes are slight and the natural drainage is difficult so that shallow lakes, sluggish rivers and bogs are frequent.

There are lush pastures and meadows on the plain but as you travel westwards the covering of soil thins, rock outcrops become common and the hedges and trees of the east are replaced by dry-stone walls. The stony landscapes of the Burren create a unique countryside with a mixture of plant and animal species found nowhere else in the world. Finally, in the Aran Islands you can see the stone-walled paddocks of rock where nature dictates a unique type of farming.

1 Castlesampson Eskers
Roscommon P
Standing before an esker, perhaps in one of the ubiquitous sand quarries, it is hard to picture the river that produced it. Eskers are the fossil beds of ghost rivers from the end of the Ice Age, which flowed inside the melting ice-sheet. They excavated a channel there and not in the ground as they would today. The icy confines of this elevated channel have melted away so the sediments stand up as a sinuous ridge. Once you have recognised one, you will see eskers in many parts of the Midlands of Ireland. The cluster north of Castlesampson are sometimes followed by roads and may rise 30 to 40 feet above the general level of the plain. They are the home of many rare flowers,

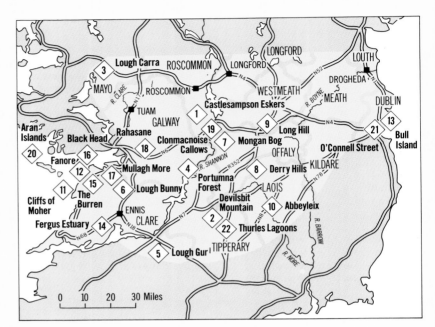

Esker near Clonmacnoise

including orchids, and make a distinctive feature in this Irish landscape, recording an important stage in its natural history • M9440 view from minor roads north of Castlesampson to Brideswell Road. ▮

2 Devilsbit Mountain
Tipperary C/FWS

A rocky ridge breached by the ice, this mountain is a landmark for miles around. It is good walking country but you must stand alone in the gap to imagine the thickness and power of the moving ice. Kestrels, wheatears and stonechats will be about but take time to look for that tiny fern, the adder's-tongue, on the western slopes as well as the wood horsetail, like a miniature cypress tree • From Ballinveny to Goldings Cross Road. ▮

3 Lough Carra Galway FWS/P
Follow the shoreline marsh looking for otter footprints in the mud below the orchids, butterworts and rushes. There is a richness of aquatic insect life and an abundance of fine brown trout to feed on it. The best example of a spring-fed limestone lake in Ireland is always used by wildfowl. Breeding mallard are joined by feeding shoveler and gadwall in winter. Lough Mask is just across the road with wild and beautiful lake scenery • M1871 from shore road on eastern side of lough. ▮

4 Portumna Forest Lough Derg FWS
Coniferous forests have been planted at the head of Lough Derg but enough of the marshy edge of the islands remains to retain the naturalists' interest in this large lough. A cormorant island offshore gives security to some of the few inland-breeding birds left in the country. Perching in the trees and hanging their wings to dry, they give the place a tropical air. Look closely among the lakeshore tussocks of sedge for skullcap, hemp-agrimony and gipsy-wort. Fallow deer, brought to Ireland by the Normans, are present in large numbers. So, too, are mallard, teal and wigeon, sheltering from the winter in shallow bays • M8403 west of Portumna on T41. ▮

5 Lough Gur Limerick P
You can read in Chapter 1 the story of the magnificent giant deer which stood 6 feet tall with antlers measuring almost as much from tip to tip. It would have been a familiar sight round this attractive lough after the ice retreated from the surrounding hills. The nearby marshes have revealed many skeletons of this monarch. Nowadays, the lake basins and marsh have several species of breeding wildfowl and you may find nearly 2000 ducks in winter • R6441 at east side near the visitor centre. ▮

6 Lough Bunny Burren, Clare P
A white, marl lake set in the low Burren limestones, Lough Bunny fluctuates in level during the year. The shoreline includes fens and sheets of rock in which dwarf willows and buckthorn find a home. Underwater, lime covers everything: plant stems, algal colonies and snail shells are all washed up with a slimy coating. On the islands a thousand pairs of black-headed gulls nest and you can hear their raucous calls as you look for alpine plants in the grassland. A splendid mixture of interest for the naturalist • R3796 from roads at south-east corner of the lough. ▮

7 Mongan Bog Shannon Valley AT
The liquid whistling song of the curlew is one of the distinctive sounds of Irish bogland. These beautiful, elegant birds breed in this classic raised bog, south of the esker which carried the ancient roadway to Clonmacnoise (see site 19). The Greenland white-fronted goose can also be found here. The bog is very wet with pools and hummocks and frogs in the safety of the sphagnum moss. Islands of cottongrass and stands of old, unburnt heather give a patchwork of habitats. Here you may meet the bright green caterpillar of the emperor moth or the russet hairy one of the fox moth. Dragonflies hunt like colourful helicopters • N0330 from roadside north of Fin Lough. ▮ ▮

8 Derry Hills Derry P
The Derry Hills represent the end of an esker, where the deposits are petering out, enveloped by raised bogs. Lime-rich water seeps over the peatland enabling the growth of a host of beautiful wild flowers that find no place on the bog itself. Butterworts are common among the bog-rush and sedges; orchids are there too and also the cranberry • N2612 west from T9. ▮ ▮

Cormorants nesting on Church Island, Lough Derg

9 Long Hill Westmeath P
The main road cuts through the esker of Long Hill at a point where it bears tall woodland. The trees are ash, hazel, whitebeam and spindle and, though not fully grown, they give one of the few impressions we have of lowland woods on good soil. Many herbs grow beneath the trees and in spring the flowers of wild strawberries, violets, woodruff and primroses brighten the ground ● N3836 from T4 and minor road to the north-west. **3**

10 Abbeyleix Leix P
The oak forest of Abbeyleix is one of those ancient woods which has been protected and managed for many centuries behind high estate walls. Well-grown oaks on each side of the Nore River produce a beautiful sight in spring as they come into leaf above a carpet of bluebells. Jays, sparrowhawks and woodcocks are some of the larger characteristic birds but you will also see long-tailed tits, redpolls and tree-creepers if you wait. With the general absence of woodpeckers in Ireland, the treecreeper has been adopted as the Irish woodpecker ● S4282 from main Cork Road south of town. **3**

11 Cliffs of Moher Clare Coast P
As the evening sun swings round to the west the light hits the rock face and the cliffs take on a magical appearance. In rough weather the scene can be most dramatic as time and again huge waves pound against the 650-foot-high cliffs. Fulmars soar on the updraft, sometimes joined by peregrines, choughs and rock doves. Nesting guillemots, razorbills and kittiwakes are neatly spaced on the ledges. Occasionally you may be lucky enough to see the fluttering display flights by several hundred puffins ● R0391 from L54 at O'Brien's Tower which is the visitors' centre. **4**

12 Fanore Burren Coast, Clare F
The rocks north and south of this beach are fretted by the sea, offering a multitude of niches to marine life. Some animals add to the dissolving action of the sea: one is the purple sea-urchin nestling here in shallow depressions, another the limpet, which returns to exactly the same spot after each feeding trip. Sea anemones, winkles, crabs and brittle-stars frequent the rock pools with sheets of crowded mussels and barnacles on the more open surfaces. Look, too, at the greyish sand for among its grains

there lies a miniature world of tiny shells, sea-urchin spines and crab claws thrown up from the deep. Something certainly attracts the stoats down to the rock pools away from their normal diet of rabbits in the sand dunes ● M1309 northwards along the beach from Fanore. **4**

13 Bull Island Dublin Bay LA
This sand-spit is the roosting ground for all the shore-birds of Dublin Bay and a feeding ground for many of them. Countless numbers of knots, dunlins, godwits and oystercatchers add to wintering wildfowl such as brent geese, wigeon and shovelers. The tameness of many of the birds is an additional attraction. From the roadside you may see 30 species and also have the chance of seeing an Irish hare on the salt-marsh ● O2338 by causeway from the coast road. **5** **10**

14 Fergus Estuary Clare P/F
The sloblands of the Shannon Estuary cover 25,000 acres, a large part of which is in the Fergus. Here at Ing the mudflats are the feeding ground for whirling flocks of dunlins, excitable godwits and the more sedate curlews. In winter, 40,000 waders, of which 16,000 may be black-tailed godwits, and 6000 ducks are a birdwatcher's delight and geese sometimes feed on the damp pastures behind. Around the shore there are narrow patches of salt-marsh where wild celery and sea-beet grow. Look out, too, for sea aster and scurvygrass—the white-flowered fleshy-leaved plant renowned for its vitamin C content ● R3467 from T11 at Dromoland. **5**

15 The Burren Clare
In Irish, the Boireann means rocky place, and so it is. Yet this rocky desert of flat limestone slabs, dry clints and grikes will draw you back again and

Abbeyleix woodland

again. For it is also a herb-rich grass-land where plants usually found in arctic or alpine regions mingle with the normal Irish flora. Species from Greenland share this time-worn land-scape with plants from Spain and Portugal. This is not just true of one or two spots but for 140 square miles the colour and variety of plant life is astonishing. The frequency of plants here that are rare everywhere else in the British Isles is extraordinary. The history of the area is mysterious and the lines of evidence, though some-times conflicting, point to a forested past and a great clearance followed by soil erosion in the Neolithic period. The result is so fascinating a mixture of plants and animals that the Burren should be regarded as considerably more important than is generally accepted ● R2299 there is a display centre at Kilfenora. **7** **1**

16 Black Head The Burren, Clare C

From the coast road the Burren rocks look particularly bare and inhospitable. Ice rode up these slopes from the north, leaving a trail of Galway rocks behind. Rocky slopes and flat pavements are everywhere and the vegetation grows deep within the cracks or in pockets of peaty soil on the limestone. Mountain avens relives the time of ice, covering the ground with its tiny oak-like leaves, its white flowers or its plumes of seeds. Saxifrages crowd their clumps on to the smallest patches of soil and the rock-cress and lettuce seem to spring straight from the stones. There are woodland plants here, too, finding conditions within the sheltered cracks moist and to their liking. A botanist's treasure trove ● M1411 from coast road, L54. **7**

Burren flora

17 Mullagh More

The Burren, Clare S/C
A dish-shaped hill in the south-east Burren, Mullagh More brings together many of the region's special features into a small area. Grassland and scrub are grazed by goats so that trees, even yews and holly, are kept flat on the ground. The flowers provide amazing colours in spring and early summer – the eye-catching blue of the gentians, the yellow of the small rock-rose and cinquefoil and the reddish purple of the bloody crane's-bill ● R3295 southwards on minor roads from Glencolumbkille. **7**

18 Rahasane Galway P/C

The largest turlough, or dry lake, in the country, Rahasane is unusual in having a river flowing through it. When flooded, it supports many thousands of birds, including large flocks of golden plover and lapwing. When dry, it pro-vides good grazing for cattle and horses which feed on grasses and sedges and the few other plants they can find. The flooding depends on the water table and its irregularity prevents the growth of bushes or trees. It encourages a blackish moss to cover the walls which often cross a turlough and look in-congruous at times of flood. The aquatic creatures have to adapt to the long, dry summer spells. The fairy shrimp is perhaps the turlough's greatest survival specialist ● M4619 on minor road north of Dunkellin river. **7**

19 Clonmacnoise Callows

Shannon Valley, Offaly P
The lordly Shannon and the old abbey at Clonmacnoise form a perfect back-ground to the colour and variety of wild flowers which flourish in these wet hay meadows in spring and summer. Wildlife benefits from farming in the traditional style, leaving most of the fertilising to the river and cutting the hay comparatively late in the year. Listen for the call of the corncrake from its refuge in the meadows. Altogether, 120 species of plants can be found and offer many different habitats for abun-dant insect life. The local birds are sup-

plemented by many species which use the Shannon Valley as a migration route ● N0131 northwards from Clonmacnoise via river-bank path. **7**

20 Aran Islands Galway Bay

These Atlantic islands show the extra-ordinary endeavours of man to survive inhospitable surroundings. An extension of the stoniest parts of the Burren, they are rocky ridges with some accumulation of sand on the sheltered sides. Their surface is covered by fields surrounded by high stone walls, but fields is a name only of convenience. They are paddocks of rock with enough vegetation growing in cracks to support a single cow or a few calves. The productive land which is gardened by hand has largely been made by bringing sand and seaweed up from the foreshore. It grows crops of fine potatoes, largely free from blight, and other vegetables. Currachs, frail canvas-covered fishing boats, are still made on Inisheer and are used for trans-port and lobster-fishing ● L9005 by boat from Doolin, Clare, or Rossaveal, Galway. **8**

21 O'Connell Street Dublin

Many birds have adjusted to living with man: the town pigeon, starling, magpie and house sparrow frequent our cities. But the oddest example of them all is the roost of 800 pied wagtails in the plane trees of Dublin's main street. As dusk gathers in winter, these birds fly in from the suburbs, in small groups, gathering in the glare of the street lights with much posturing and chattering. At Christmas time the scene is further lit by the fairy-lights strung between the trees of the birds' roost ● O1634, O'Connell Street, Dublin City Centre. **9**

22 Thurles Lagoons Tipperary P

No visit to Thurles from September to March is complete without a look at the lagoons and river below the sugar factory. Few wildfowl lived here before the factory was built but now the air rings with the sound of wigeon and the barking calls of Bewick's and whooper swans. Over 1000 wildfowl are often present, including teal, shoveler and pintail. Green sand-pipers, too, winter here, one of their most regular haunts in the country ● S1155/L119A road south of sugar factory entrance. **9** **10**

In a continuous sweep around the south of the central plain, ridges of beautiful sandstone hills, separated by deep river valleys, form a distinctive mountainous province. From the Wicklow Mountains near Dublin to the mouth of the Shannon, you can walk or drive always in sight of hills. Most are covered in blanket bog and all show signs of the ice. You cross ten river systems that give an imprint to the landscape which can only be southern Ireland. The sea is never far away. The wild Atlantic beats at the base of the Skelligs and penetrates deep into Cork and Kerry, bringing its warming influence to sheltered farmland. Lough Ine is one of the many fascinating places where we can enjoy the abundant life of the Gulf Stream.

Inland, the Killarney Valley is one of Ireland's greatest natural history treasures. It brings together two of the country's nationally distinctive features: the richness of beautiful lakes with their own relic fish and the splendour of sessile oakwoods interspersed with the native strawberry-tree.

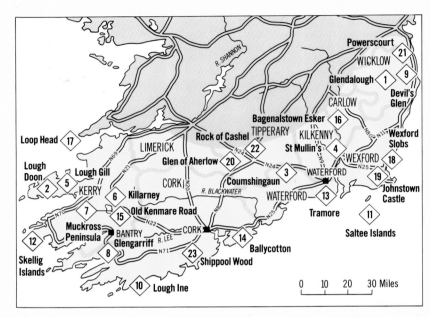

Fuchsia hedge

1 Glendalough Wicklow S/C

In the heart of the Wicklow Mountains, ice cut and over-deepened this wild valley to a flat-bottomed U-shape and lake waters accumulated on the valley floor. A stream on the south side was also cut short by glaciers and this now empties, as a waterfall, on to a delta which divides the upper and lower lakes. Penetrate beyond the sixth-century monastic settlement to get the feel of the mountains with their wheatears, skylarks and pipits—you may see sika deer and red squirrels around the upper lake ● T1096, westwards from Laragh (T61). ◼

2 Lough Doon Kerry C

Winding your way from sea-level over a hill of 1350 feet, you need a clear day to see the full range of landscapes from the Conair Pass Road. Above the fuchsia hedges and poor pastures, the effect of ice dominates the land. The road cuts through the crest and on the northern side runs close beside the corrie of Lough Doon formed in the last phase of the Ice Age. It was here that ice was first recognised as the major

formative influence on the landscape; little wonder, you may think, as you stand before the awesome cliffs above the lake. You can see the countless scratches carved into the bedrock or, below the road, clamber about the crescent-shaped pile of debris left by the melting glacier. The panoramic views of Irish mountain scenery are memorable ● Q5005 from Dingle to Castlegregory Road. ◼

3 Coumshingaun

Comeragh Mountains, Waterford C
The largest and the most accessible glacial lake in the Comeragh Mountains, Coumshingaun Lough lies in one of several ice-gouged corries on the eastern side. The char still swims in its dark waters and arctic plants grow on the cliffs above as they have done since the close of the Ice Age. These first colonists were once widespread on the lowlands, too, but have been banished to these inhospitable sites by later immigrants better suited to withstand the vigorous expansion of plant life as the climate warmed ● S3210 from T56 along stream valley. ◼ ◻

4 St Mullin's River Barrow, Carlow S
Many of the southern Irish rivers make
their way to the sea in broad, imposing
valleys but have to cut through hilly
ground in gorges as they near the coast.
Once the river flowed fast through
St Mullin's but, as the melting ice raised
sea-levels, the sea flooded inland and
slowed the flow. The river is a firm
favourite with canoeists, many of whom
enjoy the wildlife of the reed-beds as
they paddle their way downstream.
Their silent approach will not disturb
the sedge warblers, swans and otters.
The river has salmon and eels with
plenty of trout rising to feed on
a rich insect life ● S7238 from
Graiguenamanagh (L32) on east side
of Barrow. ◪

5 Lough Gill Kerry P/C
A shallow, sandy lake impounded by
the two sweeps of sand dunes which
form the Castlegregory peninsula, Lough
Gill contains abundant fish life, many
wildfowl and, along the southern shore,
interesting fen communities. In winter,
both whooper and Bewick's swans
cruise its shallows, dabbling ducks frequent its reedy edges and tufted ducks
and pochards dive in its open water.
The machair, or grassland, is a feeding
site here for flocks of up to 50 choughs
in winter. The lake has breeding natterjack toads, being one of the centres
of their very limited south-western
range ● Q6014 from Stradbally or
Trench Bridge. ◪

6 Killarney Kerry OPW
The Killarney Valley is a very special
place, happily accommodating both the
tourist and the naturalist in the country's
oldest National Park. The beautiful
scenery has rocky streams, waterfalls
and lakes set in an ice-cut valley, with
spreads of the largest oakwoods in
Ireland. The upper lake has harsh, rocky
shores with blanket bog and woodland
running down to the water. Muckross
Lake sits half on limestone and its water
supports many more plants, insects and
fish. Lough Leane is vast in comparison
and rich in life. Mallards dabble around
its sandy margins for seeds and small
animals, while mergansers fish for
trout, char and shad offshore. Sand-
pipers flit anxiously from stone to stone.
The Killarney shad is an isolated form
of sea-fish that normally breeds high

up in estuaries. At Killarney the shad
must have been cut off from the sea by
some quirk of the ice-sheet.

The evergreen strawberry-tree, as a
native in Ireland, is confined to the
edges of splendid sessile oakwoods.
Despite centuries of management for
timber production, these forests are
probably close to the natural wildwood of south-west Ireland, with the
trees covered with mosses and lichens
● V98 from N71 south of Killarney,
especially at Ross Island. ◪ ◪

7 Muckross Peninsula Kerry
The path around Muckross Lake
traverses such a variety of habitats
that it is ideal for the naturalist
who enjoys walking. The dark, twiggy
yew-wood, the windshorn scrub of
arbutus, whitebeam, juniper and hazel,
the marshy hollows of ash and the
moss-filled oakwoods all create a picture
of the diversity of the greenwood that
once covered the land. Man's hand
can also be seen in the frequency of
rhododendron–the green blanket that
threatens to engulf the entire area
beneath its sterile shade. Only the sika

deer, themselves an introduced species,
find these bushes to their liking ●
V9686 from Muckross House or at
Dinis Cottage off T65. ◪

8 Glengarriff Cork FWS
The oakwoods follow the sheltered
valleys close to the sea. Trees and ground
are festooned with mosses, ferns and
lichens, each supporting a community
of tiny animals within them. The place
hums with the sound of insects; hoverflies, bumblebees and butterflies are
everywhere. Beetles chew away at
plants and wood; caterpillars eat the
softer leaves. Nesting birds gather
beakfuls of unwary insects to feed
their young. Watch for treecreepers
climbing the mossy trunks and listen
for the screeching of jays ● V9157,
from west side to T65. ◪

9 Devil's Glen Wicklow FWS
Old oakwoods, deciduous plantings and
modern forestry make this a delightful
area in springtime, alive with the songs
of birds and the new growth of spring
flowers. Here you can experience the
sound recordings of a woodland at first

hand: the thrushes, blackbirds, wrens and blackcaps seeming to compete for attention against a background of chiff-chaffs, willow warblers and wood-pigeons. You may wonder how such a beautiful place could be called the Devil's Glen ● T2498 from Glenmore Castle, west of Ashford (N11). **3**

10 Lough Ine Cork FWS
Twice a day, rapids develop in the narrow channel that joins this landlocked bay to the sea and it is here that some of the more bizarre forms of marine life occur. Sponges, starfish, sea-slugs and sea-urchins crowd among the forest of large seaweeds. More than 60 varieties of fish swim over sediments in this sea lough which show that it was once a freshwater lake, before the rise of sea-level. Among the more exotic fish are red-mouthed goby, trigger-fish, tompot blenny, 15-spined stickleback, lump-sucker and the Lough Ine pipefish ● W0928 from road at north or west. **4**

11 Saltee Islands Wexford P
This is probably the most accessible sea-bird colony in the country. On the Great and Little Saltee you can look 18 species of these ocean-going birds in the eye. Puffins, razorbills, shags and gannets nest on the low cliffs which are constantly patrolled by fulmars. Colonies of gulls cover the flatter land, posing for your camera against a background of bluebells and young unfurling bracken ● X9579 by boat at weekends from Kilmore Quay. **4**

12 Skellig Islands Kerry Coast S/IWC
Words cannot convey the spectacle of the Skelligs, those pinnacles of rock set in a heaving sea. Viewed across 7 miles of the Atlantic the islands look the least habitable place on earth. But 1400 years ago monks lived in stone cells on Great Skellig and built a stone stairway of 600 steps from the landing place. Now their walls conceal storm petrels by the thousand. Puffins nest here too but it is the 50,000 gannets on Little Skellig that must rate as one of our noisiest, most exciting sea-bird spectaculars. It is amazing to think of this isolated rock as equivalent to a fishing port, of truly remarkable size, landing at least this number of fish every day ● V2461 by boat from Portmagee or Ballinskelligs. **4**

13 Tramore Waterford F
At the far end of the tourist beach, the Tramore sandhills rise layer upon layer. Young dunes are actively growing on the point while erosion by wind and waves takes place on the landward side. Both the strandline and the high dunes have a varied flora and fauna. Woody plants are, unusually, quite important and wild privet, dewberry and the burnet rose predominate. Small blue butterflies and burnet moths skip over the summer flowers while kestrels hunt pygmy shrews or lizards. The back strand is a good area for wintering wildfowl and waders including brent geese ● S6101 along beach, east of town. **5**

14 Ballycotton Cork F
A long, shingle ridge swings north-eastwards away from Ballycotton town, creating several bird-filled brackish wetlands. In the harsh conditions of drought, wind and salt spray, plant life has to be specially adapted to survive; fleshy leaves, wax, prickles, a dense hair covering, deep roots are all used. Annual plants that survive the winter as seeds, grow fast in the more favourable conditions of summer. You will notice many tenacious garden weeds amongst them. In winter this site is the most southerly location for wintering Bewick's and whooper swans ● W9964 northwards from town, along the foreshore. **5**

15 Old Kenmare Road Kerry OPW
Blanket peat and moorland, the summer range of the native red deer, now cover this hilly area above the Killarney valley. You can see the traces of old sheep pastures, farmsteads and potato ridges around the site of a deserted village. Wet pools, springs and streams will repay attention today and you should not miss the large Kerry butterwort or the many dragonflies. The native herd of red deer is very difficult to find, though, because of their remarkable camouflage in these uplands ● V9683 from N71 just south of entrance to Muckross House. **6**

16 Bagenalstown Esker Carlow P
Eskers are the beds of rivers that flooded through the melting ice-sheets. They consist of stones and sand mixed together in long ridges that were once used as trackways. Generally they are lime-rich and the hazel scrub and grassland are full of flowering plants. Wild thyme, marjoram, trefoils and clovers are prominent as well as selfheal and several orchids. These grasslands are small-scale communities where a square yard of turf may contain 20 different plants ● S7461 south side of L33 road to Myshall. **7**

17 Loop Head Clare P/C
The clay pastures of south Clare respond poorly to drainage and many have been left as damp hayfields or grazing land. Grasses and rushes are the dominant plants but they are brightened by the yellows of marsh-marigold, ragwort and buttercups, and the pinks of ragged-robin, purple loosestrife and orchids. Towards Loop Head, sea spray begins to affect the fields and the pasture plants fall off in numbers. Sea plantains and thrift appear and become more frequent until they form a low, shining sward above the cliffs, much used by choughs. A good spot for an autumn sea-bird watch ● Q6947 beside road west of Kilbaha. **7**

18 Wexford Slobs Wexford S/IWC
Crops were first planted on the reclaimed polders of the North Slob in 1850. Today the tillage and grassland interlink in large open fields intersected by drainage channels. Geese have taken to this habitat with enthusiasm, first the grey-lag and now the white-front. This man-made site carries a majority of the Irish population of Greenland white-fronted geese in winter. Bewick's swans, ducks and waders add more to an outstanding birdwatching area. A wildfowl collection makes a summer visit worthwhile too ● T0824 from Wexford to Castlebridge Road. **7** **8**

19 Johnstown Castle Wexford S
An experimental farm set in an old estate, Johnstown Castle offers a very good combination of agricultural land, woodland and garden to attract most of the wildlife which will adjust to living on farmland. A nature trail beside the lake and an agricultural

museum provide insights into the practices that have shaped the landscape and nature ● T0217 turn off T8, 1 mile south of Wexford. **8**

20 Glen of Aherlow Galty Mountains P
Lying in the shadow of the lofty Galty Mountains, the Glen is an agricultural region with tall hedges, trees and pastures that should be explored on foot or by bicycle. Look along the hedges for scrambling plants such as the wild rose and honeysuckle and in gateways for the special types that withstand trampling and winter mud ● R9030 westwards from Bansha on T13. **8**

21 Powerscourt Wicklow P
Powerscourt is well known for its classical garden set against mountain scenery but there is so much more. Estate woodland leads upriver to a waterfall where the Dargle falls into a glacial corrie. Here oakwoods cover some of the slopes, their trunks rich in lichens. The planted woodland is now well grown and includes many interesting conifers from around the world. The bird fauna too is rich, with siskin, redpoll, treecreeper and blackcap as well as the commoner species. In autumn, look for fungi such as edible chanterelle. It was from here that the now successful spread of sika deer in Ireland took place, following their introduction from Japan in 1860 ● O2116 off Enniskerry to Roundwood Road, waterfall section all year, garden open Easter to the end of October. **9**

22 Rock of Cashel Tipperary S
The ecclesiastical buildings of Cashel crowd a tiny outcrop of limestone overlooking the Tipperary plains. The round tower, castle and cathedral offer lodgings to jackdaw, starling and town pigeon. Stonecrop and pellitory grow on the walls and the early or late visitor may catch those winter annuals such as whitlowgrass and rue-leaved saxifrage that have flowered and set seed before the summer sun reaches its height ● S0740 from Cashel town (N8). **9**

23 Shippool Wood Cork FWS
The coniferous plantings of the lower Bandon River mix into the older hardwoods at Shippool and the contrast is clear to see. Darkness on the forest floor prevents the growth of most woodland plants and limits ground-feeding birds such as the thrushes, blackbirds and robins. The brighter canopy overhead, however, is filled with the sound of goldcrests and tits hunting for food, and the far-carrying cries of hooded crows, wood-pigeons and jays ● W5755 from Inishannon to Kinsale Road (L41). **10**

Powerscourt gardens (top) and The Rock of Cashel

BIBLIOGRAPHY

Angel, H. *The Natural History of Britain and Ireland*, Michael Joseph, 1981
(This review of the main habitats of the British Isles is enhanced by Heather Angel's perceptive photography)

Briggs, A. *A Social History of England*, Weidenfeld and Nicolson, 1983
(Unpedantic human history that counterpoints the natural history of this land)

Fairbrother, N. *New Lives, New Landscapes*, The Architectural Press, 1970, Pelican, 1972
(Stimulating account of the impact of our own way of life on the modern landscapes of this country)

Godman, N. *History of the British Flora*, Cambridge, 2nd ed, 1975
(A classic work for professional and amateur botanists)

Hale, W. G. *Waders*, Collins 'New Naturalist' series, 1980
(Revealing insight into the world of wading birds)

Hardy, A. *The Open Sea*, Vols 1 and 2, Collins 'New Naturalist' series, 2nd ed, 1970
(Still unrivalled as an introduction to marine ecology)

Hoskins, W. G. *The Making of the English Landscape*, Hodder & Stoughton, 1955, Pelican, 1970
(A pioneer study of the evolution of the English landscape since iron-age times: a vivid history)

Mabey, R. *The Common Ground*, Hutchinson in association with the NCC, 1980
(Richard Mabey's unsentimental but sensitive analysis of nature conservation in Britain; a very readable and informed contemporary view)

Macan, T. T. and Worthington, E. B. *Life in Lakes and Rivers*, Collins 'New Naturalist' series, 1951
(Uncluttered account of our freshwater habitats)

The Macmillan Guide to Britain's Nature Reserves, Macmillan, 1984
(The most comprehensive of the gazetteers for Britain)

Mitchell, F. *The Irish Landscape*, Collins, 1976
(Excellent account of the shaping of Ireland's landscape by natural forces and by man)

Rackham, O. *Trees and Woodland in the British Landscape*, Dent, 1976
(Scholarly history of our woodland – particularly that of south and east England, by the author who first adopted A. A. Milne's romantic notion of the 'wildwood' to describe the primeval forest)

Simmons, I. and Tooley, M. (eds). *The Environment in British Prehistory*, Duckworth, 1981
(Academic but fascinating review of our knowledge about the physical nature of the British Isles in pre-history – from Ice Age to the Iron Age. Its extensive bibliography leads the reader to a new perspective on natural history)

Stamp I. Dudley. *Britain's Structure and Scenery*, Collins 'New Naturalist' series, 1946
(Still one of the best introductions to the geology of our islands – one of the many excellent titles in the 'New Naturalist' series that is now available in paperback)

Steers, J. A. *The Sea Coast*, Collins, 4th ed, 1969
(Vivid account of how our coastline has been, and still is being, formed)

Streeter, D. *The Wild Flowers of the British Isles*, Macmillan, 1983
(An up-to-date catalogue of the wild flowers of our islands – well illustrated and succinct)

Tansley, A. G. *Britain's Green Mantle*, Allen and Unwin, 2nd ed, 1968
(Very readable description of the contemporary habitats of Britain)

PICTURE CREDITS

INDEX